WORKING WITH
PARENTS

Learning from other people's experiences

Edited by Ann Wheal

Russell House Publishing

First published in 2000 by:
Russell House Publishing Limited
4 St. George's House
Uplyme Road
Lyme Regis
Dorset DT7 3LS

Tel. 01297-443948
Fax. 01297-442722
e-mail: help@russellhouse.co.uk

British Library Cataloguing-in-Publication Data:
A catalogue record for this book is available from the British Library.

ISBN: 1-898924-59-7

Text design and layout by The Hallamshire Press Limited, Sheffield

Printed by Cromwell Press, Trowbridge

Russell House Publishing Limited

Is a group of social work, probation, education and youth and community work practitioners and academics working in close collaboration with a professional publishing team. Our aim is to work closely with the field to produce innovative and valuable materials to help managers, trainers, practitioners and students. We are keen to receive feedback on publications and new ideas for future projects.

WORKING WITH
PARENTS

Contents

SECTION THREE   Health

SECTION FOUR   Education

Dedication

This book is dedicated to the memory of Rhod Napier.

Rhod was Service Manager for young people in Perth and Kinross. At the time of his death he was about to write a chapter for this book.

Throughout his working life, Rhod's priority was young people. He brought a great sense of humour, fun and commitment to all those with whom he worked.

Rhod will be greatly missed by his wife Lorraine, his family, young people, work colleagues and all those whose lives he touched.

Acknowledgements

My grateful thanks must go to:

Sue Blundell for her tireless effort and 'sharp learning curve' in helping to get this book to the publishers.

My husband, Peter, for his patience, dedication and love.

Most of all to the contributors to this book whose wealth of knowledge and experience is so evident in their chapters.

Contributors

Rosemary Bazley has worked with communication impaired children and their parents in health centres, family centres, special schools and nurseries. She currently job-shares a pre-school specialist post in Portsmouth, working in a special nursery.

Ann Buchanan is a lecturer in the Department of Applied Social Science and Social Research, University of Oxford. She is an experienced researcher and has published widely in the area of children and families.

Alison Cathles is Planning Manager at Gloucestershire County Council Social Services Department.

Mair Dyer is the parent of an ex-pupil and governor of The Willows Special School.

Gerry Emson is a teacher at The Willows Special School, working half-time as an advisory teacher for visual impairment seconded to Portsmouth LEA, and half-time outreach worker.

Frada Feigelson has been director of the Schusterman Centre in Jerusalem since its opening in 1992. She has been actively involved in the fostering of knowledge about children at risk and their families in Israel. After immigrating to Israel in 1971 she worked in hospital settings with developmentally handicapped children and their families and taught courses in child and family welfare at the School of Social Work, Bar Ilan University.

Peter Ford trained as a Probation Officer and subsequently worked as a Court Welfare Officer and for Southampton Counselling Service. He has practised as a family mediator with Hampshire Family Mediation for the past eighteen years, and was a founder member of the service. He is currently Director of Studies in the Department of Social Work Studies at the University of Southampton.

Jaz Galloway is a recruitment worker, Community Foster Care Limited, Gloucester.

Stewart Greenwell is the Area Manager, Gloucestershire County Council Social Services Department.

Carol Henderson is the Social Work Manager, Community Foster Care Limited, Gloucester.

Cathy Hill is a senior lecturer in community child health at the University of Southampton. She has eleven years' clinical experience in the field of paediatrics and child health including neonatal intensive care, general paediatrics, child guidance and care of the chronically disabled child. Currently she is specialising in social paediatrics, working alongside social services departments in the field of child protection and looked after children.

Joy Howard has worked for social services departments in London and West Yorkshire since 1982. She has experience in residential, youth work, area social work and family placement, specialising in the 11-plus age group. The innovation and development of the Support Care scheme in Bradford has been her ambition for a number of years, and her full time occupation since 1996.

Suzanna Jacoby is a Business Manager at Community Foster Care Limited, Gloucester.

Yitzak Lander has been director of the Elvire and Lucien Levy Treatment Centre in Beer Sheva since its opening in 1994. He teaches courses focused on innovative theories and techniques of intervention with children and their families at the Schools of Social Work and Education, Ben Gurion University of the Negev. Prior to his immigration in 1994 he was faculty member at the School of Social Work, University of Victoria, Canada.

Lisa Lewer is currently Clinical Charge Nurse at the Park Hospital for Children. She has worked in child in-patient mental health settings since qualifying in psychiatric nursing seven years ago. She has interests in multi-disciplinary team dynamics and milieu therapy.

Meriel Mann is Deputy Head of The Willows Special School for pre-school children.

Pat Mood has worked in palliative care and hospice work for 20 years, working with children and families. She is currently a team leader in the social work department of a hospital in Stoke-on-Trent.

Eileen Murphy is a consultant to social services and education departments. Based in London, she trains teams including social workers, teachers, and youth offending teams in their work with difficult, vulnerable and resistant young people as well as her direct practitioner work with crisis families.

Rosie Nichol Harper has been a qualified social worker for 12 years and has worked within a variety of settings in different local authorities. These include children and families fieldwork teams, a palliative care unit, child protection development, family placement and child mental health. She is currently employed by Oxfordshire Social Services at the Park Hospital for Children.

Val O'Connor is a Co-ordinator at Coney Hill Neighbourhood Project.

Hazel Osborn was a medical social worker and worked for 17 years in London teaching hospitals; she set up a social work student practice teaching unit in a Portsmouth hospital; managed health based social work in South-West Hampshire; taught in the Department of Social Work Studies, University of Southampton. Throughout her career she has been involved in teaching both social work and medical students in pursuit of best standards of practice.

Karen Postle is a qualified social worker. She has trained and worked as a counsellor and as a family mediator, working for Hampshire Family Mediation for six years. She works as a research fellow in the School of Occupational Therapy and Physiotherapy and as a teaching fellow in the Department of Social Work Studies, both at the University of Southampton.

Kate Rose is a qualified social worker employed by Salford Social Services. Her current project in Salford, Greater Manchester, concentrates on the issues for children and their carers following sexual abuse.

Maria Ruegger is a senior lecturer in social work at De Montfort University. She is also a Guardian ad Litem on the Hertfordshire Panel of Guardians Ad Litem and Reporting Officers. Since joining the University she has maintained strong links with practice. Her recent research interests include Children's Perspectives of the Guardian ad Litem Service and Mentoring in General Practice.

Peter Sandiford is a Development Manager for the Children's Residential Care Unit at the National Children's Bureau. He is currently managing a project which is looking to develop models of working that unite services for children and young people in public care, and establish partnerships within local authority services, other agencies, parents and families.

Anne Savage is a qualified social worker, employed by the NSPCC. Her current project is in Salford, Greater Manchester, and concentrates on the issues for children and their carers following sexual abuse.

Anne Scowen was a nursery nurse at The Willows special school, and is now working full time developing outreach work.

John Stevens trained as a teacher. He then worked in agricultural research at Bristol University for a number of years, gaining an M.Sc. He started teaching in Southampton in 1974 and was Head of Science for five years before moving into vocational and then pastoral work. He has been a Year Head for the past seven years.

Alison Stokes is a recruitment worker and foster carer, Community Foster Care Limited, Gloucester.

Bernice Thompson is a Co-ordinator at Hesters Way Neighbourhood Project.

Marian Thorpe has managed Derbyshire Young Carers for three years. She has worked in hospital social work and has extensive residential care experience, particularly in managing secure accommodation.

Paul Tosey is Director of the Human Potential Research Group and a lecturer in the School of Educational Studies, University of Surrey. His research is in the field of experience, learning and change in organisations. Currently he is focusing on two themes: a) evaluation of organisational change and the effects of change interventions through appreciation of the learning (especially 'transformative learning) experienced by participants; b) exploring and representing people's experences of organisations in terms of 'energy fields'.

Ann Wheal is in the Department of Social Work Studies at the University of Southampton. She previously spent 17 years teaching young people in inner-city, multi-racial schools and colleges. She has a commitment to working in partnership with young people, children and families, involving them in the decision-making process.

John Whiteside is the manager of the Adolescent and Family Support Team for Tameside M.B.C. social services. He trained as a teacher and taught in secondary schools and in further education before turning to residential work with young people. He helped develop the Adolescent and Family Support System that operates in the borough, and is currently involved in developing this service to encompass the needs of children of all ages.

About This Book

This book has been written by people across a wide spectrum of disciplines. Each chapter has been written in the author's own words in their own way.

The book will help anyone working with parents to:

- Better understand the work of others.
- To learn what works and what doesn't work in order to inform practice.
- To realise the effect their actions may have on others.
- Realise the importance of interagency working.

- See how working in partnership with parents can help the parents and especially their children and young people.
- See the necessity of evaluation and monitoring of all their work.

Each chapter can be read alone but, if possible, the book should be read as a whole, as the full impact of the chapters will become clear.

The eclectic flavour of the book ensures it will be useful for anyone studying or working with parents in the areas of health, education, social care, child care law, the police and youth justice.

Introduction

Ann Wheal

Parenting has become a major topic of social policy discussions in the media and in government. The aim of this book is to help anyone working with parents as well as students, academics and policy makers to develop successful ideas that will really help parents, which in return will improve the quality of life for the parents and their children.

Many of us will have heard professionals presenting papers, that include discussing issues or working with parents as an important component of their work. How many of us ask them – what was the thinking behind this working with parents; what was the ethos; the rationale; what training had they had; how did they measure success? Certainly from my experience as a teacher the answer was that very little preparation was given for working with parents, it was just something teachers did.

This book is the result of asking people to record their experiences in the hope that they might help others. It is about what works and what does not work for the authors of the various chapters. It gives an insight into the knowledge and skills required within the different disciplines and shows how these may be transferred to a variety of situations.

The second chapter is by a father who has been through the system who offered to write a chapter of his personal and harrowing feelings and experiences of being on the receiving end of the court/social services system. When reading Paul's chapter it was difficult for me not to become emotional as it reflected too closely my own family's experience of the health service during a family crisis. This chapter is a clear opportunity to learn; to review our own practice and to ensure such experiences do not happen to other parents.

I have also been able to learn from three pieces of work that have entailed meeting parents to find out their views of the services offered and the support available. Quotations from these projects are included throughout this chapter. These pieces of work are, Children in Need Research Project for Southwark Council, 1996, University of Southampton, Identifying the Training Needs of Friends and Family who are Carers for the NFCA on behalf of the Department of Health, 1998, Identifying the Information Needs of Families in Wiltshire, Wiltshire Council 1996.

Background

Much has been written about an apparent decline in good enough parenting; the lack of extended family networks and, if the media is to be believed, out of control children roaming the streets at night with parents out enjoying themselves totally disinterested in their child. But there would actually appear to be very little hard evidence to support these perceptions. As John Hudson says in his paper *Working with Parents*:

> There are very few inherently bad parents. Most parents who find themselves unable to carry out their responsibilities are being affected by circumstance... such as lack of knowledge, experience or satisfactory role models; resources; stigma or social isolation or long term stress through unemployment, poor living conditions or chronic illness.

We may encounter such issues when we encounter parents:

- during divorce
- managing difficult behaviour
- as a result of child abuse
- for legal reasons
- resolving family difficulties

- resolving child difficulties
- for health reasons, both physical and mental
- coping with bereavement
- resolving difficulties at school
- when a child has been accommodated or looked after
- to improve or develop parenting skills
- as a support network
- in time of crisis

Working with parents is not an easy task but one which requires skill, care, thought, preparation and compassion.

Parenting Help and Support

The vast majority of parents are very capable people. We should be empowering them to take control of their lives. This may be in helping them to develop parenting skills by:

- Actively involving them in decisions that affect their children's lives such as in health and education.
- Providing opportunities to share responsibilities for the welfare of their child if this will help to maintain family life.
- Providing opportunities for them to help others by using their own skills to care for other people's children.
- Teaching them how to cope in times of illness or bereavement or at other times of stress in their life.
- Letting them know that support is there if needed.

In all of this we should ensure that parents are not disempowered by the system, but are confident in their own child rearing skills and knowledge. We must work to ensure that they do not come to believe that:

he who shouts loudest gets the money or service

Judy Sheba, DfEE, July 1999

Since the implementation of the Children Act 1989, children's rights have received a good deal of attention. It is important to remember that parents have rights too, as well as responsibilities.

Listening to Parents

Many professionals assume that parents need, or indeed want, educating and support. In many cases this may be true. In others the reverse. Parents have a wealth of experience, knowledge and ideas to offer other parents and professionals. I believe their views should be sought and their experience valued and utilised if appropriate. Careful listening is the most critical aspect for anyone working with parents.

A recent conversation on a train journey highlights this. The parent had a child who was diagnosed as dyslexic. He naturally wanted the best possible education and support for his son. Inter-agency working did not happen and the parent felt he had to continually fight for over a year in order to achieve his aims. He said:

> *they had no idea about project management; about working together; about meeting my child's needs. They were only interested in their particular job and not my child's welfare as a whole.*

In another instance, the parents of a disabled child went to see the Assistant Director of Social Services. They arrived in an aggressive manner and spoke aggressively. The Assistant Director quietly asked them if they always spoke in such a way. The parents were surprised at this person's calm approach. In the past they had found that the only way to access information or appropriate service for their child had been by shouting or threatening legal action. They were taken aback when they were treated calmly and well. A satisfactory outcome was achieved.

A parent in Wiltshire said:

> *I feel that we have to fight for everything. Nothing is made easy for families with a special needs child or adult.*

Clear Communication of Options and Opportunities

In the Southwark research, many of the parents interviewed, expressed feelings of powerlessness and lack of choices in the situations within which they found themselves. Social services, along with other agencies, may need to explain carefully what the different services offer – then families themselves can decide if the service might meet their need.

Communication with other professions does not always allow information exchange to occur which might enable contact to be made at a sufficiently early stage, for example in assisting expectant mothers. A considerable amount of re-education, development of trust and articulation of shared understandings about boundaries of responsibility between agencies is urgently needed.

Diversity and Expectations

Southwark Council issued service level agreements to a cross section of family support groups such as Newpin, Charterhouse, WelCare and FSU (Family Support Unit). The ethnic mix of the groups did not necessarily reflect the mix in the particular neighbourhood. As one worker said:

> *We used to have a lot of Asian referrals here but now the social worker has changed we are getting many more Afro-Caribbean as she (the social worker) is Afro-Caribbean.*

At WelCare the leader was of South American origin and most of the women attending the group were from Spanish speaking countries. The language and culture of the group apparently playing a major part in the decision of the women to participate.

The ethnic diversity and different cultural expectations between parents, professionals and children may exacerbate relationship problems and this should be borne in mind when working with parents – one's own

views and beliefs taking second place to that of the family.

Anecdotal evidence suggests that the social class of the family also has a part of play in whether a family receives appropriate services. Several delegates and speakers at recent conferences have highlighted the fact that 'middle' or 'upper' class families are often not considered to need, and do not get, help from social services when in fact help is necessary. Conversely, in education, for example, the articulate and confident parent often ensures their child gets the best support available, some times to the detriment of working class children. Research is obviously necessary here but good monitoring would also highlight areas for concern.

Monitoring, Evaluation and Assessment

Ann Buchanan in her chapter mentions other groups who are working with parents. There is a whole gambit of groups across the UK, in both the state and voluntary sector. It seems to me that continuous monitoring, evaluation and assessment is essential. The chapter by the staff at The Willows gives a wide example of different monitoring and evaluating schemes in use, including regularly asking parents what they want and think of the service. These can easily be adapted for use in other circumstances. In fact, since writing their chapter Willows have introduced two new services in response to parents suggestions – a group for fathers and a group for grandparents.

Fathers

The term working with parents may sometimes be a misnomer. What it often means is working with mothers.

The1995 report from the Department of Health, *Child Protection: Messages from Research*, picked up on this issue:

Although researchers were sensitive to this issue it was frequently easier to interview mothers in the studies than fathers, other relatives or resident partners and this should be borne in mind when interpreting results. (p17)

Trevelyan, interviewing representatives from the Institute for Public Policy Research (1996) cites their comments:

The attitude of professionals are crucial. In practice, it appears that they almost invariably target services at mothers, many are ambivalent about engaging with fathers and evidence suggests that many actively avoid them. Fathers then sense how they are 'defined out' of the childcare equation.

Linda Richards a social worker in Perth believes that the above may be generally true for fathers of children under about 10 years old. However, social workers dealing with older children, do involve fathers as their role is seen as crucial during teenage years. She also believes that social workers now acknowledge that there has been a shift in attitude of fathers. In some places this has been driven mainly by unemployment and the change in family work patterns.

Patterns of rising employment for women and declining employment for men has made it easier for men to undertake more parental tasks. However beneficial from a parenting perspective this may appear, it is unlikely to be fully valued by the father because of the circumstances. Given the choice, most fathers would, understandably, prefer to have the option of employment. The idea of the universalism of a 'new man' model who nurtures intimacy and values his emotional side still remains too difficult for some people to accept.

Social workers are not the only profession whose work with 'parents' may actually mean, working with mothers. Fathers find difficulties, for example when visiting health visitors' clinics often known as 'mother and baby' clinics. Similarly a male reported spending two hours at a 'mother and toddler' group with his child. No one welcomed him and only one mother spoke to him.

Health visitors reported in the Southwark research that they hardly ever met fathers and even when they were in the house, the fathers very often remained in another room or left the house when the health visitor arrived. It is not clear whether this was because of the attitude of the health visitor or the parental expectations of the family.

Individual interviews in the Southwark research showed that intervention by a social worker and/or Section 47 enquiries (possible child abuse) often appeared to have a huge and unacknowledged impact on fathers and other male family members. The depth of male feelings of the father, and possible accused perpetrator, went unacknowledged. A middle-aged unwaged father articulated his own distress and confusion caused by the abuse on his son. He could not share or explore this with his other family members as each person could only deal with their own pain.

Cavanagh and Cree give some insight into one contributing factor to this reluctance by some to consider fathers. They argue that:

feminists thus exclude men and non-feminists do so by maintaining gender stereotypes

(Cavanagh and Cree, 1996, p3).

One of the voluntary agencies visited was Newpin who clearly saw their role as helping mothers. However, they acknowledged that fathers also might need help. In one location visited they had obtained funding to set up a separate group for men. As one worker noted 'we have the room, we have the staff, so all we need now is the men'.

The reluctance of men to identify that they might need help or to attend groups was confirmed by a project on men's health in Bristol where getting men to participate was extremely difficult. The Lawrence Weston Family Centre where 70 per cent of the children are on the Child Protection Register have become aware of the fundamental role of fathers. They have discovered that fathers' and children's groups seem to be the most successful way of engaging fathers because fathers feel excluded from mother-focused groups. They have engaged fathers by encouraging agencies to identify the needs of the father, as well as mothers at the referral stage; ensuring fathers are involved at all introductory visits and contact meetings. They also offer fathers a range of services at this initial stage. Parenting Education and Support Forum provide materials relevant to men as well as women; respecting both different family patterns and cultural diversity.

Fathers by tradition have been willing to come into schools so the answer may be that the role of schools need to change in order to develop a greater welfare role, additional to their present educational role, if fathers are to be involved in all aspects of child welfare.

There needs to be a complete shift in mindset of many of those working with parents to ensure the needs, opinions and role of fathers are included in all work wherever possible. This may mean not just changing attitudes but also work patterns and timings to ensure meetings and other programmes fit in with the needs of all the family. It is obvious that:

> *Supporting change in gender roles, identities and relationships, and in the sharing of family responsibilities, is one of the most important challenges facing European societies. Success or failure have major implications for children's welfare, gender equality, family functioning and effective use of human resources.*
>
> Fathers, Nurseries and Childcare, The Pen Green Centre.

The Way Forward

As we move into the 21st century, the structure of the family has changed, in many cases beyond recognition, from even that of say 30 years ago. Many families have been reconstituted not just once but several times. Cathy Hill (Chapter 13) mentions the different types of parenting groups in existence. There have been changes in the structure of employment, in housing development, in transport and travel and in the role of fathers.

These changes often mean that families no longer live in close knit communities supporting each other. Families who have moved house often do not have close friends around them for support. Those who suffer financial hardship, poor housing and education may be doubly deprived.

All this means that there is a need to re-think the role of parenting. In the first instance, parenting skills should again be taught in schools, including basic child care, budgeting, managing money, simple cookery as well as making and keeping friends.

Parenting programmes should adopt preventative approaches to families, with parents who might need help being identified early and help and/or education being offered before there is a problem. However, when it is considered appropriate for parents to need parenting education and support these should be aimed at creating a supportive environment and developing coping and independence skills.

The chapters in this book show what valuable work other people are doing. The aim for the future is that we should learn from each others' experiences and work together to ensure the future generation of children have the quality of life to which they are entitled. The best way for this to be achieved is through working in partnership with parents.

References

Cavanagh, K. and Cree, V.E. (Eds.) (1996). *Working with Men – Feminism and Social Work*. London: Routledge.

Health, Department of (1996). *Child Protection, Messages from Research*. London: HMSO.

Hellincckx, W., Colton, M., and Williams, M. (Eds.) (1999). *International Perspectives on Family Support*. Hampshire: Arena.

Kahn, T. (1996). *Fathers, Nurseries and Childcare*. Corby: The Pen Green Centre.

Nash, S., Waldman, J., and Wheal, A. (1996). *Information Needs of Families in Wiltshire*. Wiltshire: Wiltshire Joint Advisory Committee for Under Five's and the Community Council for Wiltshire.

Smith, C. (1997). *Developing Parenting Programmes*. London: Joseph Rowntree Foundation/National Children's Bureau.

Trevelyan, J. (1996). Father's Day. In *Health Visitor*, Volume 69, June 1996: p 213.

Waldman, J., and Wheal, A. (1996). *Children in Need Research Project for Southwark Council*. Southampton: University of Southampton.

Wheal, A., and Waldman, J. (1997). *Family and Friends who are Carers – Identifying the Training Needs of Carers and Social Workers*. A Research Project and Report. London: National Foster Care Association on behalf of the Department of Health.

SECTION ONE
General

1   Making Sense of Interventions: Stranger in a Strange Land*

Paul Tosey

Introduction

This chapter is a personal account of the experience of being a parent in a family in which there was agency intervention. I do not know what others' experience is like, or how different circumstances may affect its quality and characteristics. Nor do I have any knowledge of the professional literature about working with families.

While I cannot and do not intend to reveal full details of the circumstances, my situation was one in which several agencies, including the court welfare service and social services, became involved as a result of a civil process. It was complex and protracted, spanning some four years.

I found the last year and a half of that process in particular disturbing, exhausting, and at times frightening, although the process as a whole was also supportive and helpful. Probably, I have as many reasons to be grateful for the intervention as I have reasons for wishing it had never happened, but I certainly would not volunteer to go through the experience again. I would emphasise the positive aspects of the experience, but the emotional truth resides still in metaphors about juggernauts, nightmares and being devoured; about wanting to stop the world and get off.

More than two years on from the last 'official' event, I am still making sense of it all. How was it that I came to feel so despairing and so constricted, even when the outcome was helpful? How did the substantial efforts of so many well-intentioned professionals, some outstandingly generous and human, often feel like an abuse?

My purpose in writing, therefore, is in one sense to tell my own story, even to find out what my story is. I will not discuss here procedures, rights or statutes – that kind of information is better available elsewhere. More significantly, my story is only one dimension of the whole experience. Another dimension, which I might call the tacit experience, receives much less attention. I suspect this might be true for professionals as well as for people like myself.

This is intentionally my own story, not that of any other family member. I acknowledge that the impact of this type of process on any child involved should justifiably be the main focus of concern, but I only claim here to speak for myself, and from my personal experience. My aim is to map out what happened. What emotions did I experience? What metaphors and images characterise the experience? What did it teach me, and what did I need to learn in order to survive?

I do have a professional interest to declare. I work in higher education and my main role is within a course for people working as consultants to organisations – people whose job it is to make comparable types of intervention, albeit in different contexts, to that which I have found so unsettling to receive. One might see it as ironic, either a cosmic joke or cosmic justice perhaps, that a teacher should experience so vividly what his students take out into the world. But this irony has prompted some fruitful questions.

*with apologies to Robert Heinlein

A Role with No Name?

The first thing that strikes me is that I am not even sure what to call my role in this process, in terms of being a member of a system that receives an intervention. Formally I was a 'parent', a term that defines my role and status from the point of view of the legal and professional system. There is a set of labels for those who introduce interventions or who, broadly speaking, are agents (e.g. social worker, solicitor, court welfare officer).

But what term expresses the role of a participant in a system into which agencies are intervening? 'Participant' itself is too bland. 'Client' implies a more freely chosen contractual relationship. 'Recipient' is accurate in one sense but also feels too benign and passive (recipients do, of course, shape interventions and influence the outcomes of the whole process). 'Victim' would be even more inaccurate, inappropriate and too evaluative. Karpman's drama triangle (Stewart and Joines, 1987) can be a helpful way of looking at this type of situation. One point of that model is partly that all participants can occupy all of the roles at various times. No-one is constantly a victim, every party can be a persecutor and a rescuer too.

It seems to me that the predominant language available for describing and depicting the intervention process is the language of the professional system. My personal experience feels elusive, difficult to articulate, and perhaps liable to be lost, if I have to tell my story in the role of parent. I feel myself resisting this fiercely. 'Parent' is a true description and yes, I acted from the same responsibility, love and determination that any parent is likely to feel. But there are powerful expectations about how parents should act, think and feel. If the human being who is affected by an intervention is seen as no more than their parental behaviour, they are in some respects being stereotyped.

The experience of intervention can then be discounted; 'of course we understand how difficult the situation is for you'…Do you?

How come you understand when I don't understand it myself?

Knowing that I have experience that is difficult to name is disconcerting. It is like a vague feeling of nausea that is not distinct enough to label as an illness; or an atmosphere one feels in a room of people, but for which there is no name. This tacit dimension includes, but is more than, parental thoughts and feelings, just as my existence as a human being includes, but is more than, my parenting. There is an undertow of emotional and psychological experience that is more difficult to articulate and which can be more risky to express – I will explain why later.

Initially the nearest I could get was to portray the experience as one of dislocation, disorientation or displacement. Writing about it feels like a process of the recovery, not only in the usual sense of regaining health, but also in the sense of the recovering of something lost. I am giving form to my sense-making to see what it looks like, to size it and weigh it, rather than proclaiming it as something I knew all along.

In Temporary Exile

Let me start with an obvious pressure for a parent: there is a great deal of work involved. Over the years I had scores of meetings and visits to accommodate, many involving significant travel during the working week. There were telephone calls to take and to log, papers to read and to write, and files of correspondence to maintain. Court proceedings meant that I had many professionals and agencies, and a series of events, to keep track of.

In retrospect it seems that I had little choice but to put my main 'work' career partly on hold to engage in this parallel life in the legal and social service systems. It is a serious process with significant consequences, and I was unwilling to risk giving it too little attention. Its demands felt comparable to those of a second career and there were real costs to me in terms of my opportunity and energy for professional and domestic projects.

There is another layer beneath that of the obvious, practical demands, and it is this layer that I want to explore in this chapter. How these systems are designed to work in a formal sense is the kind of knowledge that could be written into an instruction manual. But understanding how they work in practice, and what it is like to be involved in them, is another issue altogether. What is this machinery, this process, in which one has suddenly become enmeshed? How big is it? Which parts affect me and concern me? Where do I have legitimate influence and authority? Where will I be seen as acting beyond my powers? What levers can I pull and where do I find them? What are the implications of this, that and the other event? What are the probable consequences of this choice, or of that decision? How, above all, do I understand what is happening?

A parent, especially one encountering these systems for the first time, cannot develop as complex and sophisticated a picture of their operations as a professional. Even with the general helpfulness shown by professionals, and just about all that I met were generous with their time and patient in giving explanations, they could not, in principle, tell me how it really worked. One is inevitably more dependent on others than one might like, and this contributes to a sense of disempowerment.

I remember my first experience of a court hearing. It was quite informal, held in the judge's chambers. He listened, then summed up with a number of principles and some specific items of agreement. Good, I thought, here is a useful framework. Then the written Order came through. It contained only the specifics, and none of the principles. By this time it had become clear that the principles had either been heard differently by others, or did not suit them. It felt essential to me that these should have been recorded and I was convinced that a mistake had been made. I talked to my solicitor about getting back to the Judge. This, however, was clearly not the done thing. A barrier had sprung up, blocking my way to what had seemed a very reasonable goal. I quickly became more alarmed. The process (albeit then at an early stage in terms of the total time scale) had already taken several months. I was horrified to realise that we might have to go through the same arguments, the same issues, again, and not for several months hence. Franz Kafka's 'The Trial' – in which the central character is arrested arbitrarily and then subjected to perplexing proceedings during which it is never clear what is happening – came to mind, and continued to do so over the following months and years.

Worse than a mistake that could be rectified, it appeared that this was how the legal system operated. I learned, through repeated experience, that what is said in court is far less significant than what is written down. I learnt that waiting, and more waiting, and tolerating postponements, is endemic, although at times things happen in a flash, so the waiting sets a deceptive pace. And yes, I feel it is a failing of the legal system that not only parents but all parties can be left in a predicament where something that appears to be largely settled remains unresolved, or can be unravelled, because of inadequate recording. As a parent in the system, however, I felt that my choices of response lay between resigning myself to this reality, becoming a cynic, or imploding with frustration.

So I suggest the 'instruction manual' metaphor is wholly inadequate. One arrives in this situation largely without wishing to do so, whether to be helped or to be investigated or both. I have to acknowledge that the initial entry into this experience was made voluntarily; neither the length of stay nor the depth of involvement were in any way anticipated or desired. The experience of a parent encountering the welfare and legal systems is, I believe, far more akin to a prolonged, involuntary visit to another country. Professionals and agencies have acquired taken-for granted knowledge that is the result of having inhabited their worlds for many years. However imperfect, it is the knowledge of a native. Parents find themselves suddenly in a bewildering, foreign territory; effectively they are in temporary exile.

As a parent, therefore, one is faced with needing quickly to learn enough of the language, know the geography and understand the culture. Professionals may give advice on how to be an effective citizen, but they themselves operate through a vast amount of tacit knowledge that is impossible to convey. There is also the fallacy of believing that indigenous peoples have some perfect, valid understanding of their world. Each one can only give a partial and particular view, a fragment of a postcard rather than the whole map.

Some people seem able to quickly understand how other worlds work. I take more time, though I think it unlikely that I am unusually slow. I need to have some things explained to me more than once, or preferably I need to experience them first hand in order to understand a verbal description. My first couple of visits to a court, for example, counted much more than any prior description in words.

I realise now just how much of the learning involved is effectively about orientating to the norms and criteria of the system, or of individuals and agencies within them. As an exile, I became immersed in trying to understand this new world, learning the language and discovering the rules of the culture. In effect this was a process of allowing the culture to incorporate me, and to some extent of losing rather than asserting control, even though at the time, I am sure I would have said that I was acting autonomously, aware of my rights, and doing my best to bring a legitimate influence to bear.

The Extended Family

Imagine that in this unfamiliar land the exile is looked after by some indigenous guides. They seem pleasant enough, they take a close interest in the family and act as potential friends. But soon one realises that they are also observing and assessing. This is not a land in which the exile is free to wander at will; in this country, the territory and the routes of travel are mostly patrolled. Ultimately, it is the guides who decide where visitors go and what they see. As I will mention later, they do not want visitors to hang around for too long.

Not only has the exile's family been transplanted into a new land and culture, but also they are no longer able to close their doors on the outside world. It is as if they are cohabiting with a new set of relatives and visitors. For when agencies are involved, one lives in a particular form of the extended family, and has to cope suddenly with new stimuli and demands.

For me, in the early days, professionals appeared relatively infrequently and encounters with them were more easily containable. But as time wore on and the situation had become complex, the professionals came to feel present psychologically in our home, as if a camera were perpetually trained on us. Our life became the proverbial open book. Everything felt open to scrutiny, everything potentially to be justified. Our actions and our characters were dissected and discussed by others whom we did not know, whom we had not invited into our home, yet who would have an immense influence on our lives. Our 'normal' family privacy vanished, and we were entangled in something which devoured our time and energy but felt largely out of our control.

Incidentally, it seems obvious to say so but not all 'natives' are of the same mind. I could differentiate cognitively between agencies, between the welfare and legal systems, although at times I would not be sure whether I was commenting on the agencies or on the particular individuals I met. Yet the overall effect, in terms of the experience of exile, is that there is more similarity than difference. Ultimately, all are members of the extended family, and the fact of their presence overrides the detail of duties, responsibilities and affiliations. Professionals have different factions and different outlooks, but nevertheless appear to hold a deeper membership of their cultures. For example, I became inured and resigned to the adversarial nature of the English judicial system. I experienced being cross-examined by a hostile barrister, intimidated and undermined so far as is allowable. Suddenly in an adjournment I saw my own barrister, those in opposition, and other professionals, exchanging banter and news. These people, of course, know each other – they are on the same circuit. At one level it was heartening to see them relate to each other in this human way; at another, it was a jolt back into the realisation that I was the stranger, the exile.

The Rules of the Kingdom

There are new cultural rules to observe while adjusting to this new country and the uncomfortable experience of being observed.

The first example is that one must maintain the impression that everything is more or less normal. Of course, this is crazy. Everything is not normal. The family is stretched, overburdened, and fearful of what is likely to happen. Any family that truly acts as if everything is normal is surely oblivious to reality.

Did you play with a toy when you were a child, a balancing toy like a fat skittle with a rounded base, and with a smiling face painted near the top? Push it and it wobbles like crazy, but eventually, if you leave it alone, it returns to an upright position. The family being observed and assessed is similarly poked and prodded to see what happens but rarely allowed to return to equilibrium. It cannot be stable because it keeps being pushed off balance, and yet

somehow it is expected to behave as if it had not been pushed at all.

I remember one visit when I had been working long hours and had been ill all day. I arrived home to find a professional on our doorstep – the visit had been arranged beforehand to meet the professional's timetable and diary, a piece of co-operation and accommodation that I soon regretted. However, being seen to co-operate is an important rule. This professional seemed uninterested in making allowances for the pressures of a busy family life. They did not make clear, despite being asked, what they wanted or how they intended to proceed. We were given no clear signals – were we being asked to carry on regardless? To engage in discussion? They set up, in my view, of course, an awkwardness and uncertainty that was only typical in the sense that we might respond in a similar way to any uncommunicative stranger in our home. Later when I read this professional's report, I was outraged to find the awkwardness of the atmosphere being cited as a characteristic of the family rather than the situation. You might counter this by saying that I would define it that way as it suits my agenda. Perhaps, I thought, they would have been more satisfied if we had put on a family performance, such as going out into the garden to pick daises together.

Such visitors seek assurance, apparently, that normality reigns. Yet in a situation like this, a family will begin to produce somewhat crazy behaviour in its efforts to remain sane. Through being visited and observed so much we ended up questioning ourselves and events more than I believe was healthy. We spent much time second-guessing, trying to work out what was going on, what the professionals were doing and thinking, and what events meant. Imagine that you have spent an hour talking with a social worker. They have shown interest in what you have been saying, but have been non-committal. They leave. You remember what has been said and begin to wonder – what did they make of that? And that? What did it mean when they raised their eyebrow? I have had experiences of realising that a professional had attached significant and, for me, skewed meaning to an innocuous remark made years previously. The remark was long gone but the interpretation had persisted and was still contributing, unchecked, to the professional's construction of the situation.

There are also rules about acceptable ways of expressing the emotional experience of being involved in this type of process. Through showing anxiety too strongly, parents can be labelled as 'neurotic' or 'paranoid'. Therefore one has to manage displays of anxiety, sensitive to the parameters that the professionals would consider to bound 'normality'. I noted above that engaging with this system can be like having a second career. Here one must be aware that there is a limit to the time and effort one can be seen to be investing, for fear of being labelled obsessional. Often it is more acceptable to express anxiety about, or on behalf of, a child; but again, not so much that as to appear over-anxious. Expressing anxiety for oneself, for example about appearing in court, must also be kept within limits.

Rarely can the terror of being caught up in this frightening process safely be given full expression to others involved in the same system. Intervention engages one in an anxiety-producing experience but disciplines one's response into an acceptable form – as if one were on a theme park ghost train but forbidden to scream. Take the experience of being interviewed by a social worker whose findings will go in a report to court. They seek co-operation and disclosure but do not disclose the thinking through which they form judgements. So the first message is to co-operate and disclose. They have the power to criticise a party for non-co-operation, because the rhetoric or rule is that co-operation is in the best interests of the ultimate client, the child. But they do not necessarily disclose what they are thinking and feeling. Similarly for the parent, disclosure can be risky because it can supply a professional who is so minded with potential ammunition. But the parent must not put themselves into the position of being seen to be reluctant to disclose, or failing to co-operate, as that is likely to be interpreted negatively.

As an exile, therefore, one is faced with a complex task of maintaining one's autonomy, identity and sanity without transgressing such cultural codes. This means that being heard can be hard. Exiles generally do not speak the language and at times there seems to be no option but to ignore injunctions to 'be co-operative' and 'be reasonable'. Sometimes, therefore, they resort to shouting in their anxiety to be understood, but in doing so they can be seen as unreasonable, aggressive or absurd. They emphasise their stories to have them noticed, but thereby make themselves vulnerable to discounting and labelling.

Encounters with the 'Undertoad'

A caring profession often has a shadow side, a layer of distress and difficulty, that can be brutal and destructive to participants, regardless of the conscious intentions of the professionals themselves. In John Irving's *The World According to Garp*, this was called the 'undertoad'; it is a hazard of the country that visitors may discern gradually, through hints and occasional glimpses, but is not talked about openly and is wholly excluded from the printed tourist guides.

Many professionals present themselves as 'caring'. On the surface, one wants to be dealing with professionals who are caring rather than uncaring. But professionals are not free to be caring alone, and this presentation gives a mixed message. Features such as those discussed here could be analysed conceptually using, for example, Argyris' (1988) notions of 'defensive routines', 'mixed messages' and 'undiscussability'; or Watzlawick's (1990) 'pathogenic communication', which builds on Bateson's (1973) 'double-bind' theory. It is the professional's job to do things that are going to upset people. They have to make judgements, to form arguments, to propose courses of action. 'Caringness' can, in this sense, function as a device for defending the agent against the anxiety (e.g. Menzies, 1970) of knowing that their work can lead to pain for others. It is like being a teacher who wants to be friendly with their students but cannot come to terms with being an assessor too.

At worst this is a treacherous caring, worn as a badge that says 'I'm not going to upset anybody', denying the possibility that people can get hurt and pretending the professional could not be the agent of harm. The parent who expresses concern about this may be confronted with a response such as 'but you don't have anything to worry about – do you?' I imagine there is a parallel, in that professionals usually must not overtly threaten the participant's 'cover' of being a good parent.

This is not intended to be an anti-professional account, a tirade against those human beings who work with families. I have experienced the process as painful as well as supportive, abusive as well as enabling. I suspect that professionals have a similar range of experiences. If I accept my own argument that 'natives' generally do not understand what it is like to be an exile then, surely, I must accept that the reverse holds true. I suspect that professionals feel their perceptions and behaviours are usually strongly shaped by institutional, legal, professional and other pressures, and that they might equally feel caught up within currents they cannot control. The whole I can see as a dance, some choreographed pattern in which the roles of professionals and `clients' are complementary, and in which their behaviours mirror each other and interlock.

Some professionals, however, brought an extra quality to their involvement, a quality of irony, by which I mean a capacity to be compassionate and to own the judgemental aspects of their role. This also entailed seeing more of the `three-dimensionality' of the exile and an awareness that some underlying issues could not be resolved by the institutionally-designed processes, whether legalistic or informal. This irony helps to avoid double binds since it includes, for example, an awareness that abnormal behaviour from parents could be attributable to the intervention process, and does not necessarily reflect parental deficiency.

Even while individuals may be caring and empathetic – and want to be, genuinely – the system as a whole is not. It cannot be. It is, metaphorically, a huge, monolithic creature, taken to hiding in shady recesses but occasionally parading its size and might, generally slow to act but periodically striking with terrifying speed. There is immense anxiety in the institutions that make up this system. Just think of all the distress, anxiety and horror they deal with. It soaks into the pores and, without a way to clean and clear it again, it seeps out quite unwarily. Add to that the pressures on the system – the threat of public exposure through the media, for example, of being damned in retrospect for a failure to be all-knowing, clairvoyant and infallible.

In such a context, especially with an adversarial legal system, protecting oneself from being wrong can become important for survival. It can be achieved, it appears, through demonstrating that someone else is to blame. However this is rarely done so explicitly. We experienced a kind of constant charade, in which there existed a tacit rule that nobody should be made explicitly to appear in the wrong, as it would be unfair and not constructive.

Yet at the same time the process was steeped in implications and inferences about whose actions could be justified and whose could not. And the nearer we came to the end of our stay, the more this mask was let slip, and the more vicious and desperate became the need to place blame. The undertoad can surface suddenly and powerfully.

Facing Deportation

The start of our final court proceedings began with a farcical process in which an available court was hunted down at the last minute, and this for a hearing that had been set months in advance. After narrowly avoiding a venue some 200 miles away, for which all would have been expected to make instantaneous arrangements to attend, we were placed in the Royal Courts of Justice, Strand.

The main entrance hall of the Royal Courts of Justice is one of those buildings designed, it seems, to make one feel humble. Once through the doorway the roof soars high, footsteps echo from the tiled floor, the benches and arched roof imply that this is a sacred place. The link between justice and divinity is direct and potent. Is this a court or a cathedral? Has one come to stand before a human judge, or to meet ones' maker?

After some four years altogether, our 'case' had begun to look too complex and unwieldy to resolve. It became clear that earlier 'solutions' were not working as well as had been intended. Many professionals seemed to have recognised that their interventions were not only being ineffective, but were also potentially counter-productive. There was a kind of panic, as if the issue had given the system indigestion. It was picked up and swallowed but could not be digested.

In retrospect this was a very instructive time about the workings of these systems. The attention of some seemed to switch from finding an actual resolution to seeking the least difficult way out – an exit point. We had overstayed our welcome. Perhaps we seemed to be settling down, or draining the local economy; whichever, it was time for us to leave. Some were in such a hurry as to want to see us deported forthwith.

It did become clear throughout the process that professionals on the whole have very circumscribed choices, and are likely to be very vulnerable themselves if they are seen to get something wrong. The danger here is the potential for professionals becoming interested only in the evidence that will support their view. From my perspective, the time leading up to the final hearing involved what I felt to be an act of betrayal that demonstrated forcibly the shadow side of caring. One of the exit routes being advocated necessitated a diametrically opposite view of my character and actions to that which had been taken in the past, and a sudden forgetting of much that was known about our situation. Suddenly, a level of informality and openness I had experienced was ended. I became acutely aware of sources of power available to agencies when the accessibility, informality and the possibility of influence vanished.

It was as if I had been semi-hypnotised, watching this machinery working over several years, then awoken suddenly to find myself in its jaws. Everything I did and said from this point on became framed to add to this character demolition. It now felt far too unsafe to disclose much of my feelings, a mirror, of course, of the way others were now behaving towards me. Yet this was construed as evidence of me being unco-operative and aggressive. Damned if I did, damned if I didn't – the essence of a double bind. I found myself portrayed variously as being too emotionally involved to be taken seriously ('Paul doesn't realise what we are trying to do' – I believe I realised only too well); as being destructive, and accused of manipulating agencies and their resources. I learnt more than ever before about standing up to being bullied, thanks to the help I received and to the fact that by no means all involved were swept up in this fervour.

Even so, I understand the need to find a way to end professional involvement. In hope or innocence, one might see the whole process as a rational one of seeking to identify the course of action that is best supported by the facts. But it seems equally a reality that the system from the start is under pressure to find an appropriate exit point. When this is achieved and the outcome is demonstrably in the best interests of the ultimate client, all are happy. However, elements of the system only have so many options to try, only so many resources they can use.

Implications: A Rough Guide?

We are no longer exiles in that kingdom. Yet we were not deported as abruptly as we had feared, indeed we had the good fortune to experience a dignified exit. So we returned wiser on the whole for our experience, yet at the cost of gaining many scars. We are unlikely to choose to venture out in that way again. The memories of the trip stay with us, like photographs and souvenirs cluttering the house. Like most people we clear things out periodically.

I do not have any answers to how this system should be, nor any easy way to guide people like myself through it. But I have two recommendations which could help those who share this experience of exile, and could inform and sensitize the professionals whom they encounter.

Write Your Own Travelogue: The Iceberg Analogy

The first is for people to find their own stories, and become the authors of their own travelogues rather than characters in someone else's tour guide. As I have argued, professionals' understandings and accounts of the experiences of parents and families are inevitably different and distorted. This happens in many fields. For all the literature on organisational change, relatively little research has been done into the experiences of people during processes of organisational change. It mirrors the situation in fields such as counselling, where practitioner 'tales' are predominant. Work to elicit and represent voices has perhaps more prominence where those 'silenced' are identifiable as an oppressed or marginalised group. In my view, this difference can be reduced, but not overcome, by empathy. Professional definitions of reality seemed to attenuate my emotional experience, and to steer me

towards roles, behaviour and even feelings that are acceptable and manageable.

To produce my story, to know what is in it and to have it heard, can itself be seen as empowering, an act of defiance. Like an iceberg, a substantial, but relatively small, part of the experience is above the surface. More significant is what lies beneath the surface, the tacit experience of the undertoad, the second-guessing, the mixed messages and so on.

The prime need here is to be sharp and sensitive, alert to the subtle, jarring effect of being labelled, placed in a double bind, or encouraged to express only part of one's anxiety. This is like a fog that descends almost unnoticed, until one realises that one cannot see the way and has come to rely on others to act as guides. I found personal psychotherapy a great help, as a place where I could go to re-establish my sense of reality. It was like cleansing my perception from the fog, finding the truth of my emotional experience, and simply shedding some of the distress of the whole process.

Whatever source of such help one finds, whether through counselling, religious faith or a friend to confide in, it feels paramount to access a sense that the intervention process is not the whole of life. The help I obtained also enabled me to look at my part in the process, and my part in producing my own anxiety. For example, I realised that I wanted a solution to take away the difficulty, the fear and the conflict. The adversarial nature of the system, with trappings that for the lay person appear largely indistinguishable from those of criminal law, inevitably promotes the impression of justice as rewarding virtue and punishing malice. It can then be difficult to separate the prospect of 'loss' in that system's terms from a sense of failure and even shame. Yet it is crucial to do so; I recall Kipling's words about victory and defeat both being impostors. Perhaps exiles seek stories that allow them dignity, rather than making them right in the eyes of the system.

Excess Baggage: False Hopes to Leave Behind

Secondly, there are some beliefs or assumptions that exiles will not need – they should use their luggage space for something more useful. Professionals might consider how they could be fostering these beliefs unwittingly, or how they react when they encounter them.

1. The belief that family life is private

We live in a society in which, broadly, there is a belief in the privacy of family life. This is not an absolute – there is no ultimate right of families to privacy, or any ultimate reason why this should be the case. But an intervention into the family system, in this society, violates our sense of what is right and normal and this can compound the impact. I ask myself here, is my story that of a middle class white male bemoaning a constraint on the freedom he is used to? How many others experience such constraints routinely and daily, as a result of their gender, race or class?

2. The belief that one can rely on the system to be rational, caring or fair

This is not to say that the system, or the people within it will necessarily be unfair, merely that it is unwise to rely on that. As the Sufi saying goes, 'trust in Allah, but tether your camel'. The capacity of the system for fairness and rationality is often beyond the influence of any individual actor. I must add that many people I met gave me good cause for confidence in the system of justice.

3. The belief that professionals will take care of parents' needs

Professionals are helpful, they do care, even given the caveats I have noted about 'caringness' – but it is not their job to meet a parent's needs. They have their own needs, duties and responsibilities. Meeting a parent's needs is up to the parent, but there are pressures to assume that one's needs are being taken care of, or that one can rely on others to do this.

4. The belief that professionals understand what parents are experiencing

For the reasons I have described above, I would assume that nobody else truly understands what the exiled person is experiencing. First, there is the issue that there is no 'name' for this experience. Second, most professionals have probably not been in that position, nor in any comparable position. Third, the nature of the system is such that it could suit other people at times to pigeon-hole or label the exile, or to see them as two-dimensional. The focus of the whole system on the needs of children is a wholly desirable principle. However, this can shift from seeing other family members' needs as a lesser priority, to seeing them as insignificant, their anxieties essentially self-centred and likely to detract from children's interests.

5. The belief that professionals have the power to change things

As a parent one is dealing with individual people and with huge, cross-professional, multi-institutional, national systems, at one and the same time. The reality is that one is at the intersection of these systems. It is not a comfortable place to dwell; the friction as they chafe together is enormous and intense. If one focuses only on the interpersonal dimension and the individuals involved, one risks over-personalising the process. If one views the experience as being primarily about the wider systems, then one risks casting oneself as the 'victim' of that system. In truth all actors are dealing with a huge and often graceless vehicle, in which effective influence may take extraordinary acts of courage or turns of fortune.

Conclusion

A contemporary myth is that people dislike change. I wonder whether it would be more accurate to say that people dislike the effects of interventions. It seems that all involved, professionals and 'participants' alike, are caught in the dilemma that the cure might be worse than the disease (Senge, 1990), and that all would be happier if intervention were not needed.

Here I have tried to unravel some of the tacit experience incurred in the (undefined) role of participant in a process of family intervention. My argument is that all parties probably have comparable experience at the tacit level, but that it is routinely masked, denied or discouraged from being expressed, to the detriment of all concerned. I do wonder how the systems can change without dialogue about the human experience of all who are involved.

I have likened the experience to that of being a stranger in a strange land. The sense of disorientation, and the subsequent need for learning, are far closer to what would be involved in temporary exile to an unfamiliar country, than in the reading of a book of instructions. I acknowledge that my story dwells on, and is coloured by, what felt like a traumatic time. Even so, I speculate that the metaphor of the exile might reflect undercurrents of the experiences of many family members, and also might prove an insight for those whose task it is to intervene.

Acknowledgements

My thanks go to all those who were supportive during the experiences referred to above, those who have helped with the sense-making, and those who have been kind enough to read and comment on drafts of this chapter.

References

Argyris, C. (1992). *On Organisational Learning*. Oxford: Blackwell.

Argyris, C. (1988). *First- and Second-order Errors in Managing Strategic Change: The Role of Organisational Defensive Routines*, Review Essay.

Bateson, G. (1973). *Steps to an Ecology of Mind*. London: Paladin, Granada.

Heinlein, R. (1992 Edn.) *Stranger in a Strange Land*. Hodder and Stoughton (New English Library).

Hillman, J. (1996). *The Soul's Code*. Toronto: Bantam Books.

Irving, J. (1986). *The World According to Garp*. Black Swan.

Menzies, I. (1970). *The Functioning of Social Systems as a Defence Against Anxiety*. London: Paper of the Tavistock Institute of Human Relations.

Mezirow, J. (1991). *Transformative Dimensions of Adult Learning*. San Francisco: Jossey-Bass.

Pettigrew, A.M. (1988). *The Management of Strategic Change*, pp 342–351. Oxford: Blackwell.

Senge, P. (1990). *The Fifth Discipline*. London: Century Business, Random Century.

Stewart, I., and Joines, V. (1987). *TA Today: A New Introduction to Transactional Analysis*. Nottingham: Lifespace.

Watzlawick, P. (1990). *Münchhausen's Pigtail*. New York: W.W. Norton & Co.

2 ...You're Walking on Eggs: Findings from Research into Parenting

Ann Buchanan

Introduction

As anyone who has children knows, the moment you give birth to your first child, the world and his wife descends with 'helpful' advice. Lying in your bed, you decide in the euphoria of the moment, that is if you wanted the baby in the first place, that you are going to be the Madonna Mother...the best ever. So you listen. You leave hospital and take this tiny bundle back home. Struggling with breast feeding, since 'breast is best' despite inverted nipples, the sleepless nights and a baby who cries non stop, which is only 'colic' they say, and a partner who is hands-on – how on earth do you manage on your own? – you are quickly overcome by an increasing sense of inadequacy. Rapidly the 'helpful' advice increases these feelings. Despite your best efforts you are 'guilty' because you are not a Madonna. Guilt spreads like a disease. However hard you try, mother or father, you can never do enough. Whatever goes wrong, you are to blame... ahead of you is at least eighteen years of feeling guilty.

So what do parents do? In the difficult and demanding task of bringing up children, you quickly discover that you are not perfect and never can be. What is more, you learn that along the road you have to look after yourself. You have needs and selfish desires of your own; you are going to do what you are going to do, and somewhere along the road the children will have to take second place. We cannot cope with too close a scrutiny on our shortcomings, so we shut the door to the world, his wife and the 'helpful' advice. Behind the closed door, in the private world of our family, tensions may develop. If the going gets too rough, one of us may break out and leave. The last thing we want

is 'help' because now we know we are really 'in the wrong'.

So working with parents is like walking on eggs. The challenge is to support parents without fracturing their already fragile confidence. Add poverty, poor housing, racism, and all the other stresses that disadvantaged families face, surviving is hard enough without well-meaning professionals telling parents where they are failing.

This then is the starting point for working with parents. Whatever their additional problems, parents are parents first with all the guilt and anxieties of all parents. If we are to help them we need to obtain their trust; that they are safe to share with us the most intimate parts of their life.

The oft forgotten truth is that those seeking to help can also harm. In the US, there is the famous Cambridge Somerville study. Boys at risk of delinquency were linked to well-meaning mentors. Many years later it was found, in a highly significant result, that the boys with the mentors were more likely to have been in trouble than those without. It makes sense, therefore, that those working with families, work from an evidence-base that is cognisant of the more reliable findings from research.

This chapter will look at three dimensions of parenting research. The first section explores the government response; the second picks up some general themes from parenting research that may be helpful when working with parents, and the final section looks at the findings from specific projects that support families.

A Non-stigmatising Approach

Parents are very sensitive to the help they are offered and any approach that induces feelings of failure may mean the help is rejected. Under the Children Act 1989, parents are not obliged to accept the support offered unless there are child protection concerns.

Barlow (1998) in her systematic review of 255 studies on parent training, notes the high drop out rate seen in many studies. The average drop out from parent training programmes is 28 per cent and in one study the drop out rate was as high as 41 per cent. Those most likely to drop out were parents whose children had more presenting problems, mothers under great stress, ethnic minorities and families at great socio-economic disadvantage.

Researchers from the Centre for Research in Parenting at Oxford concluded in a recent book:

> All contributors to this book agree that a culture of 'blaming' the parents is unhelpful. Indeed the heightened sense of guilt associated with feelings of failure may, in the extreme cases, be associated with child maltreatment.
>
> (Buchanan, A. 1998.)

The present government has taken this message on board. Whereas under the previous government in the UK, family failings were seen as related to individual psychopathology, this government appears more sensitive to the stresses and strains that all parents (including the Home Secretary with his son's drug conviction) experience. The recent Green Paper from the Home Office, Supporting Families notes:

> Governments have to be wary about intervening in areas of private life and intimate emotion. The rest of the population is meeting the challenge of family life. They are not.
>
> (Home Office, 1999 (p 4))

> …parents do not want lectures from the state, or to be nagged or nannied…except in exceptional circumstances, where the well-being of family members is at stake, it must be the decision of the parents when to ask for help and advice. (p 6)

> …Parenting support is relevant to all parents, regardless of their circumstances. We want to change the culture so that seeking advice and help when it is needed is seen not as a failure but the action of concerned and responsible parents. (p 7)

There is also a greater willingness under the present government in the UK to appreciate that parenting is harder when you are poor:

> Improving family prosperity, reducing child poverty and ensuring that the tax and benefit system properly acknowledges the cost of bringing up children

is one of the five areas in which government recognises that it can make a difference.

The Government makes an exception, however, when it comes to young offenders.

> The Crime and Disorder Bill will establish a new parenting order designed to help and support parents to control the behaviour of their children…The order will be available for parents of convicted young offenders, for parents of children who have been made the subject of an anti-social behaviour order, sex offender order or child safety order and for parents who have been convicted of failing to send their children to school.

> The parenting order will require the parent to attend counselling or guidance sessions no more than once a week and for no longer than three months. If courts think this necessary, they may also impose additional requirements on parents – for example, seeing that their child gets to school every day, or ensuring that they are home by a certain time at night – which may apply for up to a year.

The evidence given for this approach is largely based on the success of 'voluntary' parenting support work such as Home Start, and Parent Network. One wonders how well a 'compulsory' Parenting Order will work?

Some General Themes From Parenting Research

The good news for the new parent, as they crumble under the bombardment of advice, is that parents do not have to be perfect for children to turn out OK. Many years ago, Winnicott coined the expression 'good enough parenting'. In the Children Act 1989 this idea is developed further. In the Act the concept of '*good enough parenting*' per se is omitted, although you could argue that this is reflected in the grounds for a care order.

The Court can only make a care order or a supervision order if it is satisfied that:

a) the child concerned is suffering, or is likely to suffer, significant harm: and

b) the harm, or likelihood of harm, is attributable to:

> *The care given to the child…not being what it would be reasonable to expect a parent to give him…*
>
> Children Act 1989 S31 (2) (b) (i).

Most of the emphasis in the Children Act 1989 in Part III, the section devoted to family support, is meeting the needs of a child whose health or development may be impaired. This implies that, rather than one universal standard of 'good enough parenting' different children have different needs at different times. The stimulation needs of a baby with Downs' syndrome, for example, will be greater than for a child without such a disability because the child who has Downs' Syndrome who has good stimulation in the early months is likely to make more progress developmentally.

Most Children Can 'Recover'

Mostly, however, and contrary to the early Freudian idea that a child's future was set in stone by their early experiences, there is now a more flexible view. Early attachments may be the prototype for later attachments but things can change. Attachment is now felt to be a lifelong developmental task and with better care and more sensitive parenting even the most 'anxiously attached' child can become 'securely attached'. (Crittenden and Ainsworth, 1989.)

Another strongly held view is that divorce and family breakdown inevitably damages a child. An important review by Rodgers and Pryor (1998) examined the findings over 200 studies. Their conclusion was that although children whose parents stayed together generally did better educationally, emotionally and in making the transition to adult life, most children whose parents separated did not, in the long term, experience irreparable damage, although there was the inevitable distress around the separation or divorce.

Research in this area is suggesting that if families cannot stay together there are better and worse ways of separating. Children do better where parental separation is amicable and possibly where they can continue to see both parents. We know that in cases of domestic violence, children, even when not directly involved in the violence, suffer. It is possible that where conflict continues after the separation and the children are 'caught in the middle' this is particularly damaging for children. In these circumstances it is arguable whether contact with the absent parent is always in the child's best interests.

Parents Are Not Responsible For All Their Children's Problems

Further good news for parents is that they are not responsible for all the troubles their children get into. Bronfenbrenner showed that children's development is an interaction between four systems. First there is the child. Every mother will tell you that each of her children is different. Maybe she has had some role in fashioning this difference, but each child is born with their own unique genetic make-up, which interacts with their environment to make them the person they are.

Secondly there is the family: parents and brothers and sisters. Families develop their own way of interacting with each other and within the family it may be different for each child. Thirdly, there is the community in which the child lives and the schools they attend. The community and the child's peers, particularly in adolescence, is as powerful an influence on a child as is the school and their family.

Finally, there is the wider social system in which the child is brought up. This may be during a time of economic recession when large numbers of people are out of work, or it may be a time of prosperity. As the child treads his developmental pathway through his growing-up years, there will be risk and protective factors within each system that will impinge on them and the person they become. Certainly the parental influence will be strong, but so are the other influences.

Both Parents and Children Act on Their World

In good times and in bad, parents and children are not placid recipients of life's adversities. They act on their world. The child interacts with his mother and father and to some extent how they get on with them will be related to the 'goodness of fit' between the two. Some parents will find a particular child hard to handle but another parent may find the same child no problem. A difficult relationship with one parent may be compensated for by a positive one with another.

Most parents also 'act' on the school and on the community. They attend parents meetings and try to better their child's educational opportunities; they seek out recreational activities to foster their child's strengths or compensate for their weaknesses.

Research validates these informal approaches. Longitudinal research shows that risks to a child's development can be compensated by protective experiences. Some parents however, may be less assertive at 'acting' on their world. Working with parents may involve supporting them to obtain compensatory experiences for their child. The severely depressed mother may need help in obtaining a place for her toddler at the local nursery so that the toddler obtains the stimulation necessary for development.

Family Togetherness Matters

Parenting research is also showing that it is not so much the outside structure of the family, whether you are divorced, step, lone, widowed, but what happens inside the family that makes the difference.

Studies from the West of Scotland have shown that 'families who do things together' ('family togetherness') are less likely to have adolescents who are involved in a range of problem behaviour such as substance abuse. (Sweeting and West, 1995.) In longitudinal research based on the National Child Development Study, children whose fathers read to them as a child, or children whose mothers took them on outings as a child, were protected against depression at age 33. It is uncertain why 'family togetherness' is so powerful. It may be that the father who read to his child at seven was taking an interest in the child's education. We know from other research that parental interest in children's education is an important predictor of academic achievement. (Mortimer *et al.*, 1998.) Spending time doing enjoyable things together may give young people an opportunity to talk to their parents who can model their life skills in an informal way. In a further study 'family togetherness' was defined as parents who ate meals together, visited family and friends together and went for walks or played sport together. Only 7 per cent of children in these families were alienated from school compared to 33 per cent in the low family togetherness families; only 5 per cent suffered from depression compared to 24 per cent in the other families and 14 per cent had been in trouble with the police compared to 35 per cent in the low family togetherness. (Katz, Buchanan and McCoy, 1999.)

Parenting Style is Also Important

Another strong message is that parenting style matters. A survey of young people's views showed that young people with high self-esteem when compared to young people with low self-esteem were more likely to have parents who listened to their problems and views; who encouraged them to make their own decisions. They were also less likely to have parents who ignored them or were who were very controlling. Young people, however, valued being given guidance and boys in particular wanted there to be some rules.

On the other hand, punitive parenting had very poor results. Low self-esteem boys were more likely to have been smacked or beaten at lot; more likely to have experienced violence. The evidence is growing that smacking does not work, and in addition actually causes children psychological harm.

Father Involvement

After the generation of Germaine Greer and superwomen like Nicola Horlicks, there is an emerging realisation that whatever your moral stance, parenting is easier if there are two to do the work. The value of the hands-on father has been discovered.

This has been reinforced by another discovery. Boys who have 'involved' fathers or father-figures, when compared to those without such involvement are less likely to be alienated from school, less likely to be involved in crime and less likely to suffer from depression or suicidal thoughts. An 'involved' father is one who spends time with his son; listens to his worries and concerns and takes an interest in his schoolwork. (Katz, Buchanan and McCoy, 1999.)

Implications for Practice

What are the implications of these findings for working with parents? Firstly, parents may find it helpful to know what research is saying. It may be helpful to explode some of the myths that fill our parents with debilitating guilt. When I was working as a practitioner I used to say to parents 'lets put the guilt out of the window…it gets in the way of being a parent and doing what you know you have to do'. So what are the helpful messages for parents from research?

Parents do not have to be perfect; it need not be a disaster if you separate or divorce. Parents are not responsible for all their children's problems, but there is quite a lot you can do to make things better for your child in an imperfect world. Doing things with children and having a good time together is as important as parenting style. Fathers, or father figures can make all the difference, especially to boys. If one is not readily available for every child, there is much those trying to help families can do by having some male father type role models around.

What Works? – Evidence From Parenting Projects

Home visiting around the birth of a child

Parents appear to be more accepting of help and advice at particular times. Despite the portrayal of the young mother at the beginning of this chapter, around the birth of a child, particularly a first child, the parent is open to help. Some of the most useful parenting projects make a personal link with the mother before the baby is born. This person then visits the parent over the first two years. In the US the Olds and Henderson study of home visiting, targeted at disadvantaged mothers, has proved a very successful model for improving the well being of potentially maltreated children. Home visits were made by nurses. There was developmental screening and a sharing of basic developmental knowledge. Practical support was also provided for family problems and help was given to develop supportive networks.

Projects for fathers

With the rediscovery of fathers, interest is heightened about work with fathers. Around the country there are now a number of projects involving fathers. A study in the north east undertook an audit of all fathers' projects. They found that there was a need for different groups and different methods to engage different types of fathers; family centres were not felt to be good venues as they could be too 'women' focused; father's groups need men facilitators who need to work on promoting the role of fathers. (Richardson, 1998.) A network of workers with fathers is developing and these workers are exchanging knowledge and skills.

Parenting support with an education focus

There is some suggestion that projects that work with parents to promote children's education may be less stigmatising and thereby more acceptable to parents. In Oxford, PEEP (see glossary) is an interesting example of an education focused pre-school project that includes the whole catchment area of a secondary school covering three highly disadvantaged areas. The project, using a structured curriculum, works in partnership with parents, who are seen as the child's first educators. Names of all new-born babies are obtained from the local maternity hospital. There are weekly *Baby PEEP* sessions when the baby is about six weeks old, then *Small PEEP* (1–2 years), *Big PEEP* (2–3 years), and finally *Nursery PEEP* (4–5 years). Each level has different toys and books to borrow, along with various ideas and suggestions for what activities can be done at home. Twenty-three languages are spoken by PEEP families. Translations are made of materials, diversity is valued.

Structured parenting programmes teaching child development and behavioural management

The research is ambivalent about the benefits for parents of unstructured parenting programmes. (Durlak, 1997.) There is however, considerable evidence that the Webster-Stratton programmes, if presented in a positive, non-stigmatising setting, can be very helpful, especially with children with behavioural problems. Using her programmes, the behaviour of around two-thirds of children taking part will improve. The programmes are fun and presented in Stratton ways that engage the child and parents.

Barlow has also undertaken a useful review of studies. She notes that broadly speaking there are two types of parenting training programmes: 'relationship' and 'behavioural'. Programmes based on cognitive behavioural principles are consistently shown to be more effective than other types of programmes. (Barlow, 1998.) This links with other research showing that change in children and parents is better effected by teaching strategies and skills rather than by unfocused counselling. (Buchanan)

Home visiting by volunteers

One of the anxieties when working with parents is that the families most in need of help are those least likely to attend a family centre or other resource for family support. In recognition of this, many family centres now run an outreach service.

One service that has been evaluated and shown to be helpful is the Home-Start initiative. This voluntary organisation trains volunteers who offer practical support, friendship and help to families with young children, who are under stress, in their own homes. Each scheme adopts the Home-Start standard and methods of practice and is managed by a multi-disciplinary committee supported by the national organisation Home-Start UK. In the evaluation more than half of the mothers felt their emotional well-being and parenting skills had been increased.

Evaluating What We Do

In the UK, very few interventions have been rigorously evaluated. This means that we have to rely on studies undertaken in the US or elsewhere to indicate what approaches might be effective in the UK. This is clearly unsatisfactory. In medicine it would be unacceptable to prescribe a medicine without that medicine having undergone rigorous trials in each country. All of us working with parents have a responsibility, in however a humble way, to evaluate what we are doing. This need not be large-scale research. It is simply a question of taking a measure before we intervene. Afterwards, simple checklists that take only 5–10 minutes to complete can be used to check out that what we are doing is producing some positive change in a child. One of these checklists is the Goodman Strengths/Difficulties questionnaire.

Conclusion

The parents with whom we work professionally are parents first, with all the anxieties, guilt and the need to keep their private lives private, that all parents experience.

In addition, the parents with whom we work may have experienced more than their share of life's adversities, which will have further bruised their fragile confidence. If we as helpers are to work effectively with such parents we need to tread carefully to gain their trust. Without this trust, no matter what approach we use, our efforts will fall on stony ground and may actually cause harm.

Once we have gained precious trust, we have a duty to ensure that the interventions

we use are those with the best chance of helping. Ethically we have no right to be involved unless we have done our homework.

References

Barlow, J. (1998). Parent Training Programmes. Findings from a Systematic Review. In Buchanan, A. and Hudson, B.L. *Parenting, Schooling and Children's Behaviour*. Aldershot: Ashgate.

Bronfenbrenner, U. (1979). *The Ecology of Human Development, Experiments in Nature and Design*. Cambridge, MA: Harvard University Press.

Buchanan, A., and Hudson, B.L. *Parenting, Schooling and Children's Behaviour*. Aldershot: Ashgate.

Buchanan, A. (1993). *Cycles of Child Maltreatment*. Chichester: John Wiley and Sons, Ltd.

Buchanan, A., and Ten Brinke, J.A. *Recovery' from Emotional and Behavioural Problems*. NHS.

Buchanan, A. (1998). A Census. In Buchanan A., and Hudson B.L. (1998). *Parenting, Schooling and Children's Behaviour*. Aldershot: Ashgate.

Chess, S., and Thomas, A. (1990). *Continuities and Discontinuities in Temperament*.

Crittenden, P.M., and Ainsworth, M.D. (1989), Child Maltreatment and Attachment Theory. In Cicchetti, D., and Carlson, V. (Eds.). *Child Maltreatment: Theory and Research on the Causes and Consequences of Child Abuse and Neglect*. Cambridge: Cambridge University Press.

Durlak, J.A. (1997). *Successful Prevention Programmes for Children and Adolescents*. Plenum.

Goodman, R. (1997). The Strengths/Difficulties Questionnaire. *Journal of Child Psychology and Psychiatry*, 38; 5: 581–586 (or in a pack from the Institute of Psychiatry, London).

Home Office (1999). *Supporting Families: A Consultation document*. Home Office.

Katz, A., Buchanan, A., and McCoy, A. (1999). *Leading Lads*. Young Voice. Arcadia, University of Oxford.

Kitz, H., Olds, D.L., Henderson, C.R. *et al.* (1997). Effects of Prenatal and Infancy Home Visitation by Nurses on Pregnancy Outcomes, Childhood Injuries and Repeated Childbearing. A Randomised Controlled Trial. *JAMA*, 278: 644–52.

Mortimer, P., Sammons, P., Stoll, L., Lewis, D., and Ecob, R. (1988). *School Matters: The Junior Years*. Wells, Somerset: Open Books.

Olds, D.L. *et al.* (1997). Long-term Effects of Home Visitation on Maternal Life Course and Child Abuse and Neglect. Fifteen Year Follow-up of Randomised Trial. *Journal of American Medical Association*, 278: 637–643.

Richardson, A.J. (1998). *Fathers Plus, an Audit of Work with Fathers Throughout the North East of England*. Children North-East.

Robins, L., and Rutter, M. (Eds.). *Straight and Devious Pathways to Adulthood*. Cambridge.

Rodgers, B., and Pryor, J. (1998). *Separation and Divorce.* York: Joseph Rowntree.

Sweeting, H., and West, P. (1995). Family Life and Health in Adolescence. A Role for Culture in Health Inequalities Debate? *Social Science and Medicine*, 4(2): 163–175.

Webster-Stratton, C. (1992). *The Incredible Years: A Trouble-shooting Guide for Parents of Children Aged 3–8.* Toronto: Umbrella Press.

3 Balancing Independence with Empathy: The Challenge of Meaningful and Purposeful Partnership with Parents whose Children are the Subjects of Public Law Proceedings

Maria Ruegger

Guardians ad litem (may be known as Litigation Friend in the future) work with parents at a time of great crisis in their lives, when they are involved in public law court proceedings that could lead to their children being removed from their care, either temporarily, or perhaps permanently. It is my intention in this chapter to share with readers those aspects of legislation, research and practice wisdom that together provide the framework within which guardians conduct their work with parents.

I will first explain the role of the guardian and describe the legal and practice context in which the work undertaken with parents occurs. I will also examine the knowledge and research which underpins the legislative framework within which guardians work, and which determines what constitutes good practice. Through identifying the context of good practice I hope to enable the reader to make sense of the practice described, to relate the issues for practice to their own work situations and to consider the wider applicability of this practice to other professionals whose work brings them into contact with vulnerable parents at times of crisis in their lives.

I will argue that effective practice requires that professionals gain a deep understanding of parents' worlds, and of their experience of the services we provide from their own perspective. To do so is not easy. It requires us to critically evaluate what we offer to families and to shift the focus from finding evidence to justify our actions to taking a broad and humanistic approach to our work. It involves setting aside the structures with

which we are comfortable and to which the temptation is to make our clients fit. Questions such as 'do they, or do they not, fit the criteria for registration or the threshold criteria in care proceedings', need to be preceded by a real understanding of families' needs, and an honest attempt to meet them; the embodiment of anti-oppressive practice. To conclude I will demonstrate the advantages for families and professionals of working in a meaningful partnership with parents from the initial point of contact to the conclusion of court proceedings, whatever the outcome.

The Guardian's Role

Children who are subjects of public law court proceedings have their interests safeguarded by an independent child care professional, the Guardian ad Litem.

The guardian service sets out to safeguard and promote the interests of the child by providing independent social work investigation and advice to the courts on care, child protection, adoption and related proceedings (Department of Health 1996).

Public law proceedings are those which arise when the state wishes to intervene in the arrangements made by parents for the care of their children. It is local authority social services departments that have statutory duties to safeguard and promote children's welfare on behalf of the state. If, in the opinion of its officers, a child is suffering harm attributable to the care he is receiving, then the local authority can apply to the court for permission to exercise parental responsibility for that child. In doing so, the local authority is usually planning to remove the child from its family, possibly temporarily, in the hope that standards of parenting improve and the child can be returned. Often, however, it is anticipated that the removal will be permanent, with the expectation that the child will be found a substitute family.

Clearly the advent of public law proceedings for any family is likely to be extremely traumatic. Parents are typically distraught at the prospect of losing their children and are often angry with social workers, family centre workers and others that are likely to have been involved in assisting them for some considerable periods of time prior to court proceedings being initiated. The children concerned will likely have suffered serious harm and may be torn between the conflicting emotions arising from family loyalty, distress as a result of their situation and fear of the unknown. The decisions that must be made will be made by judges and magistrates with whom the child is unlikely to have any direct relationship and whom they will not meet. It is the guardian ad litem's primary task to represent children's interests in the court proceedings. The guardian is also responsible for ensuring that the child's views are elicited and made known to the judges and magistrates, and that the child is informed of the process of their case through the court.

The Conceptual Framework for the Guardian's Investigation

The guardian must conduct their own investigation into the circumstances of the case and assist the court by making recommendations as to the outcome in the light of what is considered to be in the best interests of the child concerned. Guardians are guided in their practice by the principles underpinning the legal framework within which they operate. One key principle is that which is embodied in S17 (1) of the Children Act (1989). It states:

> It shall be the general duty of every local authority ...to safeguard and promote the welfare of children within their area who are in need; and so far as is consistent with that duty to promote the upbringing of such children by their families, by providing a range and level of services appropriate to those children's needs.

In support of this duty, local authorities are required to provide services to support families in their care of children, and to take reasonable steps through the provision of services to reduce the need to bring proceedings for care and supervision orders. The kinds of services envisaged by Parliament include advice, counselling, guidance, help in the home and family centres. Local authorities are further required to provide day care, after school and holiday care for children in need. They must have regard to the needs of different racial groups in making such provision, (schedule 2, paragraph 11). A further responsibility for local authorities concerns the duty to provide accommodation for children in need who require it, (S20 (1)). It is intended that accommodation should be provided as a service to all parents of children who satisfy the criteria, which they may use, or refuse, as they think best.

In legislation and associated guidance Parliament has made it clear that parents should retain the power to make decisions about their children unless local authorities successfully apply to the court for an order restricting their decision making powers. Before granting such an order the court will need to be satisfied that the child has suffered, or is likely to suffer, significant harm as a result of the care provided to him, and, that it is better for the child that an order be made in respect of him than making no order. White *et al*, (1990) point out that this 'no order' principle can be seen as 'part of an underlying philosophy of the 1989 Act, namely, to respect the integrity and independence of the family save where court orders have some positive contribution to make towards the child's welfare'.

Thus the relevant statutory guidance under which the guardian operates in work with parents upholds the principle of non-interference in family life except where the interests of a child's welfare clearly require this and the relevant criteria have been established. The legislation is based on clear and strong messages emanating from the research on which it is based which shows that children are likely to do better when brought up within their own families. Parliament has sought to ensure that where possible, children are given the opportunity to be cared for by their families by laying upon local authorities a range of responsibilities and duties aimed at supporting vulnerable parents in the care of their children. The guardian must consider whether parents have received appropriate services in the light of the clear expectations laid upon local authorities to provide such services. The guardian will want to know about the kind and quality of the services the family have received, whether there was any shared understanding as to the nature of the difficulties the family were experiencing, and if any agreement was made between parents and social workers in order to resolve them.

A study by Gibbons, Conroy and Bell (1995) which looked at the detail of what happens to children and families within the child protection system revealed that the greater proportion of social work time and resources in child protection is allocated to investigations of suspected abuse, many of which come to nothing. The estimations of Gibbons and her colleagues suggest that there are approximately 160,000 referrals for investigations of suspected abuse in England every year, 25 per cent of which are unsubstantiated and eliminated at an early stage. The remaining 120,000 receive a visit from social workers, after which a further 80,000 are deemed to require no further action. In over half of all investigations, families receive no services.

Several studies have found that geographical location is a significant factor in determining how many children are processed through the child protection system (Gibbons, Conroy and Bell, 1995), and a direct link has been identified between decisions about the threshold for intervention and the availability of resources, (Thoburn, Lewis and Shemmings, 1995). Thoburn and her colleagues found that social work teams were likely to want to avoid being inundated with work and that this was an important factor in deciding how many cases should proceed through the system to allocation. Other professionals though, such as health visitors and teachers, were conscious of the link between the allocation of a social worker and access to resources, and this led to disagreement amongst professional groups involved with vulnerable families.

All too often, having been appointed as a guardian for a child and upon examining social work files, I come across great numbers of records of investigations dealt with on a duty basis and then closed. Usually little, if any, consistent help or support is offered to these families as a result of the investigations. It is often the case that parents have interpreted the actions of the investigating social workers who close their cases as a vote of confidence in their parenting. The implicit message received by parents, though often not intended by social workers, is that their parenting is good enough. When eventually the growing number of incidents of concern leads the local authority to institute legal proceedings, parents can feel betrayed and let down by those they previously felt positive towards.

The guardian who wishes to conduct a thorough investigation will take care to understand parents' responses to social work intervention by listening carefully to their personal account of their experience of the child protection system. Efforts will be made to understand parental responses to the help offered by considering the quality of the relationships with social work staff at the point at which help was offered. If it is the case that help was offered in the context of the threat of legal proceedings, when parents were feeling confused and angry, then one cannot conclude that failure to co-operate with help offered in that context equates with non co-operation. The guardian will want to consider whether further assessment of the parent's capacity to respond to help should be made during the course of the proceedings and before any final decision is made as to the children's future.

Sadly, it is often the case that specialist help is only available late in the day to families when proceedings are underway. The expertise of such professionals as psychiatrists and psychologists is used to assist the court by determining the nature of the alleged harm, rather than assisting families to find solutions to their problems. If such help could be offered at an early stage then it is reasonable to assume that at least some families would never need to experience legal proceedings.

Parents' Experience of Our Interventions

Research by Cleaver and Freeman (1995) which focused on parental perspectives in cases of suspected child abuse describes the traumatic impact of investigations on parents accused of abusing their child. Parents reported that they felt 'frightened, ashamed, guilty or powerless', others described feelings of 'excitement, jealousy and the desire for revenge'. Cleaver and Freeman also noted variations in the ways in which parents respond when faced with the fear of losing their children. Some, particularly lone mothers, 'passively accept the stress as inevitable, others mount strategies of denial, non co-operation and marshal external support'. Coping in traumatic situations is suggested by Schatzman and Strauss (1955,1973), to be assisted by attributing events to external causes, for example by considering them someone else's responsibility. Bentovim (1987), in describing the effects of the trauma induced in parents by investigations, refers to psychic numbing,

anxiety, depression and feelings of worthlessness. Professionals investigating allegations of abuse must take care to distinguish between the facts of the situation and not interpret what might be a normal psychological reaction to the investigation itself, such as denial or anger, as further or conclusive evidence that abuse has taken place. It can be difficult if not impossible to distinguish anxiety from guilt.

The findings of the Cleveland Inquiry (1987) echoes Cleaver and Freeman's findings in respect of parental responses to child abuse investigations, and the report which followed recommended that parents be given support during investigations. Whilst it is undoubtedly the case that many parents would not find it easy to accept support at particular stages of their relationships with social workers, one would expect that professionals would demonstrate a considerable degree of empathy in attempting to understand parental behaviour, and that an effort would be made to look beyond the superficial for explanations.

Evidence from Cleaver and Freeman's study (1995), suggests that where parents feel that they have been treated fairly and sensitively, and given appropriate assistance, outcomes are likely to be satisfactory with children living safely at home. The parents in this study were either positive or negative about the professionals they dealt with, there was no middle road. Parents liked social workers better if they could relate to them as 'struggling parents like themselves, as survivors of a difficult childhood or as fellow travellers on a rocky road'.

Brown (1986), in examining parental perspectives in cases of suspected child abuse, found that parents were highly critical of social workers on the grounds that they provided little information, were insufficiently honest and that there was insufficient recognition of the difficulties they faced. Corby (1997), in a similar study, also identified the lack of information given to parents by social workers as a major source of concern, as did the Social Services Inspectorate (1986) and Prosser (1992). Other studies that have looked at parental involvement in child abuse investigations, for example Shemmings and Thoburn (1990) and Bell and Sinclair (1993) draw attention to the positives to be gained from parents attending case conferences provided that they were empowered to play a meaningful role in the process. Parents in Shemmings and Thoburn's study(1990) were more likely to view the help offered more positively if they were fully involved in the decision making process. It was thought that only 20 per cent of parents studied were working in meaningful partnership with their social workers. Whilst it is acknowledged that this is hardly surprising given the painful experience for parents of being investigated, it was shown that the skilled work necessary to bring such partnership about paid clear dividends in that it was shown to be associated with good outcomes. In another study Farmer and Owen (1995) found that an understanding between professionals and parents was likely to occur if there was agreement about whether the child had been abused, who was responsible and whether the child was at further risk.

The Guardian's Assessment of Parents

The guardian will be interested to know what efforts were made to establish a meaningful partnership with the parents from the beginning of their contact with social services. If parents' experience of social work assistance is one of being worked 'on' rather than 'with', of being denied involvement in decision making in regard to the kind of help required and refused participation in decision making bodies such as case conferences etc., then the guardian is likely to consider that further assessment is necessary before being able to come to any conclusion about parents' capacity for change.

In any attempt to understand parents' past dealings with local authority personnel

appointed to assist them, it is necessary to look beyond the obvious reasons put forward to explain non-compliance with help offered, and to consider from the parents' perspectives their own rationale for failing to avail themselves of assistance. It is important to understand something of the meaning of non-compliance in the context of that parent's relationship with the child. Is the parent motivated by a need for control that is disrespectful of the child's needs, or by feelings that are to do with a sense that they know best what their child's needs are? Were the services offered appropriate to the needs of the child and respectful of the racial, cultural and religious groups to which the families belong? Was the parent involved in the decisions about the kind of help that would be necessary and were they given full explanations of what was required of them? Did they receive information in writing and to what extent did they understand the implications of failing to comply with any child protection plan? It is only when such questions have been answered that the guardian can have a good sense of the parents' capacity to care for their child, and a picture of their weaknesses and strengths.

Not infrequently, a need for particular resources, not previously offered to the family, is identified during the guardian's investigation. In order that a full assessment of the parents' capacity to provide good enough parenting for their children is available to the court it may be necessary to arrange for such resources to be provided during the proceedings. In these circumstances, if the guardian and the local authority cannot agree on the value of such an assessment, the guardian can ask the court to order such an assessment. It is usually the case that the social services department has initiated proceedings on the basis that there is no more that can be done to support the parents in the care of their children. Such situations inevitably lead to tension between social workers and guardians. Unless investigations point to social work intervention being of high quality, with appropriate and sufficient resources offered in an atmosphere of positive assistance, the guardian is likely to be asking the social services department, and if necessary the court, to allow a period of further assessment before proceeding to a final hearing.

Further assessment introduces delay, which is stressful for all concerned, children, parents and the professionals who must continue to work with the family in the interim, but delay can be purposeful in that it can lead to the best decision being made. However, sometimes it is the case that children will be positively harmed by delay. In such situations, even where parents have not had the assistance to which they were entitled, the needs of the children must take precedence over natural justice for parents.

A recent case involving three young children serves to illustrate this point. These children were aged four, three, and eighteen months. The family had first come to the attention of social services when the oldest girl was just two days old. There were a great many referrals from a great number of sources over the intervening years and something in the region of sixteen separate investigations were conducted on a duty basis. Some spasmodic assistance was offered by way of financial assistance, family aides and family centre attendance but there was no consistent overview of the effectiveness of such resources. The case was finally allocated when it was decided to institute care proceedings following the latest investigation which was in response to an event not dissimilar from many of those which had prompted earlier investigations, but which this time led to the children being placed with foster parents. The children had been exposed to persistent long-term neglect and were delayed in many aspects of their development. They made very good progress in their placement. Such was their vulnerability due to their health and young ages that it would have been highly detrimental to their well-being if they were to be returned to an environment in which the progress they had begun to make could have

been reversed. For this family, as for many others who have not received good help in time, it was too late to begin assessing their strengths at the time of court proceedings.

Often it seems as though parents have themselves become so depleted as a result of their circumstances and difficulties, which have often persisted for many years, that they have passed the stage at which they might have used help and have settled instead into well established, maladaptive ways of coping with their lives.

It is usually possible, certainly at the early stages of the court proceedings, and notwithstanding the fact that there may be serious doubts about a parent's capacity to meet the needs of their child, to work alongside parents. Courts appoint guardians at a very early stage in the proceedings, often on receipt of the local authority's application. The guardian will usually meet the parents very soon after being appointed by the court to explain their role. National standards for the Guardian ad litem service state that 'Parents should always be treated fairly, politely and without discrimination', (Department of Health, 1996). Guardians will wish to acknowledge the parents' distress and allow them the opportunity to talk about how they are feeling, both about the proceedings and about having yet another person asking them questions about what most would consider to be their private family business.

It is important for the guardian at the first meeting to set out for parents the various components of their investigation, i.e. who is the guardian intending to interview, what, if any, experts they will appoint, what documents they will read, and how they will set about ascertaining the wishes and feelings of their children. Guardians will wish to tell parents when each stage is likely to occur, as far as it is possible to do so at the initial meeting, and should provide an opportunity for parents to provide their own account of the circumstances that have led to proceedings being initiated. To ask parents whether there are any particular matters that they would wish to be investigated, and to give them an opportunity to suggest whether there are people that they would wish to be interviewed who might support them in their account of events. This helps to convey the sense that the investigation being conducted is independent and fair. It is important that the guardian takes care to give parents confidence in their independence.

Parents often assume that all professionals are in league with one another and it is not difficult to see how this impression can be given. Generally social workers, solicitors and guardians will have worked together previously. During long waits at court is it all too easy to lapse into chat about matters not connected with the proceedings that day. It is vital to be sensitive to the feelings of parents in such situations and to remember that what is just another days work for some of us is quite another matter for those faced with public exposure of their personal difficulties and threatened with the loss of their children. It is only if parents can have confidence in the independence and fairness of the guardian's investigation that there can be any chance of joint decisions being reached between parents and other parties that are in the interests of their children.

An important task is to explore with parents the meaning of the guardian's independence.

Misunderstandings can easily occur. Parents have in the past assumed that my independence from the local authority means that I will be supporting their case. Parents who feel betrayed or let down by those they believed to be supporting them may well find it hampers their capacity to work with and trust professionals in the future. I have found that it helps parents to know at the outset that I might not agree with them, or their child's wishes, but that I will investigate with an open mind and keep them informed as the investigation proceeds. It is important to achieve the right balance between gaining parents confidence, and not leading them to expect the guardian to be the answer to all their problems. In addition to checking with

parents during an interview that they understand my role, parents have often commented positively on the written information that guardians provide and that can be referred to subsequently. In essence, the guardian should emulate the model of effective and anti-oppressive social work intervention by being honest and informative.

Many parents have told me that their solicitors had stressed to them that the guardian's recommendations were highly influential in determining the outcome of the proceedings. Their legal representatives advised these parents that the guardian was someone who had to be impressed! This was interpreted by some parents as suggesting that they tell their children what they should say and what not to say to the guardian. Fortunately, guardians are usually well able to recognise when a child is speaking to a script or has been coached. Evidence pointing to interference of this kind can backfire. It can cause the parent to be seen in a negative light in that they are demonstrating evidence of inability or unwillingness to allow their child the opportunity to talk about their situation as they see it. It is, however, important to consider whether such behaviour is borne out of a parent's sense of powerlessness and desperation. An understanding of systems theory is helpful in bringing a wider perspective to bear in such situations. A basic principle of systems theory is that the behaviour of one individual cannot be understood fully without reference to the systems to which he belongs (Ruegger and Johns, 1997). It is important to consider whether and to what extent behaviour such as this is typical of this parent's relations with the child, or whether it reflects the parent's perceived lack of choices given the imbalance in power between parent, local authority and legal system.

Ken Loach's film, *Ladybird, Ladybird* is based on a true example of a child protection case in which a mother had eight children removed from her care before being allowed to keep a ninth child. In it, Loach provides a graphic illustration of how a mother's behaviour could only be understood with reference to her previous life experience and how her behaviour had an entirely different meaning for herself than for the social workers in the child protection team. The mother, 'Maggie', had developed a mistrust of social services due to her previous experiences of having children removed from her care and she feared her new baby would be forcibly removed from her. She avoided contact with the authorities and refused to answer the door to health visitors and social workers. Her actions, rather than achieving the desired effect of getting the professionals to give up and go away, only served to heighten the social workers' concerns that she must have something to hide. This was in fact not the case, but no attempt was made to understand Maggie's behaviour with reference to the unwritten rules that governed the very different systems to which she and the social workers belonged, and the different marital system of which she was now a part. Two babies were permanently removed from Maggie and her new partner before the authorities were able to work constructively with the couple in order that they could achieve their aim of parenting their third child.

In my practice as a guardian I have come to realise how important it is to investigate the extent to which aspects of parental behaviour that appear to be disrespectful of children are typical of parents' relationship with their children, or whether they are indicating misguided but nonetheless well motivated attempts at protecting their children. If one conveys to parents an empathy and understanding of the difficulties in their situations, albeit without collusion, it is usually possible to explore with them both their rationale for attempting to influence their children to give a particular line to the guardian, and their understanding of the impact of such behaviour on their children.

Some Ethical Dimensions of Practice and Long Term Goals to Keep in Mind

It is important for guardians to remain aware of the fact that whilst their own role ends at the conclusion of the proceedings, children and their parents will usually continue their relationship with each other in some form, and both are likely to continue to have relationships with the social services department. Care must be taken to protect such relationships as far as possible from damage as a result of the proceedings.

In a recent study of children's perceptions of the guardian service (Ruegger 1998), many children reported that they experienced difficulty as to whether they could trust their guardian. Whilst most children felt they could confide in their guardians a great deal, in the knowledge that the information they gave would be relayed to the judge, several spoke of their surprise, and sense of betrayal, when they discovered that their parents had learnt of their private conversations on receipt of the guardian's report. Some children felt let down and regretted being so free with their confidences; others said that they wished they had been warned in advance. The children expressed some degree of unhappiness that things they had said without knowing they would be repeated to a parent had been later used against them. In one case a child confided that his parents had blamed the outcome of the proceedings directly on what he said to his guardian. Another commented, "I said I wanted to stay with my Nan. It was hard to say this because you have to be fair to your mum. I didn't want my mum to know I said it".

The message from children to guardians seems to be to pay careful attention to informing children about what happens to the information they give, and involving them in decisions about which of the things they say appear in reports. My own practice has been influenced as a result of this research in that I have become much more aware of the 'the need to know' principle when writing reports. Often I have found that there is a choice to be made between including information from a child that strengthens an already strong case, and protecting the child from allegations of disloyalty and blame for the outcome by disaffected family members.

The majority of children who are removed from their parents will be returned to them at some stage in the future. Those who remain looked after throughout their childhood often gravitate back to their families in early adulthood. For all these children and their parents it is important that the professionals involved at times of great stress and crises in their lives, ensure that as far as possible the conditions for them to continue their relationships are fostered. For those families who are not to be reunited, many of whose children will be placed for adoption, it is known that if children can move on with their families support, then their long-term outcome is likely to be enhanced. It is thus equally important when the plan is for permanent alternative arrangements to be made that guardians and others writing court reports stress not only the weakness but also the strengths of parents.

To convey a sense that parents have tried to meet their children's needs, even where they have failed, allows them to retain some sense of dignity which can form the basis of their future relationships with their children, and with those professionals who acquire responsibility for their future care. It is incumbent upon all involved to endeavour to record any facts which will allow children who might later read these documents to have confidence that at least in some respects their parents found them worthy of love. This demands that those who write reports are able to express empathy for parents.

The impact on parents of written statements and court reports, as opposed to discussions about their personal circumstances and histories, has almost always a highly distressing and unexpected impact. I have found that it is helpful to prepare parents for this by warning them of

their likely reaction, whilst stressing that there is nothing in my report that I have not already discussed with them. Doing so does not of course make the process of reading a report less distressing; it does however convey a sense of concern and respect for parents and helps them to prepare for the traumatic experience of court proceedings.

Conclusions

These then are some of the principles, applied from the work setting of the guardian ad litem, on which sensitive work with parents should be based. These principles apply equally to all professionals who work with parents, whether they be social workers, health visitors, family centre workers, or medical professionals. The approach outlined here is based on research and direct professional experience which both emanate from comments made by parents and children who have been through the child protection system.

It is tempting to argue against this approach on the grounds of shortage of time, shortage of resources, expediency, or even that the parents do not 'deserve' such consideration and effort. However, this would not only be unethical, it goes directly against the child's interests. For it has been demonstrated that reducing parental anxiety and hostility to public law proceedings is likely to be beneficial to the child in a whole number of ways. In the short term it will probably lead to fewer contested hearings and therefore fewer delays in the court proceedings. In the long term it will significantly raise the chances of alternative care arrangements, or rehabilitation with parents, being successful. Applying this in the wider perspective, working with parents is therefore always likely to increase the chances of being able to work effectively with children. Eventually, this may enable us to divert precious and limited resources away from 'investigating' child protection, towards promoting effective preventative work with children and families. In this context every effort to work sensitively, honestly, respectfully, anti-oppressively and empathetically with parents will be well rewarded, not least in terms of the job satisfaction to be obtained from the sense of achievement that comes as a result of a job done well.

References

Bell, M., and Sinclair, I. (1993). *Parental Involvement in Initial Child Protection Case Conferences*. University of York.

Bentovim, A. (1987). The Diagnosis of Child Sexual Abuse. *Bulletin of the Royal College of Psychiatrists*, 11(9): pp 259–299.

Brown, C. (1986). *Child Abuse Parents Speaking: Parents' Impressions of Social Workers and the Social Work Process*. Bristol University, School of Advanced Urban Studies.

Cleaver, H., and Freeman, P. (1995). *Parental Perspectives in Cases of Child Abuse*. HMSO.

Corby, B. (1987). *Working with Child Abuse: Social Work Practice and the Child Abuse System*. Milton Keynes: Open University Press.

Department of Health (1996). *Implementing National Standards. A Guide Through Quality Assurance for the Guardian Service*.

DHSS, Social Services Inspectorate (1986). *Inspection of the Supervision of Social Workers in the Assessment and Monitoring of Cases of Child Abuse when Children, Subject to a Court Order, have been Returned Home*.

Farmer, E., and Owen, M. (1995). *Child Protection Practice: Public Risks and Public Remedies*. HMSO.

Gibbons, J., Conroy, S., and Bell, C. (1995). *Operating the Child Protection System: A Study of Child Protection Practices in English Local Authorities*. HMSO.

HMSO (1988). *Report of the Inquiry into Child Abuse in Cleveland 1987*. Cm412.

Loach, K. *Ladybird, Ladybird*. PolyGram Video Ltd.

Prosser, J. (1992). *Child Abuse Investigations: The Families' Perspective*. Essex: PAIN.

Ruegger, M. (1998). *Approaching the Millennium- Children and the Guardian Service Within the Family Justice System*. Department of Health.

Ruegger, M., and Johns, R. (1995). *Using Systems Theory. Unit 7. Using Theories in Social Work*. Open Learning Foundation. Churchill Livingstone. 1997.

Schatzman, L., and Strauss, A. (1955). Social Class and Modes of Communication. *American Journal of Sociology*, 60: pp 239–338.

Schatzman, L., and Strauss, A. (1973). *Field Research: Strategies for a Natural Sociology*. New York: Prentice Hall.

Shemmings, D., and Thoburn, J. (1990). *Parental Participation in Child Protection Conferences, Report of a Pilot Project in Hackney Social Services Department*. Norwich: University of East Anglia.

Thoburn, J., Lewis, A., and Shemmings, D. (1995). *Paternalism or Partnership? Family Involvement in the Child Protection Process*. HMSO.

White, R., Carr, P., and Lowe, N. (1990). *A Guide to the Children Act 1989*. London: Butterworths.

4 Using Mediation Skills in Family Work

Karen Postle and Peter Ford

Introduction

Becky's stomach tied itself in knots as her Granddad drove her over to her grandparents' house for the day. Much as she tried to think about other things, all she could hear were her mother's words ringing in her ears, 'Don't for God's sake tell them about John coming round to help me with the garden last week!' 'Whatever you do, don't say we might go to France in the summer or they'll want to know where I got the money'. There had been other instructions, plus the usual tirade about Grandma and Granddad never seeing what their precious son was like, him being late with the maintenance again and her strong suspicion that he was now with someone else. All this buzzed in Becky's head until she thought it would burst. At the point when Granddad said, 'How's your Mum?' her chatty nature deserted her and she sat tongue-tied, muttering, 'Oh. O.K.'

It always grew worse as the day went on, like waiting for a storm to break and, sure enough, after lunch her Grandmother started to ask questions. They seemed innocuous at first and she could chat away about how she still went to ballet classes and what she'd done at school. All the usual stuff adults seemed to think kids want to talk about. Then it happened. 'Granddad said the garden looked nice. I bet Mum finds it hard doing it on her own?' and before she thought about it Becky was babbling on, 'Oh no. John came to help and he helped paint the windows and put my new wallpaper up. It's got big flowers on and I've got a duvet cover to match.' 'Really Becky. So who's John then?

Is he a new friend of your Mum's?' The awful realisation soon dawned on Becky as it always did and she felt sick, trapped and desperate. It didn't end there and by the end of the visit all of the things Becky had tried to remember not to talk about had been wheedled out of her.

There had also been the sly digs, 'Nice to get a proper dinner for once, eh Becky?' 'Where does Mum buy your clothes these days? I don't think that suits you at all'. For all she loved her grandparents and they were kind to her, Becky longed to go home although that prospect became increasingly daunting and she found the homeward journey nerve-racking. Maybe this time it would be different, but it never was. Polite but tense words were exchanged on the doorstep, she took her coat off and no sooner had she sat down in front of the TV than her mother started, 'I hope you didn't mention John. I know that look on your face! You did, didn't you?! You know what will happen now, don't you? I suppose you told them about France as well?'

Becky had heard it all before. This would be something else for her parents to quarrel about and solicitors to write letters about. Somehow, it was all her fault. If only she didn't say the wrong things, but what were the right things to say if you were asked a question? By the end of the day her mother was in tears and Becky was wondering what, at eight years old, she was meant to do and how it could be different. The feelings of guilt and responsibility were overwhelming.

Becky's situation is by no means unique. Eavesdropping in McDonald's on an average Saturday lunchtime would reveal similar situations as parents spend time with children from whom they are living apart following a breakdown of relationships. For many children, the fact that communication between their parents, and maybe members of their extended family, has broken down leaves them with feelings of responsibility similar to Becky's. The process of mediation can offer a way of enabling the adults in the family to reach an agreement without involving their children as a go-between, as Becky clearly had been and, in turn, lessening any potential negative effects of family breakdown on children. We aim to show how mediation skills are used in work with separated/divorced parents and how these skills can be more widely applied in work with parents.

We will begin by defining 'Mediation' and will then identify some of the features of the mediation process and its underpinning theoretical base. We then examine research evaluating the effectiveness of mediation, and continue by considering some of its potential applications in work with parents. Finally we give examples of mediation practice.

What is Meant by 'Mediation'? History and Definition

Family mediation has been described by a small number of authors in the UK by Davis (1983, 1988), Fisher (1992), Parkinson (1982, 1984, 1986), Roberts (1997, 1992), Robinson (1991, 1993), and researched by even fewer, (Walker *et al.*, 1989, 1992, 1994). Formerly known as 'conciliation', its development can be linked historically with the work of family court welfare officers and the rise of voluntary, out-of-court conciliation/mediation schemes from the late 1970s. From the outset its development has been informed by notions drawn from family therapy, from work with couples and from

the civil law, especially with the Family Law Act 1996, encouraging lawyers to become involved increasingly in family mediation.

The development of mediation is an international phenomenon, with an extensive literature in the USA, (Haynes, 1981, 1989, 1993, Kressel and Pruitt, 1989), and Australasia and Canada (Parkinson, 1982, 1984, 1986). Many authors use the term Alternative Dispute Resolution (ADR) to describe the process (Acland, 1992). Kressel and Pruitt examine ADR practice in a very wide range of situations which include international relations, labour/management relations, small-claims cases and decisions about siting dams and oil rigs as well as family and divorce settlements. Other authors discuss the use of ADR in neighbourhood feuds and landlord/tenant controversies. Mediation does not have to be invented and developed. It exists as a well-researched model that is ready to be applied.

The term 'mediation' has been used by UK court welfare officers for several years to describe a process by which they have sought to enable parents in conflict over their children to reduce the area and intensity of their conflict, and to negotiate agreements, as an alternative to asking a court to resolve such disputes. Such processes have generally taken place within the court precincts and have been described as 'In-Court Mediation'. A similar process, offered by independent mediators operating largely outside the courts and within charitable organisations, was initially known in Britain as 'Family Conciliation', partly to distinguish it from in-court mediation and partly to reflect a notion of 'conciliation' that is used elsewhere, for instance the national Advisory, Conciliation and Arbitration Service (ACAS), a body concerned with the resolution of industrial disputes. Parkinson's comprehensive 1986 study defines conciliation as:

> *A structured process in which both parties to a dispute meet voluntarily with one or more impartial third parties (conciliators) who help them to explore*

possibilities of reaching agreement, without having the power to impose a settlement on them or the responsibility to advise either party individually
(Parkinson, 1986 p 52)

She treats 'conciliation' and 'mediation' as interchangeable terms (ibid. p 86).

It became apparent that parties attending conciliation appointments frequently confused the term 'conciliation' with 'reconciliation'. This confusion caused particular difficulties when one party did not accept that their relationship had ended or they were strongly opposed to any idea of reconciliation. In 1992 the National Family Conciliation Council renamed itself the National Association of Family Mediation and Conciliation Services, since abbreviated to National Family Mediation. 'Conciliators' across the country redefined themselves as 'mediators'. The term 'mediation', with its connotations of taking a middle or intermediate position, is now accepted as a more accurate reflection of the process.

Mediation has attracted practitioners from a wide range of backgrounds, including counselling and social work. Increasingly, lawyers are entering the practice of mediation, a striking development in a profession long accustomed to resolving disputes by adversarial processes rather than by taking the middle ground. The entry of lawyers into family mediation demonstrates that it is not solely the province of those with a counselling, therapeutic or social work background.

Mediation is not counselling or therapy. It does, however, reflect the values of these types of work, such as self-determination and empowerment, because it aims to enable individuals to negotiate their own agreements. Like counselling, therapy and social work, mediation practice demands sensitivity and skill in, for example, seeking to ensure that agreements are not made under an unspoken threat of 'domestic' violence. Mediation aims to avoid influencing outcomes by the insensitive giving of advice, but parties may legitimately

request information from mediators. Much that is useful in social work practice is valuable in mediation, providing mediators and clients are clear that mediation is not a therapeutic endeavour. As Roberts succinctly states:

> *Mediation has emerged to fill a space hitherto unoccupied, which none of the existing services, welfare, advisory or therapeutic on the one hand or lawyers and the courts on the other, could in their nature have filled.*
> (Roberts, 1988 p 3)

Family mediation, as it developed in Britain, focused on issues concerning the children of separated parents; usually their place of residence and their contact with their 'non-resident' parent. Occasionally this was extended to include other members of the family, for example, grandparents or new partners. Since the Family Law Act 1996, mediation has been extended to include negotiation of agreements concerning matters of property and finance. Comprehensive Mediation, or 'All-Issues' Mediation, as this is now called, has introduced lawyers into mediation practice. This reflects the notion that mediation has the potential to be applied in many different kinds of conflict, as we will discuss further when considering its potential for wider use in work with parents.

While mediators have always been trained, their training is now regulated and governed by the UK College of Family Mediators and comprises elements of: principles and values, knowledge, skills and a practice component. Family mediators are members of the College or of services affiliated to it which adhere to its code of practice. In order to satisfy the requirements for membership of the College, individual mediators must have undergone training, demonstrated competence and be in receipt of regular supervision. Payment for mediation varies according to each service's practice. Since the Family Law Act 1996, the Legal Aid Board has been enabled to secure franchises with family mediation services to provide mediation for clients who are eligible for Legal Aid.

Mediation more commonly takes place between parents, without involving the children. This can avoid adding to the burden of responsibility which many children, like Becky, feel for getting their parents' situation right. However, there may well be times when it is vital to hear children's views and to give them an opportunity to voice their opinions. Providing this is done carefully by practitioners skilled in direct work with children, it can greatly facilitate the mediation process (Robinson 1991, 1993). The following guidelines apply in direct mediation work with children:

- Both parents must agree to the children being seen.

- The children should be brought to the session by a parent but then seen alone.

- Confidentiality must be maintained, with the exception of child protection issues, and children will agree what information is to be given to their parents.

- Mediators must remain neutral.

- Children must be told that, although their parents will be given their views, as agreed, parents remain the decision-makers.

- Sessions with children are for the purposes of consultation, not therapy.

Mediators can decide whether to work in pairs or alone. There are advantages and disadvantages to both ways of working and this will often be determined by an agency's resources as much as any other issues.

The Mediation Process

Haynes outlines the mediation process in nine stages as:

1. Recognising the problem.
2. Choosing the arena.
3. Selecting the mediator.
4. Gathering the data (fact finding).
5. Defining the problem.
6. Developing options.
7. Redefining positions.
8. Bargaining.
9. Drafting the agreement.

(Haynes, 1993 p 1)

Since the Family Law Act 1996 introduced mediation, wherever suitable, as part of the divorce process, the scope for 1-3 above is now somewhat limited. All couples will be offered mediation and the selection of a mediator will be limited to those services recognised by the Legal Aid Board. It remains crucial to begin the process by clarifying with the parties that mediation is a framework designed to assist them to negotiate agreements in disputed matters. It is important to differentiate it from a counselling process which aims to assist people in working through painful feelings and situations. This distinction is vital because people often bring expectations based on their counselling experiences with such organisations as Relate. Their agreement to proceed is then sought together with their assent to some ground rules:

- Focusing on the present/future rather than the past.

- Agreeing that each person will speak for themselves and not attribute attitudes or feelings to the other.

- Giving each other space to speak and listen.

- The mediator intervening if the discussion becomes too heated or strays too far from what the couple are aiming to achieve.

- Mediation terminating and appropriate further action being taken if evidence of child abuse is revealed.

- Confidentiality.

- Outline of the process with an understanding that the mediator controls the process, but not the content or outcome, which remain in the parents' control.

- Timing and number of sessions. This is usually an agreed agency policy but it is important to note that, although not a therapeutic endeavour, mediation will inevitably fail if the process is hurried and parties feel compelled to make agreements which will not work.

By asking the parties to give brief details about the background to their current situation, the mediator then gathers the basic data (Stage 4) about the dispute, identifying, as precisely as possible, what the issues are. Each person outlines the background as they see it, with the mediator checking out with the other party how this concurs with their version of events. Mediators may need to remind couples that this is solely information gathering and this information will not be used to make a judgement about who is 'at fault' in the situation. It is important that couples are encouraged to be frank and open at this stage as hidden agendas can often hinder the mediation process if they are revealed at the end of a mediation session. For example, if the parent with whom the children lives is planning to move to a distant location, but does not reveal this at the outset, plans for contact cannot realistically be made. At this stage, the skill of the mediator lies in teasing out the bargaining issues from what is often presented as the painful history of a relationship that has ended. Skill is needed in acknowledging this pain and not attempting to ignore it, but then focusing on problem resolution. We have found it helpful saying something like, 'I can see how very difficult the last six months have been for you both and it has taken a lot for you to come here today. Let's look at how we can begin to help you to move on to resolve the problems for your children and reduce some of that pain in the future'.

From this process the mediator moves to a mutual definition of the problem (Stage 5) and, for couples who may well find it very

difficult just to sit together in the same room, this requires skills of listening and attending in order to accurately reflect and summarise what each party has said. Sometimes using a flipchart to record the agreed definition of the problem is useful for focusing the discussion at a later stage.

The next stages in the process (Stages 6–8) involve the mediator in encouraging a process of constructive dialogue between the parties and resisting appeals to express judgements about who is right or wrong by keeping a focus on resolving agreed problems. Parties often appeal to the mediator to judge who is right or who is telling the truth and skill is needed in ensuring that the mediator avoids taking the role of judge and, instead, ensures even-handedness with the parties and a focus on their children's future needs. This skill cannot be underrated because it must be borne in mind that most people's experience of conflict resolution, from childhood onwards, has been the adversarial, 'Who did/said what? Whose fault is it?' and the absence of this feels uncomfortable and strange at first. Comments such as, 'We think that everyone gives their truth as they believe it and it isn't our role to judge' can be helpful.

Without giving her/his own suggestions, and using a continual process of summaries and questions, the mediator helps the parties to generate options for resolution. At this stage it often becomes clear that people have become fixed on trying to make the same option work, against all odds, and just need the chance to generate some new ideas, no matter how unusual they may at first seem. For example, if children see their father on alternate weekends and he considers this does not give him enough time with them, what are the options for seeing them at other times? Who can be trusted to help with contact arrangements if parents cannot do this themselves? How can they notify each other if arrangements need to be changed? In these days of 'phones, mobile and otherwise, answerphones, faxes and e-mails we remain surprised at the number of people who had not considered the simple process of dropping a note through a door, especially when this issue once arose with parents where the father was a postman! For all of us, fixed routines become the norm and the chance to step back and examine them can be valuable. After new ideas have been generated the parties can be helped to categorise them into degrees of feasibility.

An important feature of mediation is the skill of facilitating communication in situations of conflict where feelings run high. Success in mediation may be defined as the achievement by the parties of an agreement that works for them, or a degree of resolution of some difficulty. Thus a successful outcome might be indicated by the making of a written or verbal agreement (Stage 9), which has been reached by the straightforward process of the parties making offers, listening to each other and making counter-offers.

Described like this, mediation appears simple enough. In practice, prior to the Family Law Act 1996, people usually sought mediation because other methods of conflict resolution such as direct face-to-face attempts or adversarial legal processes had failed. Considering the situations in which people come for mediation, it is easy to see that feelings can run high and a mediation session can easily turn into a slanging match which one party may even leave because they find the other person's presence intolerable. The skill that aims to avoid such debacles is often called 'taking the heat out of situations'. However, this is an inaccurate description of a style of working which keeps focused on the agreed task and on future outcomes, clearly acknowledges emotional pain without being diverted into counselling, and positively reinforces any progress the parties make. Parkinson (1986) calls this skill 'managing open conflict'. She lists four other basic skills for conciliation or mediation work:

- clarifying and defining issues and options

- reframing, or 'positive connotation' (see Haley, 1976)

- confronting

- negotiating (see Fisher, Ury and Patton, 1982)

(Parkinson, 1986)

Skills like this are insufficient on their own, and need to be informed by such values as respect and self-determination, and by knowledge of, for example, family law and of court procedures. Mediators also need theoretical knowledge of child and adolescent development, including attachment theory. Often one parent will report that a child is very distressed after visits to the other and says that they 'Don't want to go to Daddy's again' or parents will report an increase in 'bad' or regressed behaviour such as tantrums. While care is needed to exclude other reasons for this, including the possibility of abuse, an understanding of attachment can be helpful in clarifying to both parents that this is normal behaviour in a child who cannot bear separation from either parent and lacks the sophistication of adult words to explain, 'I love you both and I hate it when I have to leave either of you'.

An understanding of various schools of family therapy, psychodynamic, structural, strategic, and especially systems-based methods is invaluable in understanding and working with families undergoing transformation and change. Likewise an appreciation of the psychological dynamics of couple relationships can be useful, for instance in recognising that commonly individuals move into, through and out of relationships at different speeds. It is often helpful to simply state this if one parent is saying, for example, 'I don't know why she hasn't accepted the relationship is over'. Both family and marital therapy offer many techniques that can be used in mediation. An appreciation of the processes of loss and bereavement may also assist mediators in understanding the difficulties of many of their clients. Parkinson's list of useful theories includes conflict management theory, communication theory and crisis theory (Parkinson, 1986, pp 124–8). Knowledge of negotiation theory is invaluable and is vital in balancing inequalities in bargaining power, such as where one party clearly has more to gain from a settlement (Robinson, 1991, p 57, Roberts, 1997 p 84, Fisher, Ury and Patton, 1982). Mediation is thus a process that is theoretically informed, and its skills are ineffective without knowledge.

Evaluating the Effectiveness of Mediation

How effective is mediation? Kressel and Pruitt's comprehensive US study of research into several different aspects of mediation asserts that:

> Mediation…gets very high marks from its users and…mediated agreements tend to stick. In most…studies, mediation generally fares better than the courts on both dimensions.
> (Kressel and Pruitt, 1989, p 3)

In Britain, Janet Walker and her colleagues have undertaken a series of studies of family conciliation and mediation. Walker comments that:

> The pioneers of family mediation may have fallen into the trap of making over-ambitious claims, sometimes promising outcomes which cannot realistically be attained. (Walker, 1992, p 18)

Hence caution is essential when claims for mediation's effectiveness are discussed. Nevertheless the outcomes of Walker's extensive studies (1989, 1992) are cautiously positive. Mediation can be successful in promoting agreements, although compliance rates two years after divorce are disappointing. However, 'mediated couples' experience less conflict and greater co-operation in those first two years than non-mediated couples. Considering the effects of reduced parental conflict for children, this is an important finding. Community-based mediation is more effective than court-based mediation. Mediation seems more effective than the traditional adversarial legal process in the short term.

The continuing need for caution is shown by research demonstrating the opportunities for exerting pressure on parties that can easily tempt mediators anxious to achieve settlements (Roberts, 1992). Recently, awareness of the significant implications of 'domestic' violence for mediation practice (see, for example, Hester and Pearson, 1997) should also urge caution. Despite mediators' attempts to balance power differences, it should be recognised that the existence of a violent relationship is a clear indication of a power imbalance which is non-negotiable. Women who have been the victims of violence should not be subjected to the risk of further abuse either during a mediation session or as a result of agreements made therein. Additionally, there is increasing recognition that children who have witnessed 'domestic' violence are placed in an abusive situation and contact with the perpetrator is, at the very least, questionable.

Nevertheless the research evaluations of conciliation and mediation practice in the past eight years have helped convince legislators and the senior judiciary of the potential value of mediation in the resolution of family disputes. The Government's Green Paper, *Looking to the Future: Mediation and the Grounds for Divorce*, placed mediation at the centre of its proposals for divorce reform, arguing that mediation should become the norm rather than the exception (HMSO, 1993).

The Potential for Wider Use of Mediation in Work with Parents

Mediation is a useful approach in resolving situations of conflict between individuals or between individuals and their wider environment. In working with parents and children, aside from the more usual mediation role with estranged parents described above, there are clear roles for using mediation in the wider sphere. There is a place for dispute resolution skills in working with conflicts between adolescents and their families, for instance. Similarly, mediation can be effective in disagreements between foster parents and birth parents, in intra-generational conflicts and in many other permutations of family life. Additionally, Liebmann suggests the following areas in which mediation can be used:

- Victim/offender situations, where victims and offenders can be helped to reach a greater understanding, perhaps leading to reparation. This sometimes takes place through the medium of community conferencing or victim/offender conferencing.

- Community/neighbour mediation, where conflict may have arisen over children's behaviour.

- Schools' conflict resolution, where children are taught mediation skills as an alternative form of dispute resolution.

- Medical mediation, enabling people to make complaints about their doctors or hospital treatment.

- Environmental mediation, which helps to resolve disputes over planning issues.

- Elder mediation, helping to resolve disputes concerning older members of the family which may be proving stressful for all generations.

(Liebmann, 1998 pp 52–54)

In each instance, appropriate knowledge of, for example, relevant legal frameworks, feasibility of suggestions generated and alternative avenues for redress will be essential. Individuals experiencing difficulty in mental health, disability, homelessness, substance misuse and poverty will often find themselves in conflict with others and mediation skills can be used in conflict resolution in these areas. Such areas exemplify the particular and individualised aspects of work with parents which have potential for the application of mediation skills. It is at this individual level that mediation is demonstrably effective.

Mediation has the potential to contribute significantly in the area of anti-discriminatory or anti-oppressive practice, which seeks to promote equality of opportunity and treatment at an individualised level by challenging discrimination wherever and whenever it is encountered, and working in ways that empower those who experience discrimination and oppression. There is an extensive literature in this area (Dominelli, 1988 and Thomson, 1993). An example of the use of mediation in this sphere would be conflicts between second-generation members of minority ethnic groups and their parents, where cultural clashes can easily produce estrangement, when a negotiated agreement would be a more satisfactory outcome. At the level of the local community, where racism affects relationships between neighbours or community groups, community development workers competent as mediators could usefully engage in dispute resolution (De Souza and Craig, 1998).

Case Studies
1. A successful mediation
Background

- Lisa and Greg had been divorced for two years.

- Their two children: Amy, 10 and Carly, 7 lived with Lisa.

- Greg and his new wife Sue lived about 70 miles away.

- Weekend contact had worked well but Greg had wanted mediation because, 'I want to stop her getting the children involved in our arguments. I want her to have an adult discussion about topics affecting the children without losing her temper'.

From the initial stage of gathering the data, it became clear that emotions ran high. Lisa had strong feelings about Sue, and Greg complained that Lisa excluded him from involvement in the children's lives. They found it hard to listen to each other and there was no trust between them. Communication about the girls was by letter and it was apparent that Amy and Carly were acting as go-betweens in disputes and manipulating their parents over some issues. The first session ended with an agreement to refer any disputes which the children raised over the weekend to the other parent rather than talking about it further with Amy or Carly.

The following session was much calmer. Lisa and Greg commented that they found the ground rules helpful, especially about listening to each other. When they came to discuss problems which the girls had raised, Lisa said that Greg only ever cooked lasagne for the girls and they said they hated it. Greg looked dumbfounded and said this was something he knew how to cook and had done it as a special treat for the girls who had never commented to him that they didn't like it. A useful discussion ensued in which Lisa and Greg were able to exchange several views about the girls' likes and dislikes and Greg was able to raise what could have been a potentially inflammatory issue, that he and Sue were moving back to the area. Lisa and Greg then discussed the implications of this calmly. By the end of the session, Lisa was viewing this very positively rather than seeing it as a threat. She saw that she might have more free time if Greg was back in the area and could look after the girls more often. Once the couple had been encouraged to listen to each other, tension reduced and Greg commented that trust was slowly growing.

The mediator needed to carefully tease out what the issues were and to balance the space each person had for talking and listening. The pace had to be slow because, if the mediator had tried to rush Lisa and Greg to reach decisions at the end of the first session, the issues would not have been fully discussed and resolved. By setting them a small task, which they were able to accomplish, the mediator was then able to build on this success.

2. When mediation did not succeed
Background

- Dave and Helen separated three years ago after Dave began a relationship with Jenny, a colleague. Dave and Helen were divorced six months ago.

- Dave and Helen's two children, Luke, 6 and Naomi, 4, lived with Helen.

- Dave lived with Jenny about an hour's drive away from Helen.

- Disputes were about contact. Helen was adamant that the children should not stay at their father's house until he was married to Jenny.

Dave and Jenny had become engaged but had no plans to marry at this stage. As Dave's job took him all over the country during the week, the only opportunity he had to see his children was at weekends and, despite trying to explore a number of alternatives, neither Dave nor Helen could see any alternative but for the children to go to Dave's house. Helen would not allow this as long as Jenny was there. Jenny had sold her house when she moved in with Dave and so, unless she left the house to stay with friends, there was nowhere else for her to go. Jenny and Dave did not think she should have to do this.

A lot of time was spent clarifying the issues. For example, Dave was adamant that Luke and Naomi should never regard Jenny as a mother figure, 'They'll only ever have one Mum and that's you'. Dave brought Jenny to one session, with Helen's agreement, so that these issues could be discussed and clarified. Helen stood her ground. In her view, Dave had broken the sanctity of their marriage by his affair with Jenny and she was not prepared for the children to spend time with her until the couple were married, seeing this as the only way that the children could learn the importance of marriage. Despite four mediation sessions in which the issues were discussed and options explored at length, Helen refused to let the children go to Dave and he refused to make Jenny move out while they were there. The couple decided to seek legal advice.

In this situation there was an impasse despite the number of avenues explored and potential solutions generated and the slow pace of the work. The mediators, however, were careful not to be drawn into the continuing debates about who was being reasonable/unreasonable or the role or significance of marriage in the late 20th century. They continually tried to re-focus the discussion by asking Lisa and Greg what the consequences for Luke and Naomi would be if the issues remained unresolved.

Conclusion

As the above examples demonstrate, mediation may not always be the best course of action for couples to take. We always remind couples that there are four ways in which they can resolve conflict:

- by talking face-to-face
- using mediation
- using a solicitor
- going to court

No judgement is implied if mediation does not work for a couple because there is no one right way of resolving disputes and what may work for one couple may not work for another, as our examples show. For couples where mediation succeeds, well-conducted mediation is found to be effective, because it helps them to achieve their own solutions, rather than trying to work with those imposed by a court or any other outside body. We are convinced that the skills of mediation, provided they are underpinned by theory, values and relevant knowledge, can be applied in many situations in work with parents.

Afterword

Some minor details in Becky's story have been changed but her story is the story of one of us (Karen). Thankfully, the process of divorce has been eased since the 1950s, when she experienced what is described above, and when divorce was as much a matter for private detectives as for the legal profession.

However, many children still act as pawns in disputes which rage between their parents, becoming inappropriately caught up in parents' continuing conflict. Mediation offers a way of reducing the likelihood of this and, in turn, of lessening the chance that children are left to carry a burden of guilt, responsibility and confusion.

References

Acland, A.F. (1992). Don't Let's Keep it in the Family: The Expanding Universe of Alternative Dispute Resolution. *Family Mediation*, Volume 2; Number 3.

Davis, G. (1983). Mediation in Divorce: A Theoretical Perspective. *Journal of Social Welfare Law*, pp 131–140.

Davis, G. (1988). *Partisans and Mediators: The Resolution of Divorce Disputes.* Oxford: Clarendon Press.

De Souza, M., and Craig, Y.J. (1998). Cross-Cultural Mediation. In Craig, Y. (Ed.). *Advocacy, Counselling and Mediation in Casework.* London: Jessica Kingsley.

Dominelli, L. (1988). *Anti-Racist Social Work.* Basingstoke: BASW/MacMillan.

Fisher, R., Ury, W., and Patton, B. (1982). *Getting to Yes: Negotiating an Agreement Without Giving in.* London: Century Business.

Fisher, T. (1992). *Family Conciliation within the UK: Policy and Practice* (2nd edition). Bristol: Family Law.

Haley, J. (1976). *Problem Solving Therapy.* New York: Harper and Row.

Haynes, J. (1981). *Divorce Mediation: A Practical Guide for Therapists and Counsellors.* New York: Springer-Verlag.

Haynes, J. (1993). *The Fundamentals of Family Mediation.* Horsmonden: Old Bailey Press.

Haynes, J., and Haynes, G. (1989). *Mediating Divorce: Casebook of Strategies for Successful Family Negotiations.* New York: Jossey Bass.

Hester, M., and Pearson, C. (1997). Domestic Violence and Mediation Processes: A Summary of Recent Research Findings. *Family Mediation*, Volume 7; Number 1.

HMSO (1993). *Looking to the Future: Mediation and the Grounds for Divorce*, Cm.2424.

Kressel, K., Pruitt, D.G. and Associates (1989). *Mediation Research: the Process and Effectiveness of Third Party Intervention.* San Francisco: Jossey-Bass.

Liebmann, M. (1998). Mediation. In Craig, Y. (Ed.). *Advocacy, Counselling and Mediation in Casework.* London: Jessica Kingsley.

Ogus, A., Walker, J., and Lee-Jones, M. (1989). *The Costs and Effectiveness of Family Conciliation.* The Lord Chancellor's Department, London: Law Commission.

Parkinson, L. (1982). Conciliating Matrimonial Disputes: An International Perspective. *The Law Society's Gazette*, p 1307 (20 October).

Parkinson, L. (1984). Mediation: A Wider View. *Family Law*, Volume 14: p 267.

Parkinson, L. (1986). *Conciliation in Separation and Divorce.* London: Croom Helm.

Roberts, M. (1992). Who is in Charge? Reflections on Recent Research on the Role of the Mediator. *Journal of Social Welfare and Family Law*, Number 5.

Roberts, M. (1997). *Mediation in Family Disputes: Principles of Practice* (Second Edition). Aldershot: Arena, Ashgate Publishing.

Robinson, M. (1991). *Family Transformation through Divorce and Remarriage: A Systemic Approach.* London: Routledge.

Robinson, M. (1993). A Family Systems Approach to Mediation. In Carpenter, J. and Treacher, A. (Eds.). *Using Family Therapy.* Oxford: Blackwell.

Thomson, N. (1993). *Anti-discriminatory Practice.* Basingstoke: BASW / Macmillan.

Walker, J. (1992). Mediation Research: Implications for Policy and Practice. *Family Mediation*, Volume 2; Number 3.

Walker, J. *et al.* (1989), see Ogus, A., Walker, J., and Lee-Jones, M.

Walker, J., McCarthy, P., and Timms, N. (1994). *Mediation: the Making and Remaking of Co-operative Relationship: an Evaluation of the Effectiveness of Comprehensive Mediation.* Relate Centre for Family Studies, University of Newcastle.

5 A Solution Focused Approach (Brief Therapy) to Working in Partnership with Young People and Families

Eileen Murphy

In keeping with the principles of the Children Act 1989 and later with the Government's Quality Protects Initiative in 1998 – 'working in partnership with families' is a term that is very popular with social care professionals.

Examining that 'partnership' term for a moment – if a social care professional was working in partnership with you, the reader, and your family – what would they work with? What is your family culture? What are your family beliefs? What is important and unimportant in your family ground rules? Is there room within that 'partnership' term to allow a social care professional to meet your needs?

It's only when we question the term that we realise that to make it more than just a phrase we have to ensure that we work to meet the mindset of the family in question.

The ethos of partnership is all important for me and I see my role as that of working as a conduit between parent and child; school and pupil, rather than attempting to be a 'fixer' of their problems. That ethos is driven by the belief that only the client is truly the expert of their problem and will therefore be the expert of their solution.

If I pose the question 'how do you know you really are working in partnership?' then I must be prepared to answer it too. I would say 'because I do not give advice, I do not drag people back into the past, I do not ask families to compromise on their family rules and I do not attempt to impose my values or beliefs but work with the families' values, acknowledging, as I must, that for an intervention to be of any success it must continue long after the professional has ceased to be involved'.

I must recognise that it is my role to draw out strengths and competences that the client possesses, helping the client to make the existing family unit stronger, in their version of family unit not mine.

Using the Solution Focused Brief Therapy (de Shazer 1985) I invite the client to look at and talk about the day after the problem is solved rather than only concentrating on the day the problem began. I ask about exceptions to their prevailing problem such as, 'are there times when this problem isn't happening or times when you cope better? – how come? what's happening differently at these times? who is doing what differently?' – the list of questions are all part of a structure that allows the worker to question rather than analyse; to talk about the future rather than only about the past; to talk about when the problem is solved rather than only when it began – thereby actually raising awareness of the possibility of solving the problem which is often overlooked when we work with families who are facing crisis. Using only 'problem' language all the time is like climbing into the problem with them rather than working to pull them out.

Because the Brief Therapy model is a non-damaging therapeutic method, social care professionals from all fields, including education, are able to use it. It allows for good practice and is an ethical method of working because it has respect for and works with not only the ethnic and socio-economic culture of the client but also their unique, individual family culture.

The visuals of my own *Examine, Repair and Move On* approach are basic, crude drawings that are attractive to both young people in their simplicity and to adults because, according to feedback, they do not feel as if they are being 'therapied'. These visuals and their accompanying language allow the client to identify *what* needs to happen and *who* needs to do what to bring change about. Families feel encouraged to use them because they are not being asked to blame anyone but identify who is part of the change. Using cartoons and drawings they are asked 'What can mum, dad, or teacher etc., keep on doing, start doing, stop doing…to help the change take place?'

Often it is not change itself that is difficult to instigate, no matter how long the problem has existed, but the belief that change is possible. Often it is not creating the 'watershed' that is difficult but the idea that people will respond to it.

My experience is that offering a watershed excites change. Accepting that change is possible and describing it in small steps as in 'what will be different?, or who will notice?' allows change to be imagined. By inviting people to rehearse in their heads how they will achieve change, with the questions 'what happens then? or how did you do that?' people are able to see their strengths, coping abilities and strategies in preparation for change.

The key element of this approach is recognising that it is futile to attempt to change the essence of people's culture and more productive to help that family change within their own lifestyle. Offering them an intervention which allows them to examine where they went right as well as where they went wrong, what they don't need to change as well as what they do, reminds people, parents especially, that there have been successes in the past and that those successes can be repeated. The alternative is to reinforce the mistakes of the past and the failure of the present.

When I train professionals in these approaches, the issue of showing intense courtesy and respect in real ways is also examined. If we think of ourselves in any stressful situation, whether its a problem with our child's teacher or a meeting with a medical professional, we are always grateful when they treat us as a *person with a problem* rather than a problem person. If we recount the story of our meeting later, we usually relate a positive meeting as 'she just listened to me' or 'he looked me in the eye when he was talking' and a negative meeting as 'she was writing all the time' or whatever tiny detail it was that made us feel less than comfortable, small things that in professional interaction is easy to get wrong.

In 1993, I devised a format, 'The Prevention and Intervention Service' incorporating the Brief Therapy Method and my own *Examine, Repair and Move On* approach specifically for implementation with young people and their families who were referred to social services either at preventative level e.g. a young person challenging the family rules or at crisis intervention level, where the problem is so extreme that the parents are requesting their child be accommodated by the local authority.

Whilst training local authority social services staff, both field social workers and residential staff, and later during their actual practice with families, it was increasingly becoming clear to the teams that often it was in the early part of the sessions, before any talk of the presenting problem, that progress was made. This is because of the courtesy and respect shown to clients; the acceptance that they are the experts of their family culture and that our job is to share with them our professional knowledge rather than our 'non-existent expertise'.

One occasion I remember most vividly was when I entered the room to meet the family for the first time, after they had asked for social service intervention to help them cope with their 15 year old son's adolescent behaviour: he was challenging their rules, staying out late etc.

The young person and his father both stood up as I entered, and I remarked how wonderfully courteous that was. I asked the young person, rhetorically, how he managed to maintain those manners as he entered the 'dreaded adolescence', whereupon the whole family laughed, including the young man and we talked for about 20 minutes about the parents other successes with the children and how they managed to instil positive values.

That one early focus on how much they had achieved as parents, and focusing on where they went right before we even talked about what had gone wrong, meant that the family were able to see that the actual problem of their son withdrawing from them and challenging their rules was a 'normal' reaction, given his developmental stage. With their willingness to adapt to his changing needs and his being aware of their 'normal' concerns as parents, they could continue their successful parenting during this difficult time. A simple interaction between people rather than a diagnosis and treatment.

There follows two case studies, which I hope illustrate how I have used the two methods. The first of the case studies is family based whilst the other is school based.

When is a tantrum a 'lack of self-discipline'?

Malcolm, aged 14, was referred by the duty social work team who expressed concerns about his violence in the home following an extremely violent outburst. Malcolm's Referral Form listed five professional agencies that he had been referred to previously, two of which were mental health teams, and one a psychiatrist who had been engaged privately by the family. All, apparently, had failed to 'stop' his violence. The violent outbursts were referred to as 'tantrums' throughout the Referral Form. Malcolm was accompanied by his parents Colin and Cassie.

On introducing myself, I explained the ethos of the work as helping to find solutions rather than concentrating only on the problem. They gave a brief outline of Malcolm's 'tantrums', including one incident where he had kicked his mother so hard in the leg that she had had to be hospitalised. I asked what the family did in response to these 'tantrums' and was told that they used pin-down techniques.

I asked Malcolm was there ever a time when he had controlled his temper and he was able to describe one occasion when they were all on holiday together and he hadn't wanted to spoil it all. He had shouted, used bad language and threatened his parents with violence but had not smashed things up or hit anyone. I asked how he had done this and he said that he just stormed off, calmed down and came back.

I noticed that while he was describing a recent 'tantrum' he used expressions like 'left hook' and 'pulled back punch' and I recognised them as boxing expressions. Enquiring whether this was so, he confirmed that boxing was his big passion.

We then discussed the 'tantrum' word that everyone kept using. I felt it was slightly embarrassing talking with a young man of his age and obvious strength in those terms feeling more comfortable using 'a lack of self-discipline' knowing he would recognise the term as a very important part of the boxing sport. He smiled and agreed that he would prefer that.

I then asked him the miracle question. 'Imagine you left here today, went home and while you were sleeping a miracle happened and the problem that brought us all here today had been solved. When you woke up tomorrow morning, how would you know, who would be doing what differently and what would you be doing differently to tell others this miracle had happened?'.

Malcolm replied that he would be controlling his temper, while his mother would accept his apology straight away and not nag him all day about how apologies are not enough. Dad wouldn't interfere when he was arguing with his mum, or threaten Malcolm with his older brother who, apparently, now possessed a 'good left hook' of his own. Finally, he added that the family would be spending more time together!

I then asked Colin and Cassie the same question, to which Cassie replied that Malcolm would get up the first time he was called in the morning.

Colin said that Malcolm would do things in the house without asking how much money he was going to be paid in reward.

Both parents presented themselves as non-aggressive.

In conversation with Malcolm about smaller steps of 'who would be doing what on the day after the problem was solved?' he suddenly became very tearful and said that:

> *Dad wouldn't hold me down while Brian (his older brother) hit me while Dad told him where to punch,* (during these pin-down times).

Colin looked uncomfortable and tried to interrupt but Malcolm continued,

> *and don't say you don't Dad because you do and I'll never forgive you for that. You think Brian can take me on now but he can't and neither can you…*

In order to assess 'learned behaviour' I conveyed a sense of bewilderment and asked Malcolm 'where does all this violence come from?'. Malcolm pointed at his parents and said,

> *them two – they hit me when I was little and it was all right for them but now they don't like it when it happens to them.*

The whole family, it appeared, communicated through slapping, punching and play fighting, which often got out of hand.

I advised the family that I would have to share that information with the referring social worker who would then discuss her concerns with them separately. I would need to know that no such further violence would occur towards Malcolm in order to ensure his safety within the home, and they all agreed.

I shared my own view that slapping children just tells them 'I don't like what you're doing so I'm going to hit you, so when someone does something you don't like, you should hit them'. Everyone murmured their understanding of the view.

I asked them to indicate on a scale of 1–10 their desire for change (with 10 very much and 1 not at all). They all scaled 10. I called a break at that point noting that perhaps they could reflect for a moment on what they thought they had achieved so far in the meeting and that I would put together some tasks to reflect the solutions they themselves had expressed.

I drew up some monitoring charts to allow them to monitor their achievements.

1. 'Malcolm's self-discipline' chart (for Malcolm to complete)

Malcolm was asked to scale himself each evening on his ability to achieve self-discipline that day. If he walked away when he was angry, thought through what he wanted to say and returned to the scene and expressed his feelings, he marked a 10. If he didn't achieve self-discipline that day and had been violent he marked himself with a 1.

Because of his age, I motivated him with a 'bonus' mark. This he should mark when he had achieved a 10 even though he considered he had been provoked.

2. 'Accepting apology the first time' chart (for Cassie to complete)

Daily chart again with a 10 for her ability to accept an apology the first time it was given. 1 – if she didn't accept apology straight away.

3. 'Fair referee' chart for both Cassie and Colin

10 – if they were fair in sorting out disagreements within the family, and listening to all sides. 1 – if they were unfair and just assumed it was one person's fault without listening to the whole story.

4. 'Family laws' chart for whole family

I gave the family a blank flip chart sheet with the words 'Family Laws' as a heading. All the family were asked to contribute to this, writing their needs within the family, e.g. 'No swearing, no violence in home' or whatever they decided.

5. '5 minute dialogue' for whole family

The whole family were asked to sit together at some point every evening, and using a watch each had to talk for five minutes on one 'bad thing' and ending on one 'good thing' that had happened to them within the family that day. No interruptions were allowed.

6. Anger control

Malcolm was invited to attend a 1:1 anger control session where he could use visuals to pin point his anger triggers and assess what his personal control techniques are in more detail.

7. A presentation

Malcolm was asked to put together a presentation about 'self-discipline in boxing' and to present this to myself and his family at a separate session using the overhead projector if he wished, and concentrating on the difference between 'boxing as a disciplined sport' and 'boxing as a show of strength alone'.

I then asked the family if, for the purposes of the work, they could suspend all physical play fighting and violence of any kind in the home and possibly invent a family code to stop it happening if it broke out. Malcolm suggested Dad's 'end of story' catchphrase, which I agreed was a brilliantly apt code. I asked them to note what was different in the home between now and the next time we met and that they invite Brian to the next session.

One week later, the family returned with Brian and their completed charts.

In reply to my question "what's better?" Malcolm said he had kept his self-discipline lots of times. Mum disagreed, relating an incident when Malcolm had lost his temper because of something she did and in retaliation he went upstairs and filled in his chart with 10 in every box for days in advance.

Recognising this action as a considerable move on from hospitalising his mother, I enquired how he had been able to control his temper to that extent? He replied that "in the new way of doing things, It's the only way I knew would upset her". I congratulated him on his achievements (the real scoring was three 10s and two 3s) in that there had been no violence in the last week and that he had been creative in finding new ways of retaliating.

Cassie achieved several 10s on her chart as did Colin. He told me that it was Cassie who had tried to break the 'no physical stuff' and that she had sulked when he stressed the 'end of story' catchphrase.

Brian, the older brother, invited to give his account of the changes he had seen in the family that week, said that the house was quieter, there had been no violence and that people spoke more.

The boxing presentation did not take place – Malcolm had studied it but had not quite found the confidence to make a presentation.

The family were invited to continue with the efforts made and invited to attend again in two weeks' time. Although during later sessions, the family relayed how difficult they had found it to keep to the 'no physical stuff' and how this had sometimes spilled over into real fights, Malcolm's 'tantrums' had gone and he continued to work on his 'self-discipline'.

By reframing 'tantrum' to 'lack of self-discipline', Malcolm was able to see the language and goals as pertinent to his own life and as something 'strong' to be achieved given his own passion for boxing, strength, winning etc., rather than a concentration of 'stopping' something.

By a 'new viewing' of Malcolm's violence, he and his parents were able to realise that the violence was a technique he had learnt directly in the home, and therefore was neither odd nor a sign of a deeper problem, thus allowing for the possibility of change.

The tasks and monitor charts that the family were asked to complete were specifically devised so that they reflected what the family themselves identified as the change that needed to, and could, happen. This gave them ownership and control over the change rather than what a professional identified should happen.

The language of the monitor charts and tasks, particularly 'the end of story' catchphrase, again reflected the family's own language, recognising and respecting their unique family culture whilst meeting statutory goals.

Through the miracle question all were allowed to hear small steps that were needed to make the change towards a non-violent home and that change was possible and, most importantly, they could control the change themselves.

'Why is he facing the wall versus How does he face the front?'

Luke, aged nine, was a client referred by the family's allocated social worker in conjunction with his school, following a particularly difficult divorce between his parents, resulting in Luke living with his father. With his parents' permission, the school asked if I could make a school visit to talk with both Luke and his teacher, Mrs Robinson, in order to deal with his problems at school.

Mrs Robinson consequently relayed the problems. Luke was extremely disruptive in class, rarely completed his homework or came equipped for school, and found it difficult to settle down after breaktimes. This meant Luke sitting at the top of the classroom facing a wall during lessons, in an attempt to prevent him from being distracted or from distracting others.

I asked Mrs Robinson whether there were any occasions, at all, when Luke had not been disruptive in the classroom; and she thought there might have been a day in the previous month when he seemed to be getting on with his work without any disruption.

Further, could she remember an occasion when Luke had completed and returned his homework, and the teacher remembered a day last week when he had returned it and placed it in the special tray that she kept for returned homework.

As to whether he ever returned to the classroom in a calm and appropriate manner, she could not remember there ever being an occasion when he had.

It was time to see Luke at this point and Mrs Robinson asked if I needed to see him alone. I advised her that I was sure that she was going to a very important part of the solution and asked her to stay.

When Luke arrived, I shook hands and said that I had been having a very interesting conversation with Mrs Robinson about him and said "Mrs Robinson tells me that last month you had a good day in class and got on with your work and I was wondering if you could tell me how you did that?"

Luke looked puzzled, since he had imagined that he was called to discuss his behaviour problems and it took him a moment to take my question in.

He eventually answered "Yeh, I didn't get told off or anything". I leaned forward and asked him to talk me through as much as he could remember from that day. He could only remember odd bits – "I didn't get told off or anything and I did my work good". Mrs Robinson also remembered that day and said, "Well it was just a quiet working day, Luke was sitting working well and I didn't have to move him; he put his hand up to ask a question…"

I interrupted and asked Luke "How did Mrs Robinson respond to you when you put your hand up? Did she see you straight away?" Luke said that she didn't but he waited for her and then she saw him. I asked him "How did Mrs Robinson help you to have a good day? What was she doing? How was she talking with you? How come you were able to stay out front for the whole day?"

Luke gave what seemed to be clichéd answers, "Because I was good – she didn't have to tell me off or put me back on the wall…" and then he said that it had felt good back out in the classroom away from the wall for the day.

When I said that Mrs Robinson had told me that recently he had done his homework, walked back into class and placed it in the tray, how he had done that? "Take me back to the night before – what did you do differently at home that meant that you were able to do the homework?" He explained that his father turned the TV off and had sat down to read his newspaper and Luke had been bored so got his homework out of his bag and did it.

I asked Luke how he calmed himself down after breaks. Mrs Robinson, thinking I had misheard the earlier discussion, attempted to remind me that he wasn't able to calm himself down after breaks and I conveyed my deliberate mistake to her by non-verbals and asked the question again.

Luke said that he just came back into class but that "Miss said I'm still noisy". I suggested that it must be very difficult for people who are playing football, running races and having fun to suddenly stop and put on a different feeling to go back into class and he agreed. I said that I wondered how children could 'put on that different feeling' as if it were a mask or something; how they could 'get ready for class' and at what point the 'getting ready for class' would happen? which bell? – the first or the second? and whereabouts it would happen – in the queue?

Luke said that he thought saying 'calm' would be a good way of getting ready to come back into class and that the first bell would be the best way because then you'd get extra seconds for the 'calm' to work.

I asked Luke what would be different in the classroom when he came back from the playground and he said that Mrs Robinson wouldn't have to keep telling him to be quiet – I asked what she would be saying instead and he said she would be "saying nothing not even saying my name just smiling at me and tell me to sit down at my place". I asked where his place would be and he pointed to the seats in front "somewhere out here, near my friend James".

I then asked "On a scale of 1–10 Luke, with 1 being 'I'm never going to get off that wall' and 10 being 'I could face the front' what number he was on?". Luke replied "a 10 for me but not for Mrs Robinson". I asked what number he thought Mrs Robinson might be on and he replied "maybe a 1". I then asked Luke what needed to happen so that Mrs Robinson could get to a 2 and he said that he needed to stop 'astracting [distracting] everyone'. I asked Mrs Robinson what number she was actually on and she replied "much higher than that – I would like my wall back!"

I then asked Luke "if you went home tonight Luke and went to bed and while you were sleeping a magic thing happened and the reasons why you had to sit at the wall had disappeared – when you got to school tomorrow how would you know?"

Luke replied that he would come into class and put his bag on one of the front chairs and Mrs Robinson wouldn't stop him. Then he would put his homework in the tray and sit down and would work and not 'astract' people. "How will Mrs Robinson know this magic has happened?" I asked, and he replied, "Because she wouldn't have to move me back".

I then talked him through the day, with me asking him all the time "and how are you doing that Luke? and then what? and who is helping you to do that? – what are they doing differently?". We discussed the breaktime, the 'calm' mask, putting his hand up if he wanted to ask a question, and leaving school and going home and repeating the homework incident. Mrs Robinson was asked to telephone Luke's father and thank him for his 'clever strategy' of turning the TV off so as to encourage Luke to do his homework. I suggested, if they all agreed, that the magic day could start tomorrow or was there a reason why it couldn't? Neither Luke or Mrs Robinson could think of any reason and it was agreed that as from the next morning, Luke could come in and sit out front to start the day off and I wished Luke well and he left the classroom.

Mrs Robinson said that she was greatly encouraged to hear the part she could play in the solution rather than be left with a problem and that she would take a full part in the 'magic' day tomorrow.

By focusing on the times when he had met expectations, it encouraged Luke to see that he had strengths and had achieved in the past and could achieve again. In talking through 'who will be doing what the day after the problem is solved?' Luke could identify what small things he could do, what Mrs Robinson could do and what could change at home that would help.

In normalising the difficulty of making the change of mood from playground to classroom for all children, Luke was able to see the normality of it and think of a strategy for children to use that would allow them to 'get ready for class'.

Most importantly during this session, a watershed was instigated thereby offering the possibility of change, of starting something and achieving something rather than stopping something.

By offering Mrs Robinson the opportunity to see herself as 'part of the solution rather than part of the problem' she was more involved and motivated to see change.

Luke's father would be asked to help subtly and without recriminations as only he would really know whether his turning off the TV was a 'creative decision' or a random exception.

I was contacted three weeks later by Mrs Robinson to say that the 'Magic Day' had been happening every day with Luke sitting out front and getting closer to his ultimate goal which was to sit next to James. The 'calm' mask was working very well and Luke was 'conforming to expectations whilst in class' but would I be able to come in and do a similar session between Luke and the dinner ladies who said that Luke was ill mannered at lunchtime. I suggested to Mrs Robinson that she invite Luke and the dinner ladies to describe the 'Magic Day…'.

References

Murphy, E. (1993). *Examine, Repair and Move On.*

De Shazer (1985). *Solution Focused (Brief Therapy) Keys to Solutions in Brief Therapy.* New York: W.W. Norton.

SECTION TWO
Care

6   Working with Parents in Israeli Emergency Centres for Children at Risk

Frada Feigelson and Yitzak Lander

The Emergency Centre for Children at Risk and their Families (ECCRF) is an initiative born into the context of latter 20th century Israeli society. This post-Holocaust, immigrant state is of late characterised by a number of significant tensions. Most prominent is the chasm between:

- longstanding continuity and fast paced modernisation and Americanisation
- religious traditionalism and secularism
- ethno-cultural divisions
- peace and militarism
- economic development and prosperity
- mounting socio-economic privation

The nature of Israeli society has far reaching impacts on its institutions, including the family. The current reality is highlighted by families in frenzied economic competition and occupational transition, removed from natural support networks, alienated from anchoring religio-cultural values and ritual, and exposed to a hostile geopolitical environment. This reality exists precariously alongside the espoused paramount values attributed to family, family life, children and childhood in Jewish civilisation and Israeli society in particular.

Within this challenging context for parents, parenting and children, there exists hundreds of thousands of youngsters whose development and functioning are defined by the society as falling unacceptably far outside acceptable norms. These 'children at risk', whose potential seems often to be thwarted primarily by deficient parenting and parent-child relationships, experience physical, sexual and emotional abuse as well as profound neglect. Awareness in Israeli society regarding children at risk and the challenges they face has increased dramatically during the past decade. This increased attention was sparked initially by the highly publicised case of a pre-school girl who died as the result of horrific physical abuse.

An organised child welfare system began to evolve even prior to the formal declaration of statehood in 1948. This system, a central component of which was group childcare, whether in the Kibbutz, residential school or foster and adoptive home – focussed on facilitating the socialisation of masses of immigrant children into Israeli western-European culture. There was the special challenge of raising a large number of children who arrived in the new state as orphans of the Holocaust (Weiner 1986). Israeli child protection evolved into a system highly focussed on child rescue, removing the youngster from a stressed environment to one presumably more healthy. Parents did not seem to play a major role in case planning and intervention. Legislation regarding the role of parents in their children's treatment was absent with existing legislation supporting the near exclusive focus on the child at risk.

The crystallisation of such an approach was facilitated by the nature of the organisational structure of the Israeli child protection system. That is, funding, supervisory and policy development functions are seated at the central government level though actual casework is carried out by local social welfare authorities. Another contributing factor to the approach is a prevalent underlying assumption in the child welfare, and specifically child protection system, that parents who put their children at risk were to some extent to be blamed and punished for their actions, or in many cases, lack of actions.

World developments encouraging family based child welfare and child protection practice during the last twenty years began slowly and hesitantly to influence Israeli child welfare by the end of the 1980s (Colon 1978, Dore 1995, Korittko 1994, Maluccio *et al.* 1994, Scannapieco 1993, Schnur 1995). There became a substantial appreciation of the unalterable importance of the child's roots in his biological family and the subsequent necessity to engage the child's parents, siblings and extended family in the therapeutic process (Boszormenyi-Nagy and Spark 1973). New found efforts were made to work with parents in order to increase the well-being of the child and all family members. A new realisation was made that a caregiver could not successfully nurture until they are nurtured. It is into this fledgling experimentation with family based child welfare that the nation wide network of seven Emergency Centres for Children at Risk and their Families (ECCRF) was born in 1992 with the opening of the Jerusalem Centre, following at least two years of intensive planning and preparation

Each ECCRF is either regionally or sectorally based and is comprised of three units – the shelter, the internal residential unit and the ambulatory care or external unit These serve up to 5, 10 and 30 children and their families respectively. Admission to the Centre is done both on an emergency and planned basis in partnership with social workers from the local municipal social welfare departments who remain case managers. The function of the shelter and residential units is:

- protection and instrumental care
- assessment, short term therapy
- case planning

The ambulatory care unit provides assessment, therapy and case planning and in addition is active in professional training and consultation. Notwithstanding the focus of this chapter is on work with parents and families it must be kept in mind that much therapeutic effort is aimed directly at the child's inner emotional world and in particular his perceptions and feelings regarding those most significant for his growth and development. This work may be done in individual or group treatment sessions or alternatively in the child's naturally occurring environments including school, recreational settings and the like. The Centre thus serves a wide range of constituencies, ranging from children at risk and their parents to social workers, educators and interested community leaders. Moreover, it operates as an integral part of the existing social service network.

The essential tenet of the philosophy of the ECCRFs is zero tolerance for child maltreatment and the critical importance that abuse and neglect be arrested immediately upon disclosure, particularly within the family, but also without. Alongside exists the strong belief in the unalterable and fundamental importance of the family, in particular the parents, for the child's normal development and functioning. Parents are seen as being an integral part of their child's daily life notwithstanding physical separation and children are perceived as being fundamentally emotionally dependent on their parents. Highlighted is the importance of rehabilitation of family structure and relations to a level where child well-being would not be seriously compromised if he was to be returned home. There remains a strong belief in the possibility of parental and family change, expressed in the ability to shape more positive experiences for the child within the family context.

The therapeutic leverage for this change is viewed as being primarily the engagement of parents in a therapeutic experience similar to that which their children undergo in the Centre (Cirillo and DiBlasio 1989). Central to this experience is the provision of a 'holding environment' where trust, courage and confidence in the care giving environment are strengthened and maximised. Parents may come to the Centre with what they perceive to have been a less than satisfactory, even painful, experiences with child welfare workers and system.

There is a belief in the importance of espousing a strengths perspective, and the need to be positive about the relatively strong parental and family functioning that do exist. There is an acknowledgement of the overwhelming complexity of parenting and also the complexity of change of parenting behaviour. Parents are seen as most often doing the best possible with the resources at their disposal – which often do not include sufficient models for the task. A central element of the practice philosophy of the ECCRFs revolves around the necessity of genuine engagement of parents in the therapeutic process. It should be noted that although the Centre supports the notion of the importance of the family and listens to parental opinions, for some children out of home placements are necessary. If this is the case the child should be placed geographically close to the parents' home and the parents should be involved with the child upon placement.

This parental-family centred practice philosophy can be seen as being applied in the Centres in each of six major activity domains:

1. assessment
2. provision of a therapeutic milieu (environment)
3. therapy
4. parent training
5. case decision making and recommendations
6. service system mediation and advocacy

Whilst there exists a common operating policy for all the ECCRFs and there is significant similarity in their operation, regional population and the background of families will affect the practice of individual centres.

Description of Work with the Parents

The critical importance of the ability to build a working alliance with parents and other family members must be emphasised (Barnard and Kuehl 1993). This skill is based on the expression of acceptance, trust and caring for parents and translates into such organisational policies and procedures as off-hours therapist availability, intensive frequency of therapeutic involvement and home-visit based therapy. Blaming is downplayed whilst understanding is embraced.

Assessment

Parents are involved in the ECCRF assessment process both as sources and recipients of information. With respect to the former, parents may be:

- observed by staff in informal activity both with and without their child
- observed by staff in formal activity both with and without their children
- interviewed by staff
- administered psychological tests

There exist abundant opportunities for both PST and child care staff to observe parents in spontaneous interaction, with their children and with others. Of importance here is the observation of parents waiting for scheduled appointments in the Centre or outside, such as with the child's ECCRF therapist or the child's physician in the community. There may also be the observation of parents at their child's birthday party or holiday celebration both inside the Centre and at home, not to mention the observation of the parents in actual interaction with the child's physician, schoolteacher or tutor. ECCRF staff will also commonly observe parents in structured formal activity both on their own and with their child. Most prominent here is the observation of parents in interaction with their child in staff authorised visitation and phone calls. There is additionally the observation of parents in interaction with their child around structured tasks designed to tap parental skills in the areas of nurturing, boundary setting, education and sensory stimulation.

Interviewing of parents for the purpose of information gathering most often takes the form of social histories. Here there is a special focus on past exceptions to the problems and treatment successes. Parents are also often asked about their view of the nature of the problem free state for their child and themselves. Evident is the influence of Narrative theory in assessment question development (White and Eon 1990).

Parents may occasionally be asked to complete a battery of psychological tests by PST staff. This is particularly the case when there is a complex discussion of parental competency before the courts. Parents are not only sources of information but also recipients of such information. It is common practice in the Centre that prior to any sharing of assessment results with colleagues, including with the court, these results are presented to and discussed with the child's parents. There will be a deconstruction of these findings with a focus on implications for the child and the family's treatment plan.

The involvement of parents in assessment at the Centre is illustrated in the case of 'N', a 7 year old boy whose parents were initially encountered by ECCRF staff during a case consultation attended by representatives from 10 education and social service agencies. The purpose of the consultation was to find a solution for the immediate out of home placement of 'N'. He had not attended school for the past six months and previously had been expelled from three schools. This was despite his participation in both a community-based therapeutic play-centre and a day care boarding school. 'N' was the sole child of the union between 'S' and 'G' with mother 'G' having five children from a previous union, all currently residing in out of home placements. It was the first marriage for 'S'.

During the course of the initial case consultation the parents had described 'N' as having been difficult to care for from birth. They had also made clear their longstanding resistance to any kind of therapeutic residential placement. At the conclusion of the meeting the parents were invited by the Centre PST staff to tour the facility and consider the child's admission. As of late the child was totally uncontrollable and mother particularly was feeling increasingly helpless to protect her son. Consequently there was some openness to the idea on her part. However even at this very early point in the therapeutic process the ECCRF worker was able to discern the father's marked opposition to son's admission. The father expressed his hostile attitude in words but most acutely in body posture and facial expression. Though the parents did not bring themselves to admit 'N' after the initial visit the court did order the boy's admission for a period of three months, a short while later.

Staff stayed in telephone contact with 'N' and his parents from the initial consultation through to actual admission and were briefed by municipal social workers about the court room proceedings, in particular the parents behaviour and expressed thoughts and feelings. Beyond creating an initial linkage with the parents this telephone contact allowed ECCRF to build initial hypotheses about the reasons associated with father's resistance as well as the strategies which mother utilised when faced by her partner's stubborn opposition. 'N's' parents accompanied him to the admission meeting at the Centre. Here was occasion for plentiful observation of their informal interactions with each other, their son and with the social service personnel in attendance.

As part of the admission procedure it was decided to allow 'N's' parents to enter the residential unit both in order to assist the boy in moving in and to reassure the parents that he was adjusting. Observation of the mother's behaviour during her brief visit to the residence clued staff to the paramount importance attributed by her to orderliness and cleanliness in her parenting repertoire – a finding later reinforced by results of formal psychological testing. It should also be noted that 'N' also completed a battery of psychological testing while in the Centre. They highlighted his fear of being abandoned, as well as feelings of rejection and lack of trust.

While in the Centre there were numerous assessment meetings where the child and parents were interviewed and at these meetings there was also abundant observation of informal interaction between child and parents. For instance it was noted that mother's hugs, though plentiful, were smothering in nature. The child's reaction to such affection seemed to be one of apprehension and confusion. In addition, the parents displayed hypersensitivity when they found so much as a scratch on 'N' and became infuriated. Staff understood this as an attempt to demonstrate that only they were adequate caregivers for the boy.

Staff also monitored all of 'N's' phone calls with his parents while he was in the facility. The major theme of these conversations was the very strong desire and promise of the parents to rescue 'N' from the Centre. There were also suggestions made by the parents as to how 'N' might shorten his stay by means of the display of exemplary behaviour. Father stressed repeatedly his 30 day countdown. In interviews with 'N's' father emerged hints of his difficult upbringing. He declared to PST staff that what happened to him as a child would not happen to his son. He disclosed having been raised in out of home placements since age seven. Additionally highlighted in interviews with father were his endless efforts to convince 'G' to bring her five children back to her home to live.

One of the most telling meetings was between 'N's' parents and the ECCRF worker on the subject of 'N's' medications. The father was on the verge of engaging in physical abuse throughout the interview. In general, thoroughly dominating the discussion – actively denying the child's emotional distress and making highly

inappropriate and impractical promises of the assistance he would provide for the child once discharged from the Centre. After 90 minutes, a compromise was nearly reached with agreement to go to the family's own trusted physician for reconsideration of the boy's medication. When the compromise almost fell through as the father insisted he had no time to go along to meetings with the physician, the mother suggested the taping of these meetings and the father readily agreed. This observation assured the staff that 'N's' mother might well be very effective in problem solving vis-à-vis her husband, including quick and creative thinking. Moreover, that she does this sensitively allowing the father at the same time to retain his authority and place as head of the family.

Contact with the therapeutic milieu

Parents are involved with the ECCRF therapeutic milieu to different degrees and in a variety of ways. This can range from abandonment through to intrusiveness and may depend on such factors as:

- the personality, make up and emotional well-being of the parent
- the nature of the parent-child relationship prior to admission
- the meaning of the child's apprehension for the parents
- the extent to which parents tend to use involvement with their child as a tool in their battle with child welfare authorities
- the underlying attitude of the Centre staff toward parent participation in the therapeutic milieu

Parent involvement in the milieu may occur in a number of realms:

Facilitation of the child's transition from home to the Centre. Parents are strongly requested, particularly at the time of admission, to assist in making their youngster's move to out of home living as smooth as possible. This will include the bringing of familiar clothing, family pictures and personal hygiene products. There will be an attempt to procure from the parents detailed information about the child's likes and dislikes as well as strengths and weaknesses. The nature of phone and personal contact with the child while in the Centre will be explained and a specific schedule for this type of contact, especially in the transitional period, will be established.

Visits. Significant efforts are made by PST staff to encourage parents to visit their child while in the Centre and to see these visits as opportunities to apply newly acquired knowledge and skills. Visits may take a number of forms and much consideration is given to matching child and parents with the type of visit that will be most productive for them. For instance, visits may range anywhere from a number of minutes to several hours, may be with or without full or partial staff supervision and visits may take place in or outside of the facility. There is an active effort made to schedule parent-child visits at times that are mutually convenient and more importantly, at times that will be productive for both the child and parent.

Home visits. The sending of children home for periods of time that may range from a few hours to a few days is seen by ECCRF staff as an opportunity for the application of new skills and knowledge by both parents and child. These visits are also seen as a valuable tool for reducing the commonly experienced separation trauma of the child. Furthermore the visits assist substantially in maintaining continuity with the child's naturally occurring social environment and support system. It should be added that PST staff, make a concerted effort to prepare both child and parents for these visits and to support them during the actual visits. That is, parents and children are worked before and after the visits, to verify the absence of danger in the child's home. Centre staff are available on a round the clock basis for

consultation. During visits child care staff are sent along with the child both to ensure his protection and more importantly, to facilitate that learning which can occur on a home visit. A particular challenge for parents is the planning of their child's time and activities while at home. This receives a good deal of attention prior to and after home visits.

Telephone contact. Telephone contact with parents is usually encouraged as it is seen as another opportunity for the practice of newly learned communication skills. There are a wide range of phone calls permitted with decisions made as to the type of calls allowed to a specific child undertaken by the Centre PST staff. Calls may last in duration from a few minutes to a half hour, may be fully, partially or not at all monitored by staff, and may be placed to parents, friends, siblings, or other figures important to the child. It should be noted that the decision to monitor phone calls has been affirmed by the Israeli courts in recognition of the potentially aversive effect of parental-child phone contact.

Centre staff often work with parents as how to best utilise the opportunity of phone contact with their children. It should be noted that in addition to calls directly with their child, parents may call 24 hours a day to the Centre staff to enquire about their child's wellbeing. This occurs particularly in the initial transitional period and when the child is not feeling well.

Decision making about daily living. Parents participate with the Centre residence staff in decision making regarding their child's health, grooming, education and recreation – whether the question is to further a certain course of medical treatment, to have a trendy haircut, or to take swimming lessons. Parents are encouraged to accompany ECCRF child care staff and child in carrying out these decisions. In addition to the above formal realms of parental involvement it should be stressed that parents often appear to be significantly nurtured themselves through contact with this 'holding' environment.

Indeed staff, see it as a high priority to directly be of service to the child's parent. This may include the serving of a hot meal, provision of advice or a listening ear or the supply of toys and clothing to homes where there is a need, particularly on the part of siblings. Such 'holding' of the parents often will occur in the well supplied and aesthetically pleasing coffee corner which is strategically located to encourage parent and staff interaction.

The involvement of parents is illustrated in the case of 'A', a 10 year old boy admitted as a result of profound neglect on the part of his single parent mother 'I'. She had arrived in Israel six years previously from the former Soviet Union with 'A' and a 16 year old daughter. Four years ago she bore another son from a causal relationship. Her first husband did not come to Israel and has no contact whatsoever with her or the children. 'I' lived and worked in a small town approximately two hours car ride from the local centre.

From the beginning of the admission process ECCRF staff made very significant efforts to encourage 'I' to be part of her son's daily life in the facility. Indeed 'I' would manage to talk to her son every three days as long as staff reminded her to do so. Moreover staff would prepare the mother on how to communicate in a loving and affectionate manner during the calls as this was a major challenge for 'I'.

The mother had great difficulty in even beginning to understand the potential difficulty in the move for her son despite a good deal of support from staff both on the telephone and on home visits. Staff ensured some possessions were brought from 'A's' home to the facility and indeed helped mother write a version of a 'goodbye' note which would allow the easing of the boy's guilt over not being near his mother to help her with the household tasks that were usually his. 'I' found organising herself to visit the Centre to be extremely difficult, partially because of the cost involved and partially because of her extremely long hours at work. This was despite the frequent heartfelt requests to her on the phone by 'A' to do so. Every two weeks staff would transport 'A' home and return using the opportunities at the start and end of the home visit for preparation and therapeutic debriefing.

A major emphasis was on assisting mother in building a timetable for the boy's home visit. This would provide a suitable balance between structured activities with his family, time with friends and alone in his own room which he sincerely missed. Much work was also completed on providing boundaries for 'A' should he attempt to engage in acting out behaviour both in the home and in the community at large. Mother was taught to apply the token economy of the Centre on home visits and more importantly to approach possible deviant behaviour in a manner similar to ECCRF child care staff. Of most importance was ensuring 'I' worked directly with ECCRF psycho-social staff in processing a six hour 'run' of 'A'.

In this instance psycho-social treatment staff, despite the late hour at night on the start of the Jewish Sabbath, insisted that 'I' make her way to the Centre. When she finally arrived she was put into a room with her son and a child care staff member. PST staff informed them that as a result of 'A' absconding which was seen as seriously endangering his well-being, they would have to stay together in that same room for 24 hours. This was to ensure that 'A' might remain in the Centre in a manner that would not again see his well-being seriously jeopardised. Mother and 'A' would spend the time discussing, with the assistance of the accompanying child care counsellor, the disadvantages and costs of running away. There would also be a series of therapeutic meetings with psycho-social staff during this 24 hours in the 'holding room'. It should be noted that it was to be mother and not the child care counsellor who would attend to 'A's' needs during the 24 hour period.

Therapy

All parents whose child is admitted to the Centre must participate in an ongoing therapeutic process conducted by PST staff. This may include individual, family, couple and/or group therapy and will always be focused on the achievement of therapeutic outcomes which will ultimately enhance the child's well-being. That means that any direct therapeutic benefits of this process for the parents, while seen as very important in and of themselves, are seen fundamentally as a means to further the 'best interest' of their child.

The involvement of parents in a therapeutic process usually begins immediately after the child's admission and is explained to the child as a necessary component of the work to be done at the ECCRF. The child is informed that not only will he be therapeutically challenged while in the facility but also that his parents will be, at least to the extent that he is, and most often times, to a greater extent. Soon after the assessment process begins and hypotheses evolve about the child and parent's relative strengths and difficulties there will be decisions made by the psycho-social staff as to what therapeutic methods will be of greatest benefit to the child's parents. The most common method provided appears to be family/couples therapy with therapeutic meetings most often including parents, child and siblings. Extended family members are often invited to participate.

There exist within the ECCRFs the conditions for live supervision and videotaping of therapeutic meetings and this may be done. Therapy may well also occur in the home of the child. Here it is seen as important that co-therapy be undertaken in the light of the particular challenge of maintaining the focus in the client's own environment.

The theories that underpin this work are the general systems theory with the concepts of holism and reciprocity particularly embraced (Worden 1994). The concepts and techniques of the structural school with special emphasis on boundaries and boundary making and the transformation of enmeshed and disengaged systems (Minuchin and Fishman 1981) and the influence of strategic family therapy (Papp 1983, White and Eon 1990). Alongside this clear influence of general and family systems theory there is the very strong influence of psychodynamic theory and technique. Kohut's notions of object needs is also receiving increasing attention by PST staff (Sable 1995). In addition there is the influence of Rogerian, Gestalt and cognitive-behavioural therapeutic approaches.

It must be noted that such theoretical and technical approaches can and are applied not only with respect to the verbal but also the non-verbal dimension of communication. There is widespread use in the Centre of drama, art and music in therapy meetings with parents, especially those which include the direct participation of children. Furthermore there is a prevailing belief in the importance of giving parents incrementally more challenging and complex tasks to perform between therapy meetings.

The participation of parents in therapy can be illustrated by the case of 'E', an 11 year old boy who was admitted as a result of physical abuse on the part of his single parent mother 'N'. Mother would hit her son with open hand, fist and later with kitchen objects after other more educational and moderate efforts to control his minor stealing and chronic truancy failed. 'E' and 'N' have lived alone since his parents were divorced when he was less than one year old. 'N' permits no contact with the father despite the boys frequent and strong expressions of his desire to build a relationship with dad. Father has lived overseas since the divorce.

The participation of 'N' in therapy took several forms – individual therapy, therapeutic meetings with herself and her son, and therapeutic meetings between herself, father, and ultimately son – by means of the telephone. Highlighted in the approximately 15 individual therapy meetings with 'N' was her early inadequate attachment experiences with both parents, particularly her father, and the likely implications of her consequent attachment style on her relationship with 'E' and on her attitude regarding 'E's' desire to be in contact with his father. In the 20 therapeutic meetings with mother and son the focus was on the following issues:

- mother's difficulty in understanding son's developmental and gender appropriate needs

- son's strong and mounting desire to forge a relationship with father and to receive basic information about him and his family of origin

- son's difficulty in accepting his parents' divorce

- both mother and son's essential social isolation and particularly their almost total lack of contact with their very small local extended family

There were two therapeutic meetings which were conducted on speaker phone with father overseas. The initial portions of both these meetings involved attempts to settle unfinished business between 'N' and her ex-husband. The last part of both calls involved the boy and both his parents as the ground rules for the development of some kind of relationship between father and son were worked out. In addition, the boy had a chance for the first time to ask basic questions about his father such as what he looked like, where he lived and what work he did.

Parent training

Parents are involved in parent training in the Centre. This training may be primarily formal or informal depending on the treatment goals of the particular child. With respect to the former for instance, evident is the use of Jernberg's Theraplay approach which involves the facilitated interaction of parent and child around highly structured tasks, with the intensive accompaniment of PST staff (Jernberg 1977). These predetermined tasks are designed to help the parent improve his skills in each of the four critical areas of nurturing, discipline, education and sensory stimulation. Teaching of parenting skills is through the directive use of play and toys.

At times parent training may occur in the parent and child's own environment at the initiative of the PST staff with the home offering abundant opportunities for learning and also honing new parenting skills. Similarly, skills needed to ensure children are sent off to school successfully will be taught in the home in the early morning hours.

In addition to formal parent training there is much parent training which is done informally by PST and child care staff, for example, when staff supervise parent-child visits or when parents take their child from the child care staff before weekend home visits. There is also informal parent instruction by staff, for instance, the parent who shows whilst visiting the Centre a lack of skill with respect to affection exchange may well receive appropriate tips by the supervising child care staff.

The involvement of parents in parent training in the Centre can be illustrated by the case of 'T', a six year old boy admitted because of profound parental neglect. Mother 'E' seemed to be overwhelmed attempting to cope with the care of 'T's' two younger siblings and the management of the home's finances. Father was occupied with friends and the taking of narcotics.

The involvement of 'T's' parents in learning new parenting skills was by means of both formal and informal instruction. They participated in an 11 meeting series of Family Theraplay. In the first three meetings there was an assessment of existing parenting strengths and weaknesses in each of the four critical realms of parenting. The basis of the assessment was an interview of the parents regarding their parenting and their child including observation of each parent in turn attempting to relate with his child. 'T's' father was assessed as being very weak in all four realms while his mother was assessed as being weak in all but the nurturing domain.

During the next four sessions PST staff worked with six-year-old 'T' by means of structured tasks in each of the critical realms with parents observing the professional staff in interaction with their child. The parents received a running commentary from a second psycho-social staff member who sat on the other side of the two way mirror with them. An example of one of the tasks was the playing of a board game whereby it was organised so that the boy would lose. The therapist coping with the boy's response to the loss was observed and thoroughly discussed with the boy's parents.

During the 8th through 11th sessions it was the parents who played the same board game, initiating the same loss by the child and dealing with the child's response. This time PST staff were on the other side of the mirror for parental consultation and support if so desired. The informal teaching of parenting skills to 'T's' parents was also of significance. They benefited greatly from child care worker input during supervised visits with their child at the Centre.

Of utmost importance here was the necessary modelling of staff regarding child discipline with a focus on the application of natural consequences for unacceptable behaviour. In addition staff modelled to parents the importance and actual ways in which to stimulate a child. Here there was a focus on the use of the child's favourite medium of music, especially song, with child care counsellors modelling the singing of beloved nursery rhymes to the child.

Recommendations/case decision-making and partial parenting

Parents are meaningfully involved in case decision-making about their child's long term treatment plan and the processing of ECCRF recommendations through the court system. PST staff discuss with parents their tentative then final recommendations and most importantly share with parents that

data which supports these recommendations. It is found that an emphasis on the explanation of recommendations greatly increases the likelihood of parental support.

Though PST staff do not as a rule do the actual presentation of the recommendations in court, this being the role of the child protection officer, there is often considerable debriefing of the courtroom experience by staff. Often this takes the form of stressing to the parents the possibility and importance of partial parenting while their child is raised in 'out of home' placement. Quite often parents' thinking in this regard involves a dramatic split – that is that if the child is in out of home placement they by definition will have no important part to play in his upbringing.

Typically, staff stress the error of this splitting of reality into all or nothing and spend considerable efforts exploring with parents the opportunities for partial parenting. The Centre has run groups on the topic of partial parenting for those parents whose children are on the way to out of home placement or already in such placement as a result of a recent court order. The involvement of parents in the domain of case recommendations and decision-making regarding long term treatment plans is illustrated by the case of 'M', an 11 year old boy admitted because of profound instrumental and emotional neglect on the part of both parents, though particularly father, who was most times in a neighbouring city in the company of his mistress.

After three months of ongoing assessment and treatment efforts it was decided that the knowledge gathered necessitated 'out of home' placement. Most prominent here was father's virtual absence; the child's continued tremendous anger over father's betrayal of mother; the mother's significant difficulty in completing necessary instrumental household tasks and the hostile relationship between 'M' and his two younger siblings.

The ECCRF recommendation and supporting data was presented to 'M's' parents by PST staff in a series of 15 meetings where the resistance, primarily of father, to out of home placement was processed and slowly modified. Staff in this case decided to accompany the parents to all court proceedings where the recommendations were to be discussed and there was a debriefing meeting with parents after each of four court hearings. Moreover, staff accompanied the parents and 'M' on all of their visits of potential out of home placements, finally convincing parents of a particular option based on the similarity of that facility to that in which father himself grew up.

Service system mediation and advocacy

There is substantial involvement of ECCRF PST staff in assisting parents in manoeuvring through the social and health service delivery system. This may take one or more of four forms:

1. assisting parents in locating and recruiting resources

2. advocating for resources on parents' behalf

3. assisting parents in presenting themselves in a more positive light to their municipal social worker, who remains the case's formal case manager

4. assisting parents in seeing service deliverers, in particular their municipal social worker, in a more co-operative light

The involvement of the Centre in mediation and advocacy on behalf of parents is illustrated in the case of 'A', a ten-year-old girl who was admitted because of serious educational and medical neglect on the part of her parents. These parents were chronically unemployed Israelis of Oriental descent who were raising eight children, aged 6 to 24, in their medium sized flat. Father 'Y', a rehabilitated narcotics addict worked 14 hour days as a labourer in the local market for less than minimum wage. The mother worked morning to night as a homemaker in order to keep the household clean and its members fed and clothed. She

also provided the children with substantial love and affection. Mother's tasks often overwhelmed her. The family had been known to the municipal social welfare department for at least the past ten years and they had received modest aid from time to time. Father was seen as a troublemaker for his outbursts around refusals for additional assistance. 'A' had failed to attend school for approximately six months prior to her referral and she was in serious need of medical treatment for asthma which her parents failed to organise for her.

The PST staff, shortly after beginning their assessment process, began to sense the large gap between the ability of 'A's' parents to care for their daughter within the home and their availability and ability to further their daughter's well-being vis-a-vis the educational and medical care systems. Consequently, PST staff worked hand in hand with the parents, in particular 'A's' mother in initiating a series of meetings with key players in the local educational and health systems. 'A's' parents attended these meetings along with Centre PST staff who significantly aided the parents in articulating their needs and presenting themselves in a manner which fostered a more positive understanding of them by the social service staff. PST staff followed up with 'A's' parents to be sure services promised to 'A' were delivered both in the school and hospital setting.

In addition 'A's' father requested help from the PST team in procuring for him special permission from the local government to open a small fruit and vegetable stand of his own in the local market. After preparation of a positive presentation style and attitude in 'A's' father by the PST team there was a joint submission made to local government officials by the father and the ECCRF team. 'A's' father was given permission to open his own booth in the market. He could now more easily support his family and be much more available to his wife and children in the evening hours.

Discussion

In each of the above ECCRF activities there remains complex dilemmas and questions regarding parental involvement. Prominent is the difficulty of ascertaining, from the many variables in the literature as well as those which emerge from practice regarding parenting, the most salient points upon which to focus. To confound matters, that which seems to be relatively insignificant in the estimation of the professional may be especially relevant in the client's own perspective. The opposite may also be true. Moreover, the in-depth and comprehensive Centre assessment is tailored to the demands of the larger social service and legal systems which envelope the ECCRF.

Another obstacle in the assessment process may be the apprehension of many parents to fully and honestly participate in the light of their perceived fear that findings may be used to their detriment either in the social service decision-making forum or in the courtroom. Periodically the time necessary for PST staff to build the trust necessary to full involvement remains in contradiction to the short amount of time allotted to complete assessments.

There also exists the challenge of determining the possible effect of the assessment itself on parents. This influence can be seen to affect parents either positively or negatively. That is, parents may feel so significantly fearful and anxious that they are unable to effectively organise their presentation of themselves and their family. Alternatively parents may find themselves so unusually highly motivated that they will be capable of making a highly effective, though once only, presentation. The setting may also affect the assessment process with parents reacting more apprehensively in the Centre than when it is undertaken at home or in another setting.

A further ongoing challenge to the integrity of the assessment process is how to consider and weigh conflicting information regarding parents, parenting and parent-child relationships, particularly subjective influences in data compilation completed by colleagues outside the Centre. Children at risk can arouse strong emotional reactions both amongst members of the larger public and helping professionals alike. Related here is the complexity of differentially weighing data revolving around individual, spousal and parental aspects of the client system.

Lastly, as relates to assessment, there is the complex question of understanding parenting and parent-child relations within the context of an increasingly pluralistic and multicultural society. A large number of ECCRF clients are new immigrants who often lack even the basic linguistic skills needed to engage in a meaningful assessment process. With regards to parental involvement in the therapeutic milieu, prominent here is the dilemma between the possibility of allowing and even unwittingly encouraging continued maltreatment and the significant therapeutic potential associated with renewed parent-child contact. Such a dilemma is exacerbated by the relatively short stay of the child at the Centre.

The concern over risk associated with parental involvement in the therapeutic milieu appears to be relatively strongly ingrained in the surrounding mental health and social service community, as well as in the public at large. There is little sympathy for the idea of providing perpetrators of sometimes heinous acts continuing contact with their victims. It is important to note that there was initial widespread resistance to the notion of the location of the Centre being known to the parents. There was much genuine concern that children might not be able to be protected under such circumstances. Such scepticism is not limited to those outside the ECCRF. Child care staff often have significant difficulty with ongoing parent-child involvement.

One of the most disturbing aspects of parental involvement in the therapeutic milieu is the effect on those children whose parents are not yet prepared to be involved in a meaningful way. Much effort is expended by Centre staff in attempting to compensate these children. Related here is the significant challenge of dealing with the effects on other children of a particular child's behaviour following contact with his parents – starting from the moment of scheduling and preparation for the visit through to post-contact summary. These periods are often marked by intense emotions in the child from which it is very difficult to insulate other children.

It is seen as an important premise at the Centre that children of different ages have different needs and capacities with respect to parent involvement in their daily lives. The mundane issue of the financial cost of parental involvement is highly relevant and worrisome, especially in light of the limited resources of many ECCRF parents. Included here are the expenses associated with lost work hours, transportation and also telephone billing.

With respect to the 'holding' of parents, there exists a relative lack of organisational and public support for what can be seen as unnecessary catering to individuals who have perpetrated criminal acts on innocent children. To complicate matters there remains a relative lack of professional knowledge and skills regarding how to best nurture those parents who often seem to be suffering from severe attachment disorders. Noteworthy is the special challenge faced by ECCRF staff in caring for a parent while being extremely tuned into his child and the damaging effects of the maltreatment on that child.

Lastly with respect to parental involvement in the therapeutic milieu, there is at times a clash between the principle of parental participation in decision-making, especially around the tasks of daily living, and parental availability and actual current competency. It remains a fairly common occurrence whereby parental involvement in decisions may be seen by Centre staff as clearly detrimental. However, it is in many cases precisely the strong parent-child bond encouraged and nurtured by the staff which makes non-acceptance of this parental

opposition a less than realistic option. It should be added that in a small number of instances parental involvement in decision-making may be resisted by the child himself.

An additional challenge facing parental involvement in therapy are those conceptual and practical obstacles involved in maintaining a viable therapeutic process. In addition there is the obstacle of some remaining scepticism by professionals about the possibility of successfully treating parents who abuse and neglect their children despite the investment of large numbers of hours in intensive therapeutic involvement.

The Centre is also commonly faced with client resistance and lack of readiness for therapy, especially in the light of the short time frames involved at the Centre. Particularly important is the difficulty of engaging parents who are new immigrants who may not have rudimentary mastery of the Hebrew language and who are not used to the sharing of feelings with those outside the family.

Lastly there is the challenge of involving the municipal social worker, who remains case manager, as a co-therapist at the Centre. Difficulties may arise when there does not exist a therapeutic tradition between the two workers or there is case overload or long travelling distances. It is important to note here the contribution of the municipal social worker in recruiting assistance for the parents which may facilitate their participation in the therapeutic process. There also remains the ongoing and special challenge of working collaboratively in therapy with professionals from the juvenile justice and mental health systems where there is often an initial need to build a common therapeutic language.

With respect to parent training, often there is the difficulty of convincing parents about the need to invest time and energy in learning skills which they invariably believe should come naturally to them. It is often hard for parents to come to terms with a realisation that they may lack such a basic commodity. In addition there is the frequent risk that parent training, at least initially, further alienates parents from their children. This risk emerges from the child's increased exposure to his parent, yet unskilled, and also his increased exposure to PST staff whom the child often use as a standard for evaluating the parenting by his father and mother.

With respect to case recommendations and decision-making there exists the challenge of dealing with parents who do not accept the Centre recommendations and in particular the rationale and data on which these recommendations are based. Moreover, there is often initially fairly widespread parental inability to accept the concept of partial parenting, which is not an infrequent part of ECCRF recommendations. With respect to service system mediation and advocacy on behalf of parents there remains the ongoing prevalence of misconceptions often held both by workers in the child welfare system and their clients, one about the other.

Conclusion

The Emergency Centre for Children at Risk and their Families has had a meaningful influence on the Israeli child welfare system and in particular the subsystem dealing directly with children at risk. The most important impact of the Centre has been to the direct benefits it has brought to Israeli children and parents. It has brought to the fore the previously underestimated needs of these children and their families. It has also revealed the relative difficulty of the service delivery systems in fully meeting these needs. Furthermore ECCRF activities, along with other developments, have gone a significant way in impacting on the practice philosophy of social workers, particularly at the level of the municipal social welfare office.

A decade after the conception of the ECCRF, Israeli social workers and allied professionals have much more hope for their most challenging child welfare clients. They have moderated some of their ideas of just what is 'good enough' parenting. There is a genuine shift whereby social workers are understanding that what may be perceived as just barely adequate parenting in a child's naturally occurring environment may well be of greater benefit to the development of a child than what may be seen as more ideal parenting in a foreign environment. ECCRF activity has given new meaning to the notion of the need to honour the child's roots or unique relationships. Related to this there is the growing acceptance of the need for long term professional support for children at risk in their own family settings.

The ECCRF has helped give a voice to parents in the child welfare system. It has shown that parents must be heard and permitted to participate and that this input must necessarily be valued. Moreover the link has been shown between such parent empowerment and the nurturing activities of the Centre on behalf of its parents. The message has spread that in order to nurture one must also be nurtured oneself. Moreover that if we want parents to hear their children that we must also listen to the parents. Basically that the treatment processes for maltreated children and their parents run parallel. In many respects the future of the Emergency Centre for Children at Risk and their Families is closely intertwined with the future of Israeli society itself.

There are mounting questions regarding the great financial costs of such social programs as the ECCRF. Demonstrating the cost effectiveness of these services, wholly dependent on the public purse, proves to be very difficult, particularly in times of economic recession. On the other hand however, there are growing social and economic difficulties facing Israeli society which are closely related to a rise in child maltreatment and interpersonal violence in general. There is a continuing migration from non-western countries with various notions about parenting and children. There is a growing acceptance for and occurrence of, separation and divorce, as well as exposure to spousal violence. The gap between rich and poor is widening and the proportion of children in poverty is escalating.

Complicating the society's approach to child maltreatment will be the growing appreciation of Israeli society as an interwoven quilt of nationalities, as opposed to a melting pot. This may well beckon the emergence of much more culturally sensitive approaches to child and family welfare practice. On the other hand, the massive influence of western, and especially American, social work in the field will likely continue, though alongside will be witnessed increasing evidence of indigenous theoretical and practical contributions. There will invariably be mounting opportunities to reach beyond Israel's borders in collaborative efforts in child and family welfare. That knowledge and skill being developed at the ECCRF will be increasingly shared with overseas colleagues, while the widening door to peace will hopefully allow for some beginning of sharing of interest and expertise with Israel's immediate neighbours.

References

Ainsworth, M. (1993). Attachments Beyond Infancy. *American Psychologist*, 4: 709–716.

Amundson, J., Stewart, K., and Valentine, L. *Temptations of Power and Certainty*, unpublished manuscript.

Barnard, C., and Kuehl, B. (1993). Ongoing Evaluation: In Session Procedures for Enhancing the Working Alliance and Therapy Effectiveness. *The American Journal of Family Therapy*, 23: 161–172.

Bellow, G. (1986). Self Psychology and Ego Psychology: An Historical Perspective. *Clinical Social Work Journal*, 14: 34–43.

Boszormenyi-Nagy, I. and Spark, G. (1973). *Invisible Loyalties: Reciprocity in Intergenerational Family Therapy*. New York: Harper and Row.

Bowlby, J. (1969). *Attachment and Loss*. New York: Basic Books.

Cirillo, S., and DiBlasio, P. (1989). *Families that Abuse: Diagnosis and Therapy*. New York: W.W. Norton and Company.

Cohen, S. and Egen, B. (1981). The Social Work Home Visit. *Social Work in Health Care*, 6: 55–67.

Colon, F. (1978). Family Ties and Child Placement. *Family Process*, 17: 289–312.

Dore, M. (1995). Preserving Families and Risk of Child Abuse and Neglect: The Role of the Helping Alliance. *Child Abuse and Neglect*, 20: 349–361.

Jernberg, A. (1977). *Theraplay*. London: Jossey Bass.

Kim Berg, I. (1994). *Family Based Services: A Solution Focused Approach*. New York: W.W. Norton.

Klein, I., and Janoff Bulman, R. (1996). Trauma History and Personal Narratives: Some Clues to Coping Among Survivors of Child Abuse. *Child Abuse and Neglect*, 20: 45–54.

Korittko, A. (1994). In-Home Treatment for Families in Crisis and its Supervision: A Systemic Multi-Level Approach. *Contemporary Family Therapy*, 16: 231–243.

Kufeldt, K., Armstrong, J., and Dorosh, M. (1994). How Children in Care View their Own and Their Foster Families. *Child Welfare*, 74: 695–713.

Ledbetter, Hancock, B., and Pelton, L. (1989). Home Visits: History and Functions. *Social Casework*, 21–30.

Maluccio, A., Fein, E., and Davis, I. (1994). Family Reunification: Findings, Issues and Directions. *Child Welfare*, 73: 489–504.

Minuchin, S., and Fishman, C. (1981). *Family Therapy Techniques*. Harvard: Harvard University Press.

Omer, H., and Omer, N. (1997). *Constructing Therapeutic Narratives*. Northvale: Jason Aronson.

Papp, P. (1983). *The Process of Change*. New York: Guilford Press.

Sable, B. (1995). Attachment Theory and Social Work Education. *Journal of Teaching in Social Work*, 12: 12–20.

Scannapieco, M. (1993). The Importance of Family Functioning to Prevention of Placement: A Study of Family Prevention Services. *Child and Adolescent Social Work Journal*, 10: 509–520.

Schnur, E., and Cohen, R. (1995). *No More-Yes Buts*, unpublished manuscript.

Skibinski, G. (1995). The Influence of the Family Preservation Model on Child Sexual Abuse Intervention Strategies. *Child Welfare*, 5: 975–989.

Villiotti, D. (1995). Embracing the Chaos: Moving from Child Centered to Family Centered. *Residential Treatment for Children and Youth*, 13: 41–51.

Wasserman, S. (1986). Decision Making in Child Abuse and Neglect. *Child Welfare*, 65: 515–529

Weiner, A. (1986). Institutionalizing Institutionalization: The Historical Roots of Residential Care in Israel. *Residential Group Care in Community Context*, 3–19.

Whittaker, J. (1989). *The Child Welfare Challenge*. New York: Aldine De Gruyer.

White, M., and Eon, D. (1990). *Narrative Means to Therapeutic Ends*. New York: W.W. Norton.

Winnicot, D. (1971). *Therapeutic Consultations in Child Psychiatry*. New York: Basic Books.

Worden, M. (1994). *Family Therapy Basics*. Pacific Grove: Brooks Cole.

7 Valuing Children, Parents and Neighbourhoods: So What's the Problem?

Alison Cathles, Jaz Galloway, Stewart Greenwell, Carol Henderson, Suzanna Jacoby, Val O'Connor, Alison Stokes, Bernice Thompson

This chapter describes a project in Gloucester where alternative ways of recruiting foster carers were tried and proved to be successful. This involved recruiting existing local parents and training them to become carers.

Faced with a large volume of children having to be placed outside of the county at a considerable and spiralling cost, the social services department looked at what it could do within Gloucester. What was needed were more placements for children in Gloucestershire and particularly in those urban areas from where most of the accommodated children originate. A network of neighbourhood projects has recently developed in the county which have started to put life back into those areas which have suffered the highest level of disadvantage locally.

Neighbourhood projects are independent democratic charities open to all residents. They work to relieve poverty, ill-health and disadvantage through advocacy, education, personal development and self-help. Neighbourhood projects are set up and run by the community themselves with support from others with a view to regenerating the area. The projects may help create jobs, improve the environment, provide advice and help for young and old to name a few. The projects are normally given funding in the first instance but the aim is for them to ultimately become completely independent.

The neighbourhood projects provided the arena which enabled us to think about recruiting foster carers in a different way; from a wider population than usual. The social services department had become used to its role as a purchaser of social care, but had hardly maximised the potential for using that purchasing power to achieve alternative longer term strategies, such as reducing dependence on services by investing in community enterprise.

From the inception of the idea of recruiting foster carers within the community from which most accommodated children come, we were taking on systems and people who had previously tried to bring in new ideas which had failed. They thus had an interest in proving that all available avenues had already been explored. 'It's all been tried before, so why bother!' were the familiar responses to any new and creative ideas. No doubt this attitude is replicated elsewhere. In addition we were aware that independent sector fostering agencies were waiting in the wings ready to exploit the untapped potential in the county.

Foster carers being recruited in a different way and supported in a different way could lead to new and very radical forms of organisation in foster care; removing the feeling that social workers can colonise the activity of recruiting and supporting people. Much the same debate is going on in relation to developing the idea of customer service officers replacing social workers as the point of access to the services of a social services department.

Social workers have a role to play, but so do neighbours and friends. In much the same way that baby-sitting circles provide a real source of support for lots of middle class people, moving beyond the actual respite provided from being a parent to the contact with other parents who live locally. That is a crucial ingredient of successful parenting which the project has brought out into the open. Well-trained support workers can offer the special service which foster carers need, but backed up by social workers.

Our project, which continues today, brings together community development and social work in an uneasy truce, harnessing the best principles of each discipline. Community development starts by working with people's strengths. Social work recognises the need to protect the most vulnerable people in our society. These are not mutually exclusive aims for each nor are they stated here with the intention of offending workers from either discipline.

Many will struggle to embrace both aims, but they illustrate the potential conflicts of interest. The fact that the most vulnerable people are likely, although not exclusively, to be working class and tend to be excluded from being part of their own solution presented us with another challenge. The notion of parents formally helping other families gives us the chance to build self-confidence and respect, so crucial to a community's ability to deal with future crises and to manage its own needs.

We didn't think that you would be interested in people like us.

This statement was forcibly conveyed to those of us who met with parents at the first few information evenings. Social work had failed to put across a message about the need to recruit working class foster carers to care for children. The image which these people had was of foster carers needing to live in a rural setting offering an escape from urban deprivation. In all probability they would be families with two cars, at least one partner in a professional well-paid job accessing pursuits like horse riding.

This caricature serves to prevent parents living in working class neighbourhoods from seeing themselves as suitable to offer care to accommodated children. They are used to being seen as people who are only likely to be on the receiving end of social services. People unable to provide services, and as parents, likely to have their competence challenged rather than valued.

Three of the newly appointed foster carers now successfully providing care to accommodated children provide a glimpse at this background:

My family were gypsies. They lived and travelled on the River Severn barges. I am one of 22 kids – 'cos my brother 'ad 'is kids taken off 'im. I'm 46 –a widow in a three-bedroom house and have six grandchildren.

I live on my own, but I have a spare bedroom, so why can't I be a foster carer?

I don't have any qualifications or much money, so why would you want me as a foster carer?

The perception, partially about the relationship with statutory services, coupled with people's poverty of both wealth and apparent experience means that the potential of a whole neighbourhood to contribute to their own solutions has been severely limited. It limits the contribution of people with real parenting experience, often under difficult circumstances, to share what they have learned with others, as well as to share how they have achieved a great deal, often against the odds.

So What is Fostering About and What Will I Have To Do?

The first step in recruiting parents from within the community as foster carers, was providing information in a form that told people what fostering is about. The vulnerability of the children and young people was stressed as was the need to provide safe care. At this stage we did not want to rule anyone out, but we did make it clear that safe care meant that people with a history of particular offences would be ruled out. This did not, however, include having shoplifted as a teenager.

Also, we pointed to the fact that carers get paid for caring. This in itself produced some interesting reactions, from current foster carers in particular, who suggested that this was misinformation, clearly not seeing the allowance which they receive as income or remuneration. It is easy to see why, when many carers receive very little and the level of allowances are determined by the individual local authority, leading people to receive very different allowances even though they are doing the same job. It is also a fact that generally foster carers are not invited to consider themselves as 'doing it for the money', that statement leaving a nasty taste in the mouth. Fostering is seen as the optimum expression of altruism. Many of the parents we met in those early days did not have the privilege of considering how to make a contribution to their local community, as they were too preoccupied with surviving, yet they had done so and with pride.

Interestingly, the move which a number of carers have made to independent sector agencies across the country suggests that money can be a factor in determining with whom they want to be associated and that it does not make anyone less compassionate in carrying out their job as a carer.

A significant part of the project was to invite people to consider becoming part of a community business, which would offer foster placements to the local authority, generating real income within the neighbourhood and giving people a sense of control over the business of which they were part. Expecting anyone to hold on to all of this when also being asked to consider becoming a foster carer may have been too much to expect, but we have held firm in our belief that a different form of agency could emerge which delivers high quality care as well as providing people with real income for carrying out socially worthwhile jobs.

How Did We Get the Message Across in Our Recruitment of Parents as Foster Carers?

The recruitment campaign involved the production of a special issue local community newspaper, produced in one week, in each of the three neighbourhoods. This was followed by door knocking on each house in each neighbourhood to see if they had read the newspaper. If interested, they were invited to attend an information evening. This kind of personal contact in itself is not radical, but in the area of foster care recruitment may be

unusual, in that social services departments might be more concerned about avoiding the people who they do not want to recruit, rather than widening access to a highly valued job and indeed in some cases an income. The fact that the contact was made by community development workers rather than social workers is also significant. The workers were all people who lived in the neighbourhood, so were likely to be known and not have the door immediately shut in their face. A worker said:

> *Having been involved with mental health in the community for many years, starting to work for Community Foster Care has opened a new avenue to me, empowering people who thought they had nothing to offer. Recruiting people, supporting them through the training, seeing them proud that they have something to offer, and seeing them change for the better, is so rewarding.*

The recruitment workers were paid for by a grant from the social services department to carry out the task. Another important way of getting the message across has been through carers talking to their friends, neighbours and relatives about doing the training and being approved and most importantly taking the first child on placement. These kind of networks, which are basically ordinary people exchanging ordinary information, are influential in helping people to think of alternatives for themselves.

'Training Sounds Frightening'

> *I like the way you explain and listen to our views. I know that I can ask questions and trust that you won't make me feel stupid* (foster carer in training).

There is a real danger that we forget the damaging experiences which a lot of people have had from their own education. Even the word 'training' made some people withdraw, as it sounded as if all of their worst nightmares may be repeated. The quote above suggests that a way was found around that, but this involved a great deal of time being devoted to allow people to talk about their fears, but time that has been a good investment.

Even when parents have not gone on to being approved as foster carers after completing their training, the workers have observed the benefits to the individuals and noted how they have grown in confidence and self-esteem. One young mother dropped out of the training to go into a women's refuge following her experience of domestic violence. When contacted by one of the recruitment workers she explained how she had gained enough insight and strength to change her own situation. She had also become aware of the impact of her circumstances at home on her own child. These may be unintended outcomes from someone starting and dropping out of foster care training, but they cannot be ignored and should be seen as an overall community benefit rather than a loss. Sadly, it is just these kinds of opportunities that social work can miss if it fails to look searchingly at what it is encountering.

The National Foster Care Association was sufficiently interested in this initiative to choose it as a pilot site for testing out the 'competency-based' model of training and assessing foster carers. The attraction was the way in which the model builds upon people's previous experience and their strengths, particularly those around parenting. Initially, those workers who carried out the training were also involved in the assessment and this helped make the connections, so that the training was brought back home and shared with the family.

Parents were given the time they needed to understand the implications of the training for them and other members of their family and were helped to build a picture of how their previous experiences had led them to consider foster care. As indicated, for some it was informally caring for children within their extended family, childminding, often unregistered, but nevertheless a significant experience, and in other cases having been on the receiving end of social work some years previously. One foster carer, with her own children grown up and moved away, sums it up eloquently:

> Community Foster Care has acted as a springboard for me to rediscover and explore my strengths and weaknesses. I'd never thought about it like this before.

and another:

> I went into fostering, because I was a recruitment worker on the project. I felt that you begin to learn about yourself and what you could offer a child. What you learn over the years, your inner-self knows what you can give. You don't have to live in a high-class area. It's about what you feel about yourself and what you can offer. I was lucky or unlucky enough to have a very difficult first placement. It threw me in at the deep end, but at the end of the seven weeks' placement, both the child and myself and my family had a greater insight into what fostering is all about.

This shows that the approach adopted was one of continuous learning, not one of simply being approved and assuming that is where it ends, but being approved and helping people learn through their early placements so that they can take on new challenges. Parenting has begun to have a different meaning for people, not necessarily intellectualising the ordinariness of it, but making sense of it in a way that builds self-esteem and confidence and being prepared to learn from mistakes.

One important difference for people was the effort put into de-mystifying the whole process. This included what the training was trying to do, what the assessment was likely to uncover and how to prepare for that. In addition what might happen at the approval panel and how to prepare for that, knowing that most people would find the whole idea intimidating became an important topic leading up to the fostering panel. This is particularly so when people's common experiences of assessment by social workers are more likely to be around questioning their capability to be adequate parents for their own children.

'I Will Pop In at the Weekend'

What does being professional mean? This may seem a strange question to ask. Is it the same for community work as for social work? Is it OK for people to just pop in on foster carers as a way of offering support, when usually social workers make appointments? The foster carers seem to appreciate the closeness which the project offers to their daily lives. However, these are issues which have cropped up which have had to be dealt with honestly and openly. One of the benefits of engaging with neighbourhood projects as part of this initiative is the way that we have harnessed the energy of local people to do something positive. Recruitment workers live in the same neighbourhoods and know the foster carers as friends and occasionally as relatives. That is how some of the recruitment has worked, by word of mouth and that is how support happens on working class estates. However, we have to be careful that this does not lead to exploitation of the workers, expecting them to give more of their time than is reasonable. Conversely, we have to be careful we do not put too many constraints on people offering authentic support as and when people need it.

The issue of confidentiality is a crucial one to unravel. There is a difference between gossiping, and exchanging information in a professional manner, where professional means understanding the new boundaries which a different kind of relationship imposes. It is not just one parent talking to another, the support worker is there with a particular purpose, to offer support, not just to pop in because they are looking for support themselves. The worker will have a responsibility to report back about how things are going and that may mean that they start to become regarded with some caution. Our experience is that when these issues are faced openly, they can be overcome.

Community work clearly involves difficulties around confidentiality just like social work. There is also the imperative for the children to be well protected. We have had to recognise that this can sit easily, if occasionally in tension, with widening

opportunities for people who have previously been denied those opportunities.

The issue of administration also touched on who was in control of the initiative, the social services department or the neighbourhood projects? The neighbourhood projects were well used to the administration flowing from ESF (European Social Fund) projects and showed their capabilities to respond to bureaucracy. It may be an inevitable hurdle that we all have to jump as a way of demonstrating that good ideas can also prove themselves to become well managed, reliable and regularly monitored pieces of work.

The project, now a company limited by guarantee, has presented a service level agreement to the local authority in order that proper business can begin at a price which brings in money to the local economy.

'She Just Has Not Come Back'

The local labour market is fluid, and in recruiting local parents we found that there was a lot of early turnover. This meant that at worst people were let down, but probably no worse than the way that social services let people down, whether it be through turnover of staff or simply a less than human face being provided at each point of contact. The project has learned from this, without ruling out taking advantage of the opportunities which occur in a neighbourhood project to use someone's interest and time for the collective good of the community.

> But that is where the children come from and you can't send them back there, can you?

This was expressed as a potential objection rather than a reason for pursuing the objective of the project, as if it was to be avoided at all costs. The statement came from a current foster carer, during one of the early discussions with the local foster care association. It suggested a degree of prejudice and a lack of understanding about the causes of disadvantage, for which we all have to take responsibility, rather than blaming this individual. It could stem from believing that there are families and indeed communities which are inherently dangerous and therefore they should be respectively 'done to' and avoided as potential service providers. Bringing community development and social work together can help to demonstrate that protecting children and strengthening communities are not mutually exclusive goals. We have learned a lot from the early work on 'dangerousness' and believe that the most important thing to get right is the level of trust between agencies which will avoid keeping secrets when information sharing is likely to be in everyone's interests.

> *Perhaps the most dangerous aspect of inter-agency functioning lies in the way in which agencies relate to one another.*

(Dale *et al.*, 1986, p 38)

Contact With Parents

Another important feature of the project's work has been to think carefully about the issues of contact with the child or young person's parents. The close proximity between parents and carers allows it in a way that traditionally may not have been available, although many foster carers in Gloucestershire and elsewhere now have a great deal of experience of offering contact in their own homes. Those carers who have taken their first and second placements are beginning to build up experience from which others will learn. Being only a bus ride away gives parents a feeling that their child has not 'been taken away' in the same sense that in other circumstances might require a social worker to provide transport. However, the maintenance of boundaries is something that we are all learning about and about which there is a developing clarity. The project is building some new links between families and the social services department with Community Foster Care acting as a link. An unthreatening one, that is slowly developing confidence and trust between those people on the receiving end and those who provide services.

'So What Do You Mean by a Community Business?'

A community business is one that has both social and economic goals, operates within, and as part, of the local economy and is owned and controlled by the community. A community business usually has some form of membership system and is characterised by its commitment to democracy, participation and mutuality. Central to the idea of community enterprise is a distinct set of core values that distinguishes it from both the public and private sectors. These values are characterised by community roots, accountability to local people and community benefit; all fine sounding principles which often are discounted as being too far out of reach and then discredited.

This has meant that we have had to support each other through the process of establishing the community business as others have sat on the sidelines waiting for it all to fail.

So Who Would Benefit From Community Businesses?

One and half million people currently take part in community economic initiatives in the UK. Community businesses normally trade in areas of high unemployment and often in socially and economically disadvantaged areas; hence their relevance to this particular initiative. Community businesses support the generation and sustainability of wealth within neighbourhoods, improving local jobs and services and offering the potential to build upon the skills and self-esteem of local people.

What has setting up a community business got to do with social services and foster care? In the current climate, social services departments must take a broader view of their role, and consider the causes of the deprivation which they encounter and try to tackle. The county council's anti-poverty strategy has helped to focus minds to ensure the business of employment and regeneration no longer belongs elsewhere exclusively.

> *…unemployment is, more than anything, an intensification of tribulations that are common place: powerlessness, low status, low and fluctuating incomes are the lot of the unskilled, the uncertificated, the unorganised, in work or out of it*
>
> (Harrison, 1983, p 108)

Social services departments would say that they recognise the significance of unemployment as a factor mitigating against people achieving in all areas of their lives. How many do anything about it?

'There Are Just Too Many Forms'

Groups considering becoming involved in this type of work should realise some of the problems. During the infancy of the project we were successful in obtaining European Social Fund resources particularly around the development of community enterprises. The bureaucracy and administration involved in ESF as well as fostering generally could be a big turn off for some people. We engaged people in these processes so that they understood the purpose of administration, and good administration in particular. We were lucky in attracting two people, a social worker and an administrator, for a temporary period, whose strengths are in setting up systems and making them comprehensible to all concerned. This was essential as a way of demonstrating to the local authority that there would be access to good information, well stored and well recorded. This gave people who may have been sceptical about the quality of what was being developed more confidence in the potential end product.

So What is Happening Now?

At the time of writing this chapter, Community Foster Care Ltd. has been registered as a not-for-profit community business and has a board of directors made up from community leaders. The business employs foster carers, all of whom are themselves parents, a social work manager, a business manager, two job share recruitment workers and an administrator. The company has a policy of continuously recruiting with training programmes planned over the next few months. This allows for parents to express an interest and be given time to discuss the implications for them and their own lives without the pressure of feeling that it is the next programme or nothing. Each family has continued links through the process with their recruitment worker who acts as a link with the social work manager and the social worker carrying out the assessment.

What Have We Learned?

- The need to manage and work with those interests that would seek to maintain control over the way that fostering recruitment and training and assessment is carried out.

- The need to deal with and, if possible, anticipate staffing crises as they occur in the neighbourhood projects as well as the social services department.

- How to engage the wider social services department's interest in purchasing from community enterprises and thereby not only achieving best value in purchasing the service but also in meeting some of its responsibilities in relation to the county council's anti-poverty strategy, economic development and sustainable communities policies.

- Not to underestimate the work entailed in taking on a new way of working and that in working in partnership with neighbourhood projects we are expecting a lot of them in terms of extra workload.

- That neighbourhood projects will rightly challenge the social services department's assumptions about parent's suitability for fostering and their interpretation of life experience.

- That this kind of partnership places

more responsibility on all involved to ensure that everyone knows who is doing what, avoiding assumptions about who has the authority or expertise to carry out particular work.

- That parents living in disadvantaged areas can understand what they have to offer, can benefit from self-development opportunities and can offer care to children which is relevant and appropriate.

The best testimonial is short and sweet and comes from the parent of a child placed with Community Foster Care who is able to recognise her own weaknesses, but at the same time consider her own child's needs for safety:

> *I know that we're not capable of looking after our baby, but it's so important that she is only a few streets away and we know she is happy.*

References

Dale, *et al.* (1986). *Dangerous Families.* Tavistock.

Harrison, P. (1983). *Inside the Inner City.* Penguin

8   Shared Care: Ensuring a Network of Care to Meet the Needs of Young People

Peter Sandiford and John Whiteside

This chapter details theory and practice around shared care. Peter Sandiford describes the theory which is supported by his experience. John Whiteside records the work by Tameside Social Services Department.

> *The Act (1948 Children Act) introduced the idea that children might be looked after not as a punitive response to their own misbehaviour or to the inadequacy of their parent, but as a service to families.*
>
> (Jackson and Thomas, 1999)

It has taken half a century for this idea to become the subject of debate and service delivery. In October 1998 the report of the Ministerial Group on the Family said that one area in which the government could make a difference was:

> *…improving services and strengthening the ways in which the wider family and communities support and nurture family life.*
>
> (The Home Office, 1998)

Shortly after came Quality Protects:

> *To increase the number of families of children in need supported by a series of planned short term care arrangements involving for each child the same substitute carer. This sub-objective is significant for children with disabilities but should be extended to apply to all children in need. It counters children moving in and out of 'care' in an unplanned way and substitutes planned and therefore predictable periods of short term care which supports the main carer(s).*
>
> (Department of Health, 1998)

It is the conference season, and the delegates are having an informal evening debate on issues of concern in residential child care. The debate centres around three key issues:

1. How many of us, who are all involved in providing residential and foster care, see ourselves as supporting parents – is our work far more about replacing parents?

2. How many of us have provided a residential or foster placement as part of a package of 'shared' (as distinct from replacement) care?

3. Have we not in fact customarily seen residential services used as a last resort, to only be considered when all else has been tried and indeed failed?

At this point an example of good practice might be presented. What would it look like? Perhaps an example from Tameside is relevant.

If somebody asked whether residential and foster carers believe they are doing a valued and valuable job the reply would probably be 'no'. The following quote may go some way towards explaining this:

> *Virtually all social workers appear to view admission to care very negatively. They see it as a last resort and a sign of failure to prevent the break up of families. They are also worried about what the care experience will do to children and parents. Residential care is looked at with special pessimism. This attitude only serves to increase the stigma, shame, depression and passivity in families, field and residential social workers alike. It hampers proper planning because social workers close their eyes to the possibility of admission and keep hoping that it will not have to happen. When the crisis comes, no-one is adequately prepared.*
>
> (Department of Health, 1985, p 16)

The reasons for this negative view from within the profession are not easily addressed. There are many different influences, some of which are:

The media

How often do we see anything positive about our profession in journals, newspapers, on a TV documentary or 'soap'?

Employment/qualifications

People with no formal qualifications in anything can get a job as a carer. Of course many may be highly skilled in practice, but since these skills are not signified by any formal qualification requirement, the residential social worker enjoys low professional status. This is then further compounded by the number of 'pool' or temporary staff employed in residential homes. The message given is 'anybody can do the job'. This is despite the work of 'parenting' being with some of the most disadvantaged young people in our society today.

Training

A new trolley pusher and sorter at a supermarket gets more initial training than many residential social workers.

It is interesting that those working in the area of children with a disability would be looking at the issues discussed above very differently. They would say that for many years before the Children Act they were developing packages of care in partnership with parents where shared care was the norm, and where the carers also felt they were doing a valued and valuable job.

Following the publication of a number of highly critical reports into the services provided to children and young people in public care, including *People Like Us* and the North Wales Inquiry it would be easy to see the state of service provision as being near one of chaos. Whilst this could be seen, by definition, as being a wholly negative condition, we can take hope from the management guru, Charles Handy's, *The Empty Raincoat*. He describes this state – 'the edge of chaos'– as being a time when complex systems can be 'spontaneous, adaptive and alive'. Surely this is a good description for what we need, and could be getting through to the government initiatives such as the *Response to the Safeguards Review* and the targets for improvement being

presented to local authorities in the form of quality protects.

Much of the quality protects initiative can be seen as alive and adaptive. It is also rooted deep in research that goes back a long way, so far that one wonders why it has not been taken notice of before now. *Social Work Decisions in Child Care: Recent Findings and Their Implications* (1985) contained details of four studies looking at decision-making and the experiences of children, young people and their parents.

> *The decision not to admit their children was seen (by the parents) in purely negative terms. Nothing helpful in their eyes had been offered in its place and some were left with a real sense of despair… Thus Clayport's low admission rates fostered large numbers of disgruntled parents who felt unhelped and neglected.*
>
> (Packman, Randall and Jaques p 9)

The lack of provision of services when they are needed by parents is a theme of all the studies. Another common theme was the lack of assessment at the time of referral, particularly in relation to strengths and positive attributes within families.

Many parents requiring support have received services up to the children being eight years of age but at this point little has been available. With an ever increasing emphasis on child protection, social workers have had to concentrate on rescue rather than prevention. This is mirrored in social work training where less and less time is invested in therapeutic case work skills. Many parents needing support feel they have a 'sticky plaster' stuck on the problem rather than interventions that will lead to long term solutions. Residential care and foster care are services that should be used to support parents at an earlier stage of dealing with problems. However, most social workers take a negative view of admission to residential care, seeing it as the 'last resort' and an admission of failure rather than as part of some planned continuum of care.

> *The emphasis on whether or not to admit seems to have got out of focus. It draws attention away from consideration of children's needs and how to meet them. An over-emphasis on admission may actually*

hamper the search for other options as well as inhibiting the creative use of care for children in some circumstances. Indeed there seems to be a profound ambiguity between seeing care as a service to which families and children are entitled and policies that strive to keep children out of care at all costs.

(Department of Health, 1985, p 16)

The benefits of residential and foster care provision in supporting parents and preventing permanent break-ups are now recognised. This sort of care needs to be part of a continuum of services and must be planned for with a clearly identified purpose and an emphasis on achieving the plan. Changes in the way services are provided can be made by closer working with parents rather than relying on greater resources. This in turn should lead to more positive outcomes for children and young people.

The Department of Health publication *Focus on Teenagers: Research into Practice* (DOH, 1996) highlights the 'widely accepted' belief 'that most children and young people thrive best when brought up by their families in a stable living situation which offers strong emotional ties. Unfortunately for many teenagers in need of social work services, instability and change are already common features in their lives'.

Research has shown that at the time of referral to social services a quarter of all children and young people were from reconstituted families and almost half had at least one previous experience of care, while others had moved between relatives and friends (Triseliotis *et al.*, 1995). Sadly this pattern of unstable living arrangements followed this group throughout their teenage years (Sinclair *et al.*, 1995; Triseliotis *et al.*, 1995).

While it would be wrong to assume that all movement is detrimental in its cause and effect, research suggests that it is the feelings of rejection or unplanned upheavals which are damaging. Consistent with earlier studies current research (Berridge and Brodie, 1998) has shown that the majority of children and young people were known to social services and that a high proportion of those

accommodated were emergency admissions. As a consequence social workers are often ill prepared and have little time for planning and consultation with teenagers, their parents and prospective carers.

Other research evidence suggests that effective institutions are those where young people, parents and professionals believe tangible benefits are gained from the experience, be it physical care, greater understanding and support or academic achievement (Tutt, 1974; Kahan, 1980; Milham *et al.*, 1981). In addition to these factors, flexible living arrangements can also be an important element in the support of looked after young people. The effectiveness of this sort of provision is evidenced by the fact that half of the young people who attend residential schools also spend a substantial time at home and we have already noted the stability of such placements (Triseliotis *et al.*, 1995).

Research into institutional provision has consistently shown that a more complex, though flexible caring infrastructure can offer greater stability (Triseliotis *et al.*, 1995). Social work plans may need to incorporate a number of stable 'known' bases within the young person's community and include 'contingency plans'. For example, weekly boarding at a special school with week-ends and holidays shared between foster carers and parents, or weekdays within a residential unit and week-ends at home or the placement of a residential worker in the family home during the week to support the parents or to offer support during times of stress. It is essential, however, that plans have a built-in flexibility to allow them to adjust quickly if and when a young person's circumstances change or if a crisis arises. Institutionalisation and bureaucracy should be minimised in favour of safe and flexible choice, to accommodate the variations of normal adolescent behaviour patterns and changes in family life. For a family seeking support the service provided might follow the continuum set out in the diagram below (adapted from Tameside Social Services Family Support Team).

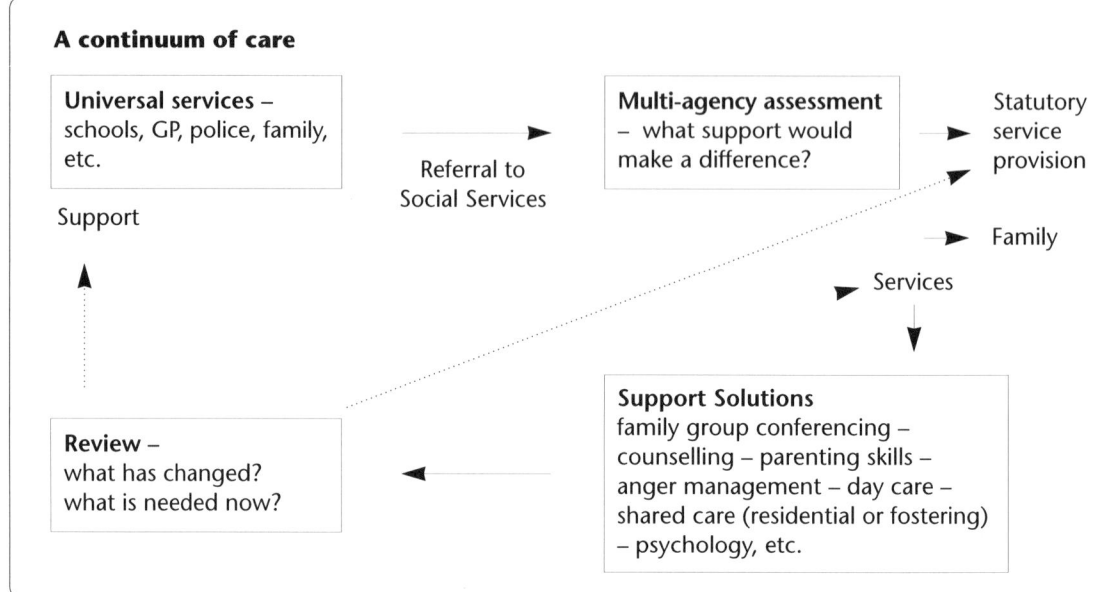

A placement plan based upon a continuous network of settings acceptable to the young person and known to each other, would offer greater overall stability. It would allow resources to be pooled and encourage responsibility and knowledge about the young person to be constructively shared. It would reduce inconsistency and unplanned changes in the young person's life and would encourage parent involvement. Thus it would prevent the total upheavals, and inevitably damaging consequences, experienced by many young people.

A continuum of care

- statutory service provision
- referral to social services
- family support services

The principle of shared care, not only between parents and carers, but when appropriate between more than one set of substitute carers, needs to drive social work thinking when planning the living arrangements and support interventions for vulnerable children and young people. This approach has many strengths, and elements of it have, or are being, introduced into the working of some local authorities, including Manchester, Wigan, Tameside, Stockport and Bradford.

The approach provides a vehicle for negotiation and planning between a set of known carers, including foster parents and residential care workers, parents of school friends, extended family or family friends. It also makes available a choice of familiar care settings throughout the child or young person's 'care career' and encourages the shared responsibility for sustaining the child or young person between the local authority, the parents and the extended family.

The Tameside Adolescent and Family Support team, AFST, was set up early in 1994. Tracking a group of young people admitted directly to the emergency reception centre indicated that 80 per cent were able to go home again within a two to six week period. It became clear that families were having to overstate their problems to obtain a service.

In response, a system was designed in order to assess adolescents in crisis quickly, pass them through to the family support panel system and on to a newly formed adolescent and family support team. Seamless transition to a service with the minimum of delay was a prime quality standard of this system.

Managers from the newly formed AFST and other related adolescent teams such as:

- duty
- assessment
- looked after children
- aftercare

were recruited to sit on the family support panel in rotation, thus spreading the load and introducing a wider structure of expertise.

The family support panel fits into a systems social work loop which consists of:

- assessing the situation
- setting outcome goals
- setting method goals
- doing the work
- re-assessing the situation

In Thameside this is a four to six week block to prevent a drift of the situation. The system is open-ended but normally the case closes naturally as the family's situation improves.

A huge amount of time and effort is invested at the beginning, with some families being seen every day. There is an expression 'Merlin's magic dust' which means workers try to find an immediate difficulty that can be resolved positively, such as helping with housing arrears or attending school to help with exclusion worries.

This builds up trust, makes families feel better and helps them cope with other difficulties.

Gradually, the service is tailored down until such time as social services no longer contact the family but the family has a worker to call in time of crisis. Often, all that is required is a call made as a gentle reminder of some of the previously agreed coping strategies.

Voluntary groups such as those for addiction, counselling and financial advice are being included in this work. This is a benefit to the family as it avoids the apparent stigma of people involved with social services. Reviewing ensures that there is no slippage. The presence of the young person and the parents ensures that clear feedback is obtained and the next service period planned with confidence.

Panel chairs may use questioning methods gleaned from systemic family therapy where family functioning can be uncovered. Often, despite huge differences of opinion, family members can be encouraged to agree to a common goal of working towards making things better. This system allows them to retain their personal agendas until the worker can target them for change. The panel, in effect, is used to turn the family members into 'customers'.

> *A customer is someone who asks for a service, perceives that they will benefit from that service and will enter into contracts and negotiations to ensure that the service meets their perceived expectations.*
>
> (Pincus and Mininhan, 1982)

In many social work arenas the family, or more especially the young person, does not meet the above definition of 'the customer'. Progress is less certain without all sides subscribing to the change process. The fast track assessment and start of this service model has allowed us to look differently at families who have previously had other young people accommodated, and the Smith family, discussed later, are a prime example.

Intensive Family Support: The Tameside Model

The aim of intensive family support is to reduce the incidences of crisis leading to admission to residential care.

The team runs a seven day service open from 7am until midnight. The service is staffed in the old residential manner with duties divided between rest days and weekends off to ensure that adequate numbers of workers are available at key times.

Workers are Case Holders and manage the wider care co-ordination and assessment duties for the family whilst they are on our service. They can carry up to seven or eight cases depending on complexity. Cases tend to last for three or four panel visits between 12 to 18 weeks. Registered children may be around longer.

The base is set out as a family house and is designed to be as user friendly as possible with facilities for refreshments and light meals to be served should this be necessary to young people or their parents whilst crises are dealt with or work is in progress.

Young people are invited in for work sessions, with workers taking care to prevent some young people at particularly vulnerable points in their lives meeting with others who may adversely affect them. We are keen to avoid a 'youth club' scenario but young people do meet during group work sessions but this is, of course, a selected and focused group.

Parents too are invited to both drop in at times of stress and for individual work or parent meetings. Our mothers' group is particularly popular as a non-threatening support and education forum. From our research into this grouping we are starting a second mothers' group run and managed by the mothers themselves for continuing support for when they have left our service. Fathers are less keen to join in but we have had some success with the 'Mr. Angrys' in group settings. The team members are all very experienced residential workers.

Professional Oversight Available

We have a clinical psychologist available for staff support and development. This includes monthly case screening sessions at staff meetings as well as the opportunity to refer young people. Two team members, in conjunction with the clinical psychologist, have developed an anger management course for young people. They are now developing two similar very practical courses, one to address and manage 'anxiety' which will be piloted with parents as well as young people and the other, 'self-esteem', which will follow as part of the quality protects agenda for young people's health and well-being.

We engaged a consultant family therapist to give us the basics of narrative therapy. We were particularly interested in the concept of 'externalising' behaviours in our quest to promote the 'unconditional positive regard theme' with adults. So often the young person is seen as the problem rather than their behaviour. This proved a revelation and all staff quickly took to this simple but powerful concept.

Positive Parenting

From Fahlberg's assertions that the most important parenting response is the provision of 'unconditional positive regard' we have developed a philosophy of Positive Parenting which follows the themes and perspectives outlined in a book produced by the people from the Leicestershire Fun and Families Centre.

Our own contributions include cognitive behaviour management work books, behaviour record charts, and cognitive effective explorations of the parents' own experiences of being parented. Our theme here is that families can be places where adults can heal and grow and family life should be embraced and enjoyed.

Our assessment system and the high 'in need' threshold in our borough unfortunately ensures that families and young people are often in quite a 'mess' when they get to us. Hence we are developing with the NCB a project to provide a complementary sub-threshold service within our assessed work. This will include the local health visitor team, child and family centre staff and teachers all focused on Positive Parenting.

We take a clear partnership role with families based on respect for them and the difficulties they are in. Nevertheless our child protection radars are running all the time. We have an arrangement with the duty team and the police family support team where they provide consultation and support for investigations when matters become serious.

Children on the Child Protection Register

Where families have been dealt with previously by the child protection teams and the children registered but not accommodated, we take over the case. The adults are by this time bruised and battered by the process and often reluctant to work. The statutory requirements enable us to take the first step in meeting the parents and then our experience and enthusiasm usually changes the parents' perspectives. Our seven day service, where we try to see all families at least twice per week, gives a positive child protection presence in the house, and re-assuring both the department and the family in this difficult time.

The Philosopher

We read all the family support research we can and have taken part in several seminars forging country wide links with others in similar teams.

We also commissioned our own survey of service users where the researcher asked 'what our service had felt like to them'. From this we have developed new ideas and practices and regularly ask the parent group what they think of our ideas. A newsletter at

times of holidays was one development requested. In this we make it clear when we are available and give advice on managing young people's time during a school break.

The survey highlighted that our service was valued for worker attitude, clear planning involving peoples own resources and above all the strengths and genuineness of the team members.

Residential child care is most effective when used as part of a planned and cohesive package of care options, a continuum of care involving parents, carers and substitute or respite care placements of various types and at various times to support the child's varying needs.

Tom: The Work With Parents

Tom's father had been in care and saw himself as having made good despite his disadvantages. He had been a fighter and saw this as an important response to any challenge. He had been violent with Tom on several occasions and Tom's mother always used the potential threat of this with us to reinforce her requests for accommodation for Tom.

Tom's worker had tried long and hard to develop his parents' ability to understand and change their management strategies when dealing with what they saw as his more difficult behaviours. Using the key principles of cognitive behavioural management she had tried to get them to accentuate the positives and ignore the negatives and above all manage him together and consistently. This was not really working and they enjoyed telling us how each strategy that the worker put forward was defeated.

I supervise Tom's social worker and we decided to co-work a family session with me as the therapist. Exploring Tom's father's own parenting revealed that he saw himself as having been parented coldly and strictly but he saw this as having been the making of him.

Tom's mother, despite having a teenage son, dressed as a teenager and behaved in a similarly immature way. I know that is a value based judgement but she was remarkably so. She set up a wall of sound in any meeting, scarcely taking a breath to develop a distressingly, for the listener, negative picture of Tom at every opportunity.

Some of this behaviour is consistent with low level mental health problems but we have difficulty getting specialist services for mothers with high levels of anxiety.

It was almost impossible to get a word in edgeways and I had frequently to apologise at the end of family sessions for the oppressive manner that I had to take to make any progress. Tom's father said little and when he did the mother always qualified it.

Using the externalising techniques I gradually drew a picture of Tom's anger and moved it outside him presenting it as something that 'washed over him and the family at times dulling their lives'. (White and Epstein, 1990).

This made anger the cause of the families difficulties rather than Tom. Tom's father got this and went with me as far as saying that he too had times that anger washed over him and that he wondered why. This was a useful shift and included Tom's father in the work.

Unfortunately Tom's mother sabotaged this in the following days as it became clear that the two men in her life, Tom and his father, were being drawn into vying for her affections. The parents wouldn't tackle this theme and Tom's behaviour was escalated by their mis-management to the point where he left.

I was concerned about the grandparents ability as carers dispensing advice to Tom when their own child, Tom's father was having such difficulties with his life. However, there is some good research on this in Pitcher's *When Grandparents Care*.

Angela

Angela Smith is a young woman of 14 years who comes from a family well known to the social services department.

Her older brother Simon had been taken into care at the request of her parents twelve months previously. In the chaotic period that followed he continually offended and ran away from numerous care situations until he ended up in a distant, and costly, out of borough placement.

Mrs Smith had been married previously, and Angela and Simon were the children of that marriage. Mr Jones had joined the family about eight years ago. Mrs Smith and Mr Jones have two children between them, Joyce, who was eight years old and Paul, who was six years old. Mr Smith had not maintained contact with Simon and Angela following his exit from the family when they were very small.

The onset of adolescence saw Angela spreading her wings, and the resulting conflicts soon escalated to the point where her parents were demanding care as they had done previously when Simon had become difficult to manage.

Meanwhile, Simon was becoming settled and finding that life in his new family suited him so well that contact was being lost between him and his family of origin. This evoked difficult feelings for Mrs Smith which complicated her responses to Angela. Mrs Smith was reduced to making chaotic and conflicting decisions when ordinary adolescent conflicts with Angela escalated into arguments. This led them to the door of the duty team with a request for accommodation for Angela. Mrs Smith claimed that Mr Jones might be reduced to hurting Angela if she wasn't accommodated immediately. It would, she said, be the fault of the social services department if Angela was injured!

The family were introduced to the concept of intensive family support and helped to present their case at the family support panel.

Mrs Smith presented as highly anxious and was frequently close to tears as she outlined the effect Angela was having on her and her partner. Mr Jones was calmer and appeared to understand what was going on in the family, and careful questioning revealed that he was frustrated by the actions of Mrs Smith whom he saw as undermining his attempts to make a relationship with Angela. He outlined how he thought that he could set her appropriate boundaries and sanctions. An agreement was reached between Angela and her parents to work on the difficulties and a review date set.

The first impressions in the panel meeting were confirmed. Mr Jones, if he had been allowed, would have set appropriate limits and sanctions for Angela. It was clear to the worker that Mrs Smith could not bear him to have anything to do with Angela and consistently undermined his efforts.

Mrs Smith alternated between wanting the social services department to remove Angela, and becoming unhealthily close to her, confiding her deep personal partnership problems with Mr Jones as well as keeping Angela off school for companionship.

Mr Jones was having difficulty ascertaining the role that Mrs Smith wanted him to assume. He began to resent the relationship the mother and daughter had and frequently went overboard in disciplining Angela. Angela began to run away, blaming her stepfather's attitude for this, whilst Mrs Smith took her daughter's side.

Intensive work by the family support social worker seemed to be making little headway in this complex situation. The situation was worsening rapidly, and Mr Jones was struggling to see the relevance of Angela's attitude and his position as a male in her life. Constant parental conflict was unsettling Mr Jones' own children which Mr Jones saw as evidence of Angela's behaviour adversely influencing them. The pressure for Angela to be removed from the home grew daily.

The family returned to the family support panel before the planned review date and a plan was agreed to suit the changed circumstances. This plan allowed Angela to be accommodated on a short term planned basis with one of the authority's foster carers in order to reduce the stress levels in the family and allow more therapeutic work to proceed. Despite this being the solution the family had asked for, it set up high levels of anxiety for Mrs Smith as she visualised losing another of her children to a substitute family.

Angela was offered a shared care place in a small residential unit catering for young people similarly needing time away from their prime carer as this was less threatening and more acceptable to Mrs Smith. Experienced staff and high staff to child ratio would hopefully ensure that Angela stayed focused and use the time usefully. Two nights per week were agreed for a six week period.

The family support worker used the time in the unit to work with Angela on some areas that she identified as important to her. They explored the role of her natural father and the position of her stepfather in the new family. They looked at her feelings surrounding the loss of contact with her brother with whom she had a strong relationship. The safety of the unit allowed this work to develop successfully.

Angela enjoyed sleeping over in a room of her own and the staff of the unit were able to give her the space she required especially after particularly difficult work sessions.

The stresses on the family visibly reduced during this period allowing work with Mrs Smith to begin. She quickly started to reveal the abuse she had suffered as a child and an independent counsellor was engaged to deal with this. Positive parenting advice, and techniques for behaviour management, benefited the family greatly and a new confidence was to be seen in the parents' handling of problem situations that occurred with Paul and Joyce, Mr Jones' children. Mrs Smith began to see the impossible position she often put Mr Jones in and began to trust his judgement a little more and to try his solutions.

Intensive work with Angela's parents to understand the complex nature of her situation and feelings was easier when their daughter was in shared care. Child protection worries too were eased as the pressure came off and Angela was able to talk. It soon became clear that there were no worries about her treatment in the family especially by her stepfather, always an area for careful examination when adolescent girls run off.

Shared care had done its job and got them through a difficult patch. Three years on Angela attends college and no other referrals have been needed. Paul and Joyce are doing well at home and at school.

Tameside has many old records of families where each successive child entered the care system in adolescence, this family will not add to that list.

The principle of shared care, between parents and carers, needs to drive social work thinking when planning the living arrangements and support interventions for vulnerable young people, extended family or family friends.

Perhaps delegates at the next national conference will be congratulating themselves on having dreamt the impossible dream, learnt from research and examples of good practice, and moved public care services on to a point where it is of high status and seen on a par with other services that are supporting families.

References

Berridge, D. and Brodie, I. (1997). *Children's Homes Revisited*. Jessica Kingsley.

Department of Health (1985). *Social Work Decisions in Child Care – Recent Findings and Their Implications*. HMSO.

Department of Health (1996). *Focus on Teenagers: Research into Practice*. HMSO.

Department of Health (1998). *The Quality Protects Programme – Transforming Children's Services*. HMSO.

Handy, C. (1995). *The Empty Raincoat: Making Sense of the Future*. Arrow.

Jackson, S., and Thomas, N. (1999). *On the Move Again: What Works in Creating Stability for Looked After Children*. Barnados.

Kahan B. (1979). *Growing Up in Care: Ten People Talking*. Blackwell.

Milhan, S. *et al.* (1981). *Issues of Control in Residential Child Care*. HMSO.

Neville, D., King, L., and Beak, R. (1995). *Promoting Positive Parenting*. Arena.

Packman, J. *et al.* (1986). *Who Needs Care: Social Work Decisions About Children*. Blackwell.

Pincus, A., and Mininhan, A. (1982). *Social Work Practice: Model and Method*. Peacock.

Pitcher, D. (1999). *When Grandparents Care*. Plymouth Social Services Department.

Sinclair, R. *et al.* (1995). *Social Work Assessments with Adolescents*. NCB.

The Home Office (1998). *Supporting Families*. HMSO.

Tresiliotis, J. (1995). *Teenagers and the Social Work Services*. HMSO.

Tutt, N. (1974). *Care or Custody*. Gorten, Longman and Todd.

White, M., and Epsten, D. (1990). *Narrative Means to Therapeutic Ends*. W.W. Norton.

9 Support Care: A New Role for Foster Carers

Joy Howard

Support Care is a fostering scheme in Bradford that offers a part-time resource to families in crisis. The intention is to be as flexible as possible in approach, so that resources can be responsive to demand. The scheme can cater for a wide variety of different requests, recognising that these reflect the individual needs of parents and young people.

Identifying the Need

During the early 1990s, Bradford's social workers had increasingly been asking for more flexibility in the use of foster care placements. Typical examples of situations driving these requests were:

- Long-standing difficulties within a family, with periodic risk of a young person being accommodated in an unplanned way.
- Return home being negotiated, but looking unlikely to succeed without ongoing support in terms of respite.
- An accommodated young person placed out of the local authority area, needing to retain family and community links through planned stays in Bradford.

The schemes then in operation at the fostering unit were not geared to the resolution of these situations. Certainly it seemed that new approaches were needed for accommodation. A report establishing demand and recommending the implementation of a new scheme based on the principle of supporting families in need who were struggling to maintain the care of their young people at home, was produced. This report identified a number of projected benefits. These include:

- Avoidance of the stigma of being in local authority 'care'.
- Earlier and properly planned intervention reducing the traumatic implications of separation for families.
- The cycle of crisis-led and increasingly damaging episodes of accommodation could be broken.
- A different dynamic between parents and foster carers would be obtained. This could facilitate experiential learning of parenting skills in a non-threatening and co-operative way.
- The opportunities for joint planning and working between area social workers and family placement workers would enhance the practice thinking of each, and improve communications.
- There should be a significant reduction in the number of children and young people looked after by the department.

It was three years before time was allocated for implementation and development of the recommendations of this report. A scheme was piloted for a year which concentrated on young people aged 9–16. This was in part a response to the demand identified in the initial report, but also because there was a recognised shortfall in resource provision for this age group. During that first year, a total of 195 referrals were taken, and over 90 placements effected. The scheme was approved by the Children and Families Sub-committee and ratified as permanent in 1997.

Principles and Values

The scheme was set up with some core principles in mind. These have driven all new developments, and are integral to the aims of all placements.

Initially, the scheme aims to ensure that the department, in this case the fostering service, has the resources available to match the needs of families and young people as identified by practitioners working with them. It acknowledges that for too long, practitioners have had to work within the constraints of what was available, not what was desirable. Social workers who are trying to work alongside families need to listen carefully to what parents are asking for in terms of help to ensure appropriate provision is offered. Often parents under stress ask for a break; quite often young people themselves do too. This has typically meant a request for accommodation by the local authority as it was the only option available but not the parents' choice.

Although accommodation is sometimes inevitable, it always constitutes a major breakdown of family stability. Once a separation has happened, the traumatic implications for the family multiply. Any return home now has to negotiate the effects of separation as well as the initial problems which led to accommodation. The family think of accommodation as an available resource should difficulties re-emerge, which may make problems more likely to happen again.

The trauma of separation for young people, and their ability to effect a constructive return home is compounded by the number of unplanned moves an accommodation often brings with it (Utting 1997). The status and future prospects of an accommodated young person are a cause for serious concern, now being taken up at government level under Quality Protects initiatives. This makes it imperative to avoid accommodation for a young person if possible. Maintaining a young person living with their parents wherever possible should always be the aim of all social workers.

Support Care

Offering alternatives to families that allow an accommodation agreement that is part time, allowing the parents to remain the primary source of care, means support care has, from the start, aimed to be a resource that has the flexibility to respond to requests as they come, to allow social workers to offer families a placement that is tailor-made to fit the situation.

In essence, support care offers the option of part-time foster care to young people in need, and respite for their parents. Most referrals are made when families are at crisis point, and accommodation is a considered option. All placements are planned, time-limited and based on a contract between all parties – parent/carer, young person, foster carer, family social worker and family placement worker.

Throughout, the emphasis is on co-operation, and joint decision-making. This starts at the point of referral, when placement options are discussed between the parents' social worker and the scheme co-ordinator. The needs of the parents and young person are paramount. However, as with all resources, there are never enough to meet every request. Sometimes this means a wait – usually not more than 6–8 weeks – and sometimes it means a compromise. No request is refused, as the scheme exists to meet demand, not to fit people into a fixed set of resources. Parents/carers and young people are always party to the discussions – if what is on offer is felt not to be useful, efforts will be made to find a more acceptable resource.

Support care placements are designed to reduce the tension that is threatening to break up families. This is achieved by offering a resource that is seen as helpful in a practical and positive way by parents. It gives them a breather. For most young people too, some time away from a household where tension is mounting is a huge relief. Having created a level of relative calm, the emphasis turns to work that can be done to improve the situation in the longer term.

All parties to the initial contract have a role. Parents and young people may be asked to engage in specific work on their relationship with each other. Carers will be expected to offer young people a positive experience within their family, and to help them build self-esteem, develop social skills and learn to accept boundaries. They should also offer parents the feeling that someone is on their side. Carers need to be able to share their skills and experience without being judgemental, so that they can enable parents to learn different ways of handling situations.

Young people are included wherever possible in discussions prior to setting up the placement, and consulted throughout. Social workers engage to continue their input, including a search for other resources that may be needed. Family placement workers act as a support to carers, and co-ordinate reviewing and time scales.

Each contract is different, as it is drawn up by the individuals concerned. The only constraint is setting a time limit – the placement has to end within a year. In fact, most end sooner – a good indication that parents do not want dependence, only constructive help. Parties to the initial contract set a date agreed together when they will meet again, and review progress. This keeps everyone on board, and in control of events. The aims of the placement are agreed from the start, and referred back to at future meetings. These may change as the placement progresses, to reflect changes that may be taking place overall.

Some Important Findings

The scheme has now been in operation for over three years. The principles and values informing its operation remain unchanged. The scope of placements has become very wide, partly because requests have been many and varied, and partly by the availability of its carers. This has produced some arrangements, born of compromise, that have been very successful and led to an ongoing development of the scheme.

The provision of day care, for example, was not envisaged. The availability of a very skilled and experienced carer, who could no longer offer overnight stays meant that day care was an option to be explored. It has proved to be one of the most popular solutions, and is now often requested from the start. Other carers have added day care to their weekend and overnight availability. It has become an invaluable resource, particularly when a school exclusion threatens to overwhelm an already troubled home situation.

The development of day care has shown that flexibility can produce excellent results. Planned short breaks are less traumatic in their effects than episodes of accommodation involving the young people being separated from the family home. Day care takes this a step further by eliminating even overnight separation.

Another invaluable resource that the flexibility of the scheme has made possible is the involvement of carers who are black or Asian. Informal time spent in someone's home has proved to be a very natural and unforced way for young people to learn about their heritage. It allows them to form a relationship, perhaps for the first time, with someone from a community other than the white mainstream, and from a community to which, though it may be unfamiliar, they also belong. These contacts are very low-key, usually occasional visits are enough to allow a relationship to build up. The scheme acknowledges that each young person will want to go at their own pace in exploring racial and cultural identity. This allows the time commitment of carers to be minimal, and they can be extended for as long as is needed.

In terms of the effect that support care has on the difficulties that led to the initial referral, there are some encouraging findings. Perhaps the most unexpected has been that many families referred at a time of crisis, when accommodation was on the agenda, have withdrawn their request after having been given a placement option to consider.

A constructive offer of help can effectively take the heat out of a situation, and allows a family to think through what they can do for themselves. A number of parents withdraw even before a concrete offer of either support care or accommodation has been made. This may be because another family member has stepped in, but it is often knowing that they are just being listened to; and knowing help is at hand, can be enough to make a difference.

Most placements have achieved their aims well within a year. Some families and young people do return for a second go – this is something which might be expected, and re-referrals are always taken. Usually the request is for something different, maybe some one-off time out, or day care.

There are some situations where it becomes clear that the difficulties are intractable, and that what is needed is a long-term shared care arrangement. Some support carers have offered this. However, the scheme was not set up to meet this need, and to achieve its aims of helping families in crisis, has to maintain a throughput. That longer term shared care is sometimes needed

there is no question; where this is an issue, attempts are made to find a resource within other schemes at the fostering unit.

Significantly, neither parents nor young people see stays with support carers as 'care', though in a technical sense they do involve accommodation procedures. The fact that parents remain in the driving seat encourages this perspective; for young people, the prospect of being away for a weekend or a day at a time does not threaten the security of their home base. Support carers are not substitute parents, and are seen more as befrienders. This is encouraging in two ways. Firstly it shows that such placements do help to avoid stigmatising families, and promote social inclusion. Secondly, it reinforces the concept that carers can be seen to be part of a wider community that should be supportive of all its members.

Support care is an aid to resolving situations between young people and parents. It can reduce tension. It can give parents a real opportunity to engage with a planned

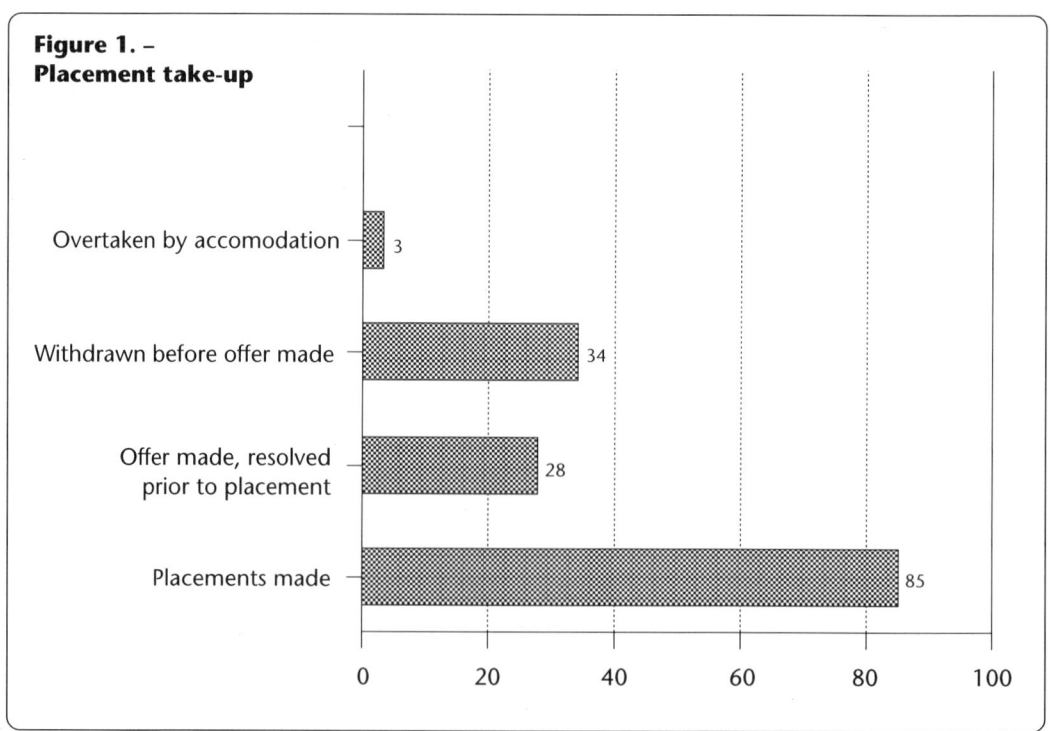

Figure 1. –
Placement take-up

resolution of their difficulties. It can offer the skills and experience of foster carers, most of whom are themselves parents, to give new insights into those difficulties. It does not in itself solve anything in the long term.

One of the benefits projected in the proposals was that opportunities for social workers and family placement workers to engage in joint planning and shared tasks would prove to enhance the practice of both. This has certainly been the case. Relations between these two sets of practitioners do not always run smoothly. This is in part when good practice has to be limited by what is available. Involving colleagues who are working directly with families by inviting them to set the agenda in terms of what they need was a plus from the outset. This has been followed up by ensuring that needs are met wherever possible, and that where they cannot be met an alternative is suggested. Some of the compromises reached have been imaginative, successful, and above all, jointly owned.

Profile of the Scheme

The number of referrals has remained relatively constant. Over the three completed years, more than 500 referrals have been taken, and between 80-90 placement agreements have been drawn up.

An analysis of families who have accessed the resource shows that by far the largest parenting group in need of this service are single mothers. There is also a significant proportion of requests from other carers within the wider family such as grandparents.

A breakdown of referrals by age and gender shows clearly that young men in their early teens are having particular difficulties within their families. As the relevant parent is overwhelmingly likely to be a single mother, a typical picture emerges of conflict arising between mother and sons as puberty kicks in, especially when there is no partner around who is willing to share responsibility.

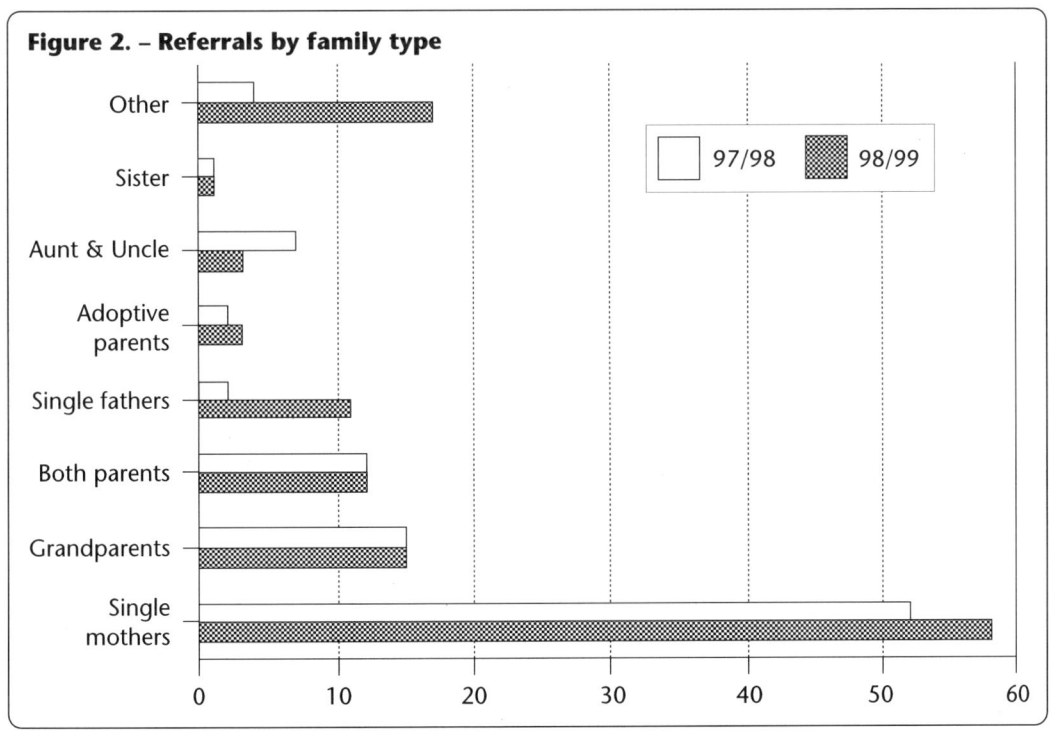

Figure 2. – Referrals by family type

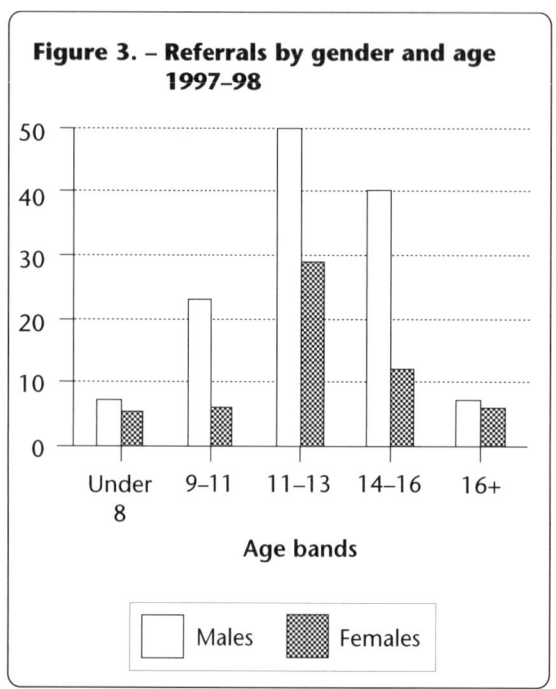

Figure 3. – Referrals by gender and age 1997–98

50
40
30
20
10
0
Under 8
9–11
11–13
14–16
16+
Age bands
Males
Females

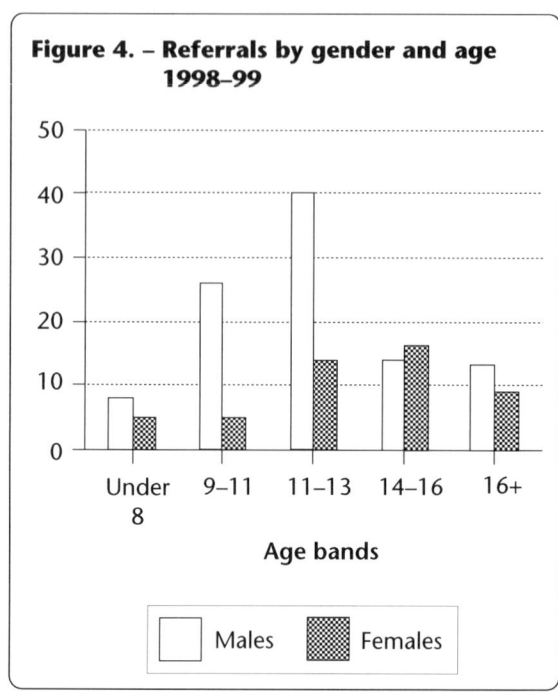

Figure 4. – Referrals by gender and age 1998–99

50
40
30
20
10
0
Under 8
9–11
11–13
14–16
16+
Age bands
Males
Females

The figure below shows the different kinds of placement that have been negotiated over the last two years. The rise in popularity of day care can be clearly seen. Demand for time out placements is high as the scheme also offers one-off breaks to long term foster

Figure 5. – Types of placements

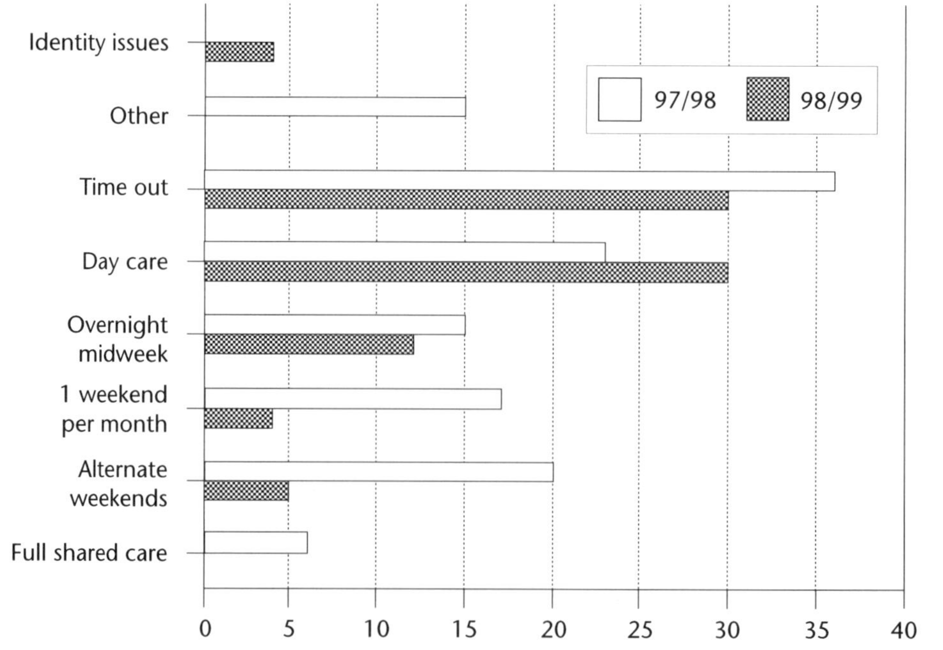

Identity issues
Other
Time out
Day care
Overnight midweek
1 weekend per month
Alternate weekends
Full shared care
97/98
98/99
0
5
10
15
20
25
30
35
40

carers who are in difficulties. It is not a resource that is usually offered to parents, as it would not be different from a short term episode of accommodation.

Analysis of referrals has highlighted some of the outstanding problems facing families who need support. The figure below shows how frequently conflict between parents and teenagers can threaten the stability of families. These categories are not mutually exclusive, so this conflict may well be exacerbated by other factors.

The Carers

At the start of the pilot year, support carers were recruited from the pool of carers working in Bradford's mainstream fostering schemes. Typically, carers would offer support care placements as add-ons to their full time fostering commitments. There are still carers who do this, and enjoy both tasks.

As time has gone on, new carers have been approved for support care only. Recruitment has largely been through the regular advertising campaigns which cover all the schemes; there is scope for more specialised publicity, as the scheme can attract a different population of potential applicants. People who have not felt able to come forward because of work or family commitments are pleased to hear there is something they can undertake on a part time basis.

A number of Bradford's carers, who have been working for the department for some years, have joined the scheme at a time when they have been thinking about giving up their fostering career. This has been of benefit all round. Carers with long experience, and a wide range of skills to offer, have been retained by the department, and their contribution has been invaluable. For these carers, too, an option that allows them to carry on with what they do so well, but without the stresses and strains that had led

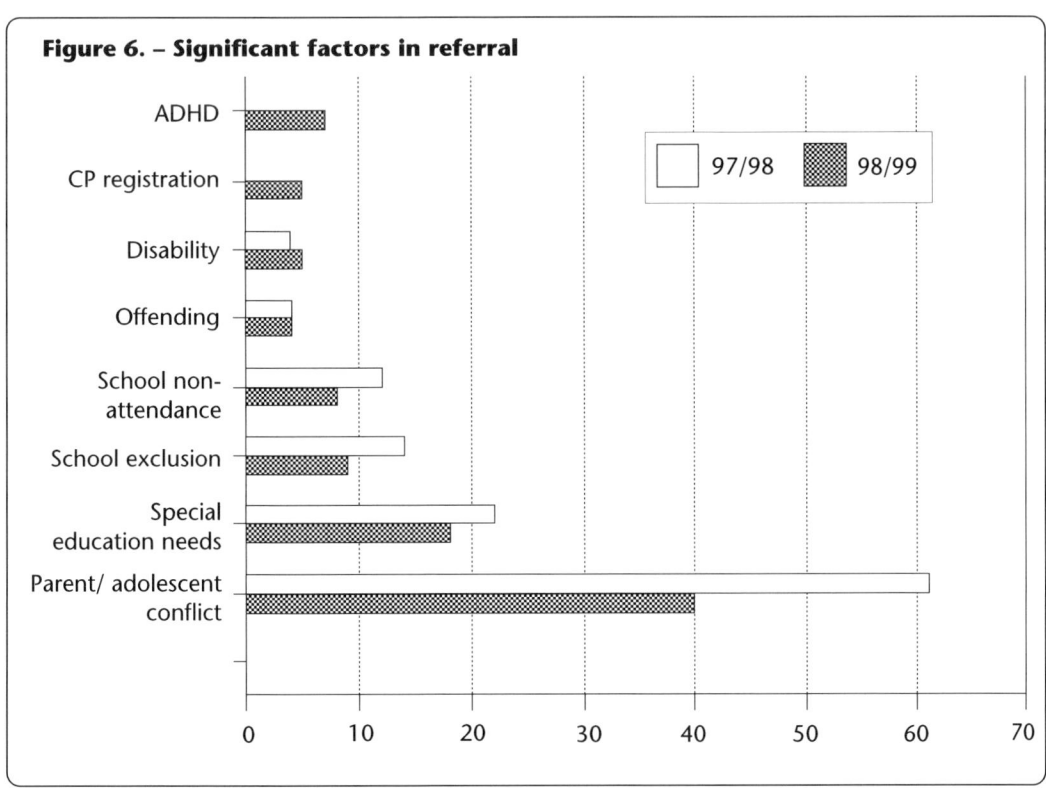

Figure 6. – Significant factors in referral

them to consider leaving the service, gives them a choice that feels positive.

Carers who simply switch roles to take up support care usually need little more than an induction visit, and a review that authorises a change of their terms of approval. Such carers have shown an ability to adjust to the new focus of work with impressive speed. Their skills with young people will have been evident already, but the tact and friendliness with which they have come alongside parents in quite a new role has demonstrated a ready sympathy and understanding of family difficulties that has been a real bonus.

New support carers undertake the same preparation and training as all other carers at present. In the future it is anticipated that more specific input will be available. Approvals are submitted to the fostering panel as for all carers, but the report is shorter and more closely focused on the support care task. As the scheme develops further, the whole training and approval package is likely to become more specialised, and the process for applicants more helpful.

Carers participated fully in the evaluation process that took place during the pilot year. Most carers felt extremely positive about the work they had done. They had enjoyed seeing young people make progress as the placement went on; knowing that parents were getting a break was also a satisfaction. They felt they had helped both parents and young people resolve their difficulties, offered what was needed, and kept families together.

Support Care in Action

Stuart (14) is a young man who has been rejected by his stepfather, and whose mother is not able to protect him from the victimisation and hostility to which he is subjected. His behaviour and general self care had deteriorated badly, and accommodation was discussed, though Stuart and his mother did not want to be parted. Then he was excluded from school, and began to spend his days on the streets and in the park, begging from shops. Accommodation was agreed, but an offer of spending just two days a week with a support carer was taken up instead. Her interest and encouragement has gone a long way to restoring his self esteem and building up his confidence, and he is beginning to take an interest in his appearance. He has started on a planned return to school, and has got himself a Saturday job. No-one is now thinking of accommodation.

Daniel (15) is a young black man, who has been brought up by his grandparents, who are white. He has only heard negative comments about his father, who was black, and was rejected by his white mother. When he was referred for some weekend care due to his grandparents infirmity, he had no real idea of himself as black, only as not fitting in, except by getting into trouble on the estate. He was reluctant to take up offers of identity work at a local African/Caribbean community centre. He refused to stay overnight with his support carer, an older black woman, but formed such a good relationship with her by visiting, even though this was only once every three weeks or so, that she has become an important source of support and encouragement in his exploration of a positive identity for himself. He now goes to the centre voluntarily, and engages in activities there. He has a girl friend who is black, and has confided his pride in this to his carer.

Kimberley (12) is a young woman with some learning difficulties whose behaviour is often hard to cope with. She isn't able to make friends at school, and has outbursts of temper that her mother can't deal with. Her mother can't really trust her to spend time out of the house, and the relationship between mother and daughter has come under severe pressure. Spending some time with a support carer, who has three daughters of her own, has helped her to observe how other young people relate, and given her some positive feelings about herself. For her mother, the break has helped her to feel less stressed. She has also developed a good relationship with the support carer, and is able to talk things through, and accept advice on handling conflictful situations when they arise.

Gareth (11) is one of five children living with a single mother who is struggling to cope. All the children are hard to manage, but when Gareth was excluded from school, this was the last straw. His mother asked for him to be accommodated, and as she refused to let him back in the house, this was done. However, the scheme was able to offer an alternative option very quickly, and Gareth returned home the following week, on the understanding that he would be spending every other weekend with a support carer. This arrangement was needed for some months, but as things became calmer, a new school place was negotiated, and other support services began engaging with the family, it became possible to reduce the frequency of weekend stays, and eventually end the placement by mutual agreement.

Conclusion

Support care has become a resource that is widely used, and social workers continue to give positive feedback. However, it is acknowledged that the direct views of people who use the scheme need to be sought. A proposal for the funding of a research project has been presented to the Department of Health. This comparative study would evaluate the different experiences of parents and young people whose difficulties were addressed by using support care and those for whom accommodation was the outcome.

The demand for this resource, and the benefits that have accrued, indicate that more is needed. The climate of change is being reinforced by new government funding, many new initiatives are, or soon will be, under way. The innovation and development of support care has been that new approaches can benefit everyone – social workers, carers, parents and young people.

References

Department of Health (1996). *Focus on Teenagers: Research into Practice.*

Home Office (1999). *Supporting Families: A Consultation Document.*

Howard, J. (1997). *A Caring Alternative: Building a New Resource for Young People in Need and Their Families.* Department of Social Services, Bradford MBC.

Utting, Sir W. (1991). *Children in the Public Care – A Review of Residential Child Care.* London: Department of Health.

Utting, Sir W. (1997). *People Like Us: The Report of the Review of the Safeguards for Children Living Away from Home.* London: The Stationery Office.

10 Working with Families with Sick and Disabled Parents

Marian Thorpe

The Young Carer's Project in Derby was set up as a response to the Carers Recognition Act 1995, to support children who are significant carers for family members who are sick or disabled, or have mental health or substance misuse problems. These are families whose whole pattern of organisation, day to day routines, the pattern of child development, behaviour and subsequent relationships within and outside the family are affected by the phenomena of ill-health. Indeed it would be true to say that the health issue becomes 'another family member', with needs and demands of its own.

The children with whom we work are aged from one to eighteen. They are from a wide variety of income groups and educational backgrounds. A minority of families in Derby, where our scheme is based, are from black and Asian backgrounds. There are, however, other schemes across the country.

Many of the families are articulate, assertive and have no experience of social services. Whilst it is true that sickness and disability affect every socio-economic group, they are more likely to affect those who are already socially or financially disadvantaged.

These two spectres will also bring in their wake additional hardships and increased financial burdens.

Aims of the Service

Much has been written about the whole issue of recognising children as carers. There is a strong body of opinion that would view the formal recognition, by the provision of a support service, as potentially undermining the sanctity of the family. By asserting the carer's – that is the child's – rights to practical help, we may be seen to question the rights of disabled parents to choose their own carer and also to threaten their parental authority.

There seems to be a largely unstated edict that these children's rights can only be recognised at the expense of the rights of the disabled parents. Rights should be seen however, not as things granted to an individual to the cost of another, but as a set of principles which lie at the basis of our society and which are fundamental to the way we organise services. There is universality about the principal of rights. As the individual grows it may be seen that we come to action these more fully, but this should not take away from the recognition that every citizen should be offered basic standards and choices that do not necessarily impinge on the rights of others.

It is the aim of the project to convey the message that we are not by any means going to change the pattern of care within the family unless the individuals involved want things to change. We try to work with all the family members so that the cared-for person and the carer are both agreeable to the situation.

However, to give a child the ability to make choices by developing their self-esteem, we provide the whole family with information about, and access to, services, but we will not impose what we may feel to be the 'right way' of coping. There is no uniformly acceptable pattern of coping and it is for each family to choose one that suits them. As long as it is a choice and not a pattern adopted because it seems there is no alternative.

We offer support by providing information, offering advocacy, listening, and facilitating the lives of every member of each family with whom we work. That does not mean to say that we are not primarily a child centred service. In reality, a parent must come to view us as a friend, a 'good thing'. We have no statutory duty to work with a parent or an individual carer and so, in order to access any sort of services to children at all, it is important to retain the confidence of the whole family and to bear in mind the power of the parental position.

We do not often meet with hostility from parents because we try to allay their fears from the outset and are usually seen as a 'family friend'. If a parent decides that the potential risks outweigh any benefits from our service, we have really lost any possibility of offering the child carer any support at all. It is important therefore, to get the early stages right.

We must be mindful that the illness will itself influence the reception of any agency intervention. All ongoing health problems bring with them concerns, worries and fears. This may make negotiating a service for the child more difficult in itself, even before we take into account the fears of any family experiencing agency intervention for the first time.

Patterns of Work

Referrals come from a variety of sources – health professionals, teachers, school nurses, social workers and other family members. It is important to ensure that the referrer has discussed the service with the parent and that the parent has had some written information from us. It is also important for us to respond quickly once the referral has been made – either by sending written information, telephoning or arranging a visit. We try to make some sort of contact within two working days of the referral. This is a fundamental priority of the service.

The majority of our families are single parents. The child who is the carer is usually a single child with no other siblings in the family.

Much of the population in the UK feel that social workers have a similar 'trustworthy-factor' to estate agents, or used car salesmen. There seems to be some notion in society that children are constantly being removed from perfectly able parents and placed with one of a large army of foster carers. If able parents have this view, then disabled parents stand no chance whatsoever of hanging on to their children, let alone those parents who have a stigmatising condition, such as mental health or addiction related problems. Fear that some outside official will come and remove children living in such circumstances is a key factor for families. No matter how irrational this line of thought, with the legal protection offered by courts, and the principals of the Children Act which promote working in partnership with parents, these fears are real and need allaying from the outset.

It is useful to work for an organisation that is separate from social services. In my case this is NCH Action for Children – a long established and respected children's charity. We state the aims of our service early on. In addition we:

- outline the need to keep families together
- support families and prevent breakdown
- encourage the idea of the need to give both child and parent a break
- emphasise our willingness to listen to what the family want from us and outline what our plans will be in attempting to fulfil those wishes
- offer to support the family, to give the child and parent access to information, services and benefits

We stress the importance of confidentiality with the single exception that if child protection issues arise we will use the all important 'get out' clause. That is, we state clearly that where a child is being harmed in some way, we will share this information with social services. Our fundamental message however, is clearly:

We are here for the whole family. Whatever you want from us we will listen and will try to provide. Although fundamentally we are here to help your child fulfil their potential wherever we can, we realise this can best be done by working with you, the parent.

In fact it is essential to address any over-riding practical problem which the parent may present in this first visit.

These clear messages are an essential part of our initial discussion with the parent. At the same time the initial visit must also be used to assess the situation. This is for two reasons. Firstly, the service's resources are limited and we clearly must provide for those who best fit the service criteria. Secondly, having established the relevance of the individual family to the service, we need to assess and prioritise the individual needs within the family.

Let us first examine the task of assessing relevance.

Assessing and Prioritising

The relevance and priority of every family must be assessed within the context of our service objectives. If we take disability as a continuum, we can say that every person has some area of poor physical functioning, or differing normality. The criteria for assessing levels of impairment can never be rigid and can be affected by economic circumstances, expectations, culture and attitude. Diagnosis alone does not determine the degree of impairment an individual may experience. Differing social, economic and psychological circumstances can affect the impact any illness may have on an individual; illnesses have a knack of not following the textbook course.

Even disability benefit may be awarded, it seems, almost arbitrarily. Some individuals are living very restricted lives because of a physical or mental condition, but may have no diagnosis, either because medical science is baffled or because there is an underlying psychological condition. No agency seems to like 'untitled disability' and there will be no support services for the individual who has 'had all the tests, but there is no organic reason'.

For the child who is the carer however, the impact on their life will be just as great with a diagnosis or without. We need to see beyond the diagnosis or non-diagnosis, to assess the true impact a debilitating condition is having on a family.

Bearing this in mind, certain factors will heighten concern. An illness or disability which is chronic but stable will usually have a less damaging impact on the family than one where the condition is of sudden or rapid deterioration. A constant physical condition will bring with it routines and adjustments that fit around that condition. A simple example of this is the parent who has always been blind. The children grow up knowing to leave gangways clear, not to leave things in the way, or how to present a drink or food and the parent will, over time, have acquired skills to cope with this disability. Some adjustments maybe viewed as unusual or even unacceptable by the outside world, such as the child who always has to sleep in the same bed as the parent. It will require a great deal of persuasion and imaginative service delivery to change such routines.

By contrast, a situation which is rapidly deteriorating will be subject to constant change and adjustments by all family members. This may lead to feelings of loss allied to those of bereavement, anger, denial and subsequent regressive and irrational behaviour. At the same time such a situation may enable participants to be more willing to accept help and even to ask for it. Although there might be an expectation that sudden and deteriorating conditions are more likely to require support and intervention, this is only a guidance as individuals cope differently with any given situation and therefore all situations must be assessed individually.

When a parent's condition has a poor prognosis with a poor life expectancy we prioritise such a family in terms of their future needs, if for nothing else. Also, some conditions, such as mental illness, are socially stigmatising and may be hidden from public view or at least expressed with a degree of reluctance. Children living with such conditions may be subject to considerable bullying at school. Unfortunately no young carer seems to be exempt. Children can be remarkably cruel even to those whose parents have a purely physical condition. Whatever the effect on the child we must prioritise accordingly. It is important to look at the impact any caring situation is having on a child's schooling, personal development and social life. It is important to ask such questions as, 'Does this child appear withdrawn?' 'Do they seem reluctant to talk?'

I am bound by contract to support children who are doing a 'significant and substantial' amount of caring, mainly those children who are doing practical tasks for the disabled person for a large part of the day. It is important to make a mental note of the particular tasks a child is doing on a regular or occasional basis, although this alone does not prioritise a case. Even so, assessing what a child does is not always an easy task. Adults may be dismissive about what the carer does and the child, thinking that the situation they are in is the norm, may not therefore highlight what we perceive to be unusually burdensome.

Some illnesses and disabilities have periods of respite. It is often easy to be dismissive of a situation because on that first visit the parent is seen to be fairly able to cope, but that first assessment may not be a true reflection of the general patterns nor an accurate picture of the impact the illness is having on the life of the young carer. Indeed the mere knowledge that somebody from an official agency is visiting, may have already had an impact on the sick parent, as for example they might double their medication in order to hide the true effects of a disability, or they might feel inspired to make a supreme effort having been given something to look forward to.

Prioritising will also look at the family structure, its isolation, both geographical and social, whether there is another parent or member of an extended family in the house and whether there are younger siblings and what their ages and dependencies are. The presence of another parent may or may not be helpful. Many fathers in particular absent themselves by choosing to work long hours. Alternatively, the other adult may not be particularly helpful but may detract from the carer getting much needed services.

Often on a first visit the parent's health problems will dominate and it may take two or three visits to glean all the information needed. It is also usually necessary to make another trip to take a child out or be able to see the child somewhere outside of the home situation. It is important to be patient throughout this entire process. Assessing a child and the family in this situation may take some time. Time is an expensive resource but it is also important to be open with a family where it seems there is no question that the support service is relevant.

Some situations are clearly not worth pursuing. The referrer may not have understood the nature of the work we do. An example is the parent described as having 'learning difficulties'. This is a hard one to assess in terms of a parent needing support. Some parents, who are so defined, may not need much support from their child at all. In another family with a similar label, there is a real role for the child as carer. This may also be associated with the shame of a parent who cannot help with the normal childhood problems with school or relationships. In reality, the impact on a child's life may be small or huge but not all children who live with disability are carers.

Alcohol related problems are another difficult area to assess. The parent may be reluctant to talk about such issues. If the parent is holding down a job, for example, and the children appear cared for, then I would wonder what the definition 'alcoholic' actually means. So much depends on the description of the referrer and we must take time to make our own assessment based on observation and listening to the child over time. At some stage we have to ask what impact any illness or disability is having on the child's life. This is crucial in prioritising the service.

At the other end of the disability spectrum to those with no diagnosis, but poor quality of life are those with a clear disability, for example, deafness. Where the disability is constant, the parent copes well and the child has grown up making some adjustment to their life, but not of a detrimental nature. A condition may be stable now, but carry with it the possibility of sudden change such as a parent with HIV. Even if things are fine today, the expectation that tomorrow the situation may rapidly become much worse, would lead to us giving a higher priority to a carer and their family.

Assessing and Doing…

The second part of the initial assessment is concerned with prioritising need within the family. This is about covering certain topics in an almost checklist fashion. Listening to those issues that concern the individuals involved and seeking to explore solutions, courses of action and underlying issues. The checklist will highlight certain basic topics. These are school, welfare benefits, domiciliary support services, respite, wishes, dreams and the future. Each one of these may lead into individual areas of planning need. However, very early on, it will usually be evident that there is some area of real crisis, which needs immediate intervention. No single item on the checklist is routinely more important than another. The need, for example, for domestic help may not be more important to the child than his need to get to football training once a week. Most young carers will say that if only they could do that special thing once a week, or once a fortnight, or even once a month, then the routine tasks involved in caring become far less onerous. Every individual needs a dream and this is no less true for children.

…With children

Who was it said 'every child needs someone to be crazy about them?' When ill health or addiction visits a family, there is less time and willingness for a child to be given the special treatment that befits childhood and is necessary for the development of self-esteem and healthy emotional development.

It is a real skill for the adult professional going into a family with such problems to keep the eyes on the prize of childhood, and not to become distracted by the truly heart-rending situation of the parents. It would be very easy to be enticed into the adult agenda and to understand a healthy child's needs to such 'frivolous' demands as the need for fun. Underlying many physical health problems are psychological factors. The parent may by nature be demanding and lack maturity. This is something we need to have insight into and acknowledge. Also, in any family where there are long-term health problems, there may have arisen an underlying culture that the way to get attention and care is by displaying the symptoms of ill-health. Many of our carers mirror symptoms similar to those of the sick parent or develop psychosomatic disorders of their own.

Parents may focus on their own agenda and will usually be supported in this by those workers who work with statutory agencies. Adults pay taxes, complain and elect political representatives. Children do none of these and so parents are far more powerful and prestigious in this respect. Even agents who have a more eclectic brief are often guilty of not recognising children as carers. This is often a cultural attitude as much as an organisational one.

As a society we have worked out systems to deal with children as victims or as problems. For children to be able to ask for services in their own right is somehow idiosyncratic. It almost seems that unless a child has a label of 'victim' or 'problem to be dealt with' they will not be covered by a procedure, and therefore do not exist and will not get a service. Social workers who spend all of their training addressing 'anti-oppressive practice' often seem to find it difficult to direct these excellent concepts to children. If social workers have adopted tunnel vision, how much more difficult is it for other professionals to have regard for, and assess, the needs and expectations of the whole family. Many people are in danger of losing sight of the 'whole picture' despite numerous edicts from health and social services departments that all professionals in both of these areas must at least bear in mind the whole family situation. This may be, for example, in devising a hospital discharge plan with the family doctor or the hospital social worker assessing the right to services for all members of a family.

Children will not complain if medical staff, for example, dismiss them as stupid and useless. Such opinions are often voiced to young carers by at least one agent or another. Adult service providers need to move away from such responses. Assessing the needs of children who are supporting families involves a lot more than merely listening to what the family says. They are children operating in an adult world and often feel bewildered and powerless. Professionals should not add to these feelings but be willing to adopt 'child friendly' attitudes and systems of assessment and service delivery. It is part of our programme to allow the young people a voice in determining what they want from our service, as well as equipping them with assertion skills and advocating on their behalf, so they can express their wants and needs to other service providers and to their parents.

It may be more prestigious to be seen to be doing 'serious therapeutic work'. Workers with adult carers do not have this dilemma. The adult carer demands the service they want. Children are not used to being regarded as service users and adult agencies are not used to regarding children as people who should dictate their own service needs. We have an educational role here with other agencies and managers. In the family, where the adult agenda dominates, our task is to

take a more 'softly softly' approach and to also make it clear that we are there principally to support the carer. It is a difficult tightrope to walk.

Some of the young carers seem to get most out of meeting others in a similar situation whereas others crave the individual attention lacking at home.

In the early days we were amazed how many of the young carers were so keen to partake in social activities with us as we clearly identified ourselves as being in the 'old boot' category, and definitely 'non-u' in the world of adolescence. The ability to listen and the willingness to take the child's opinions, concerns and ideas seriously, plus the ability to interact with children by engaging our own 'creative child' are essential tools. Adult workers need to have the confidence to be able to let their guard down, to be able to show emotion, curiosity and delight in the world around them. Amongst the volunteers who we have deemed unsuitable to assist us are those who themselves never learnt how to play in a constructive way.

In any situation children will still need boundaries set in some situations, particularly when they are in group situations. It is important however not to dominate or bully the child. Preferably, any rules will come from the young people themselves and all boundaries should be explained with a clear rationale to support them. A long time ago when I first started working with young offenders, a senior worker advised me to 'be the young people's friend but not their mate'. Children can see through falseness and hypocrisy. I was also, I remember, wrongly advised to listen to the pop charts regularly in order to have a common interest, but the music they played bored me rigid. A worker can usually find some common ground of genuine interest which is much better than faking it. It is by using such skills that we gain the trust of the child and more importantly, that the child wishes to be a part of our project. Through our work with the child we are able to develop their social skills and confidence.

So far, I have discussed the variable and often divergent needs of the parent and child carer. In reality we are often preparing a child for an independent life which may come earlier than for most children. It is part of our task to impart useful knowledge, for example on benefits, and to prepare them psychologically. However, there is also the need to see the family as a separate unit with independent needs.

And with parents…

Every individual handles their own health problems differently, and the same is true about the acknowledgement of one's own mortality. Some individuals can talk about such issues openly, others cannot. We must respect every individual's way of coping, but at the same time try to enable the parent to perceive the carer as a person separate to that world where the diagnosis and the pattern of ill health are all pervading.

Sometimes the child presents as a totally withdrawn individual, passive, timid and monosyllabic. It is as if, because the parent denies the child's individual needs and life, they come to believe themselves to be devoid of any personal opinions or experiences. When visiting such families, the parents' symptoms and medical histories are repeated over and over and the child is totally dismissed and ignored.

Sometimes parents may telephone for example, to confirm that a child will attend some function but then begin to discuss ailments and problems. If we can help, we must, in order to preserve the relationship that we have, but we must also realise our limitations in terms of knowledge and resources. We need to explain to the parent on these occasions where they can get help.

Parents who are ill often do not have the time or the energy to pursue benefit claims, housing issues or medical concerns. It is part of our job to allay fears and point the parent in the right direction if we cannot help

ourselves. By relieving the parent's stress, we help the child carer. It is about identifying the clearly achievable task and distinguishing this from the endlessly repeated and unsolved moan.

In many cases, we feel the parent could benefit from professional psychological help. It is a real problem knowing how to get such help. The Macmillan Service (see Chapter 14) will support some terminally ill patients but all such resources are fully stretched. Even obtaining counselling for the diagnosed mentally ill takes time, but many parents with, for example, a chronic physical condition, will benefit from such interventions. On occasions we have offered counselling which has been task centred. It is important that any such counselling be done by someone who is not engaged with the child and their needs. Sometimes this has been effective in enabling the parent to move on and engage better with other family members.

We have also utilised the techniques of brief therapy. (see Chapter 5) This is a focused and resource efficient way of working, particularly with parents whose psychological needs are getting in the way of their coping abilities.

From it we have gleaned the concept of how important it for us to enable parents to adopt behaviours that will help both their child and themselves. This includes giving them the confidence to move forward and to be in control of their situation as a starting point. They need to be able to perceive their children's lives as being separate from their own. To this end we must ask the questions 'Can things change for the better?', 'How can they change?', 'What is my (the parent's) role in this?' Individuals view their disabilities and their children's roles in this differently. Some parents seem to get caught up in the myths of disability and the 'poor me' syndrome. We must ask the questions 'What are you and your family achieving by this?', 'Is this working for you and enabling you and your family to get the most out of life?' The parent must find their own solutions and these issues must be addressed in a professional and caring way, but they need to be addressed.

At the same time, it is important not to neglect those areas of practical help which will improve the family's quality of life. It is important to be able to know one's way around the welfare benefits systems that affect young people and disabled people. Many issues are very complicated and it is a fact that many 'rules' that agencies have adopted seem to have been made without the thought that a carer may be a child. The worker needs to be able to fight these battles in a constructive way but to also have the knowledge of how systems work and where to go to ask for advice.

The Family Dynamic

With long term health problems there are real changes that occur in the family dynamic. A major part of our work is about enabling the family to handle these changes and deal with them. As the parent's health needs grow, the adult becomes more dependent on the child. There is then a change in the power base within the family. The child continues to care but can also feel loss, shame and anger. There are many feelings associated with bereavement and the child often feels that someone must be to blame. At the same time, the parent is less able to exercise discipline and the normal parental boundaries that have historically been in place. The parent may become erratic in disciplining the child, so that the child does not know what to expect. Both parent and child will need our support and help. The parent needs to know that we are there to support and advise them whilst at the same time giving the child the opportunity to express their feelings and offering the child ways of coping.

We must also recognise that every family will have its own culture of rules and expectations and as workers we need to respect these differences between families. We wish we could do more to enable parents to participate in fun activities together. Families need to be reminded of the good things about being a family unit, to be able to laugh together and enjoy each other.

We also need to support parents in their parental role, for example, by supporting them in meetings with school authorities and by affirming their right to set boundaries within the home. We always consult with the parent about the activities we are doing with the child, and are mindful to tell them where the child will be and the times we will pick the child up and return them.

Any formal 'family work' is best done outside the home, where issues and difficulties can be discussed, away from the caring environment. Issues of power, autonomy and extended family relationships are bound to arise and a knowledge of family therapy and the utilisation of these skills is important. Young carers who are subdued and socially withdrawn, have a real loyalty and commitment to the parent. At the same time, they may harbour feelings of resentment and anger, which they are unable to express and about which they feel guilty. Unless we can help the young carer to acknowledge and accept that they may have ambivalent feelings, which are perfectly normal and acceptable, towards the parent for whom they care, we are setting up problems for the future.

As the young carer develops in adolescence, unsupported anger and resentment can turn inward, and some children who have come to our notice in mid to late adolescence are already developing other social problems such as school failure, anti-social behaviour or even attempted suicide.

Possibly the worst scenario however, is where the disabled parent has themselves become a victim of abuse from their caring child. By giving a service to the parent we support the young carer. By giving a service to the child, we support the family.

The four steps of working with parents who are sick and disabled and their child carer:

STEP 1 – Referral

Is the referral relevant? Record as much detail as possible including details of other professionals. An important question is 'Do the family, including the child, know about the referral and the project?' It is very important that the project has been discussed with them.

STEP 2 – Contact

Make contact quickly. If a visit cannot be made for a while, explain this. It is important to be honest from the outset about the level of service that can be offered.

STEP 3 – Visit

Listen to what all the family members have to say. What are the main issues for them? Does the family fit the criteria of being a child carer because of health or addiction problems? Put the referral in some sort of priority order in terms of other work by making mental notes, to be recorded later. Address any major practical issues the parent presents. It may also be necessary to ask if you can see the child on their own by taking them out on a visit.

STEP 4 – Continual assessment

Always deliver on the plan of work promised and if there are problems encountered, inform the parents as and when they occur. The parent needs to know you are doing something and what the issues are. Continue to see the child and if appropriate, offer some sort of respite activity of their choice. Be child led in this.

Continue to review and maintain contact. A family may seem to have things 'sorted' but changes can occur rapidly and the family need to know where they can come for guidance and that we will respond.

Conclusion

Throughout this work the project workers need good and regular support and formal supervision. The work can be harrowing and, in dealing with other agencies in particular, frustrating. It is useful to have joint case discussions with other professionals and we have run training sessions for other worker groups. Schools in particular can play a vital role in identifying the young carer and offering the child some degree of negotiated flexibility in extreme instances.

The workers in the project have also benefited from training in such areas as family therapy, advocacy, bereavement work, various areas of mental health and dependency issues. They are also a strong and mutually supportive team. Much of the work we do is new and we are still learning new strategies, whilst increasing recognition for children who are carers.

11   Living with Risk

Kate Rose and Anne Savage

Introduction

Why is it, when there has been such progress in our understandings of the impact of sexual abuse on all family members, that mothers and carers are still angry that no-one listens to them? What is it about our practice that results in women feeling as though they are 'fighting' with professionals for the right to be heard?

The progress that has been made in the last twenty years has produced a wealth of new understandings which have influenced policies and practice. This predominantly focuses on the offender and survivors. Significantly less attention has been paid to the conflicts and dilemmas for the non-abusing carer, which in most situations is a woman and usually the children's mother. Even less energy has been given to issues for siblings, but that is another chapter! Yet even when we find material specifically for mothers and carers, it is often focused at women who have left the relationship with the offender at some stage following disclosure. These women have claimed for themselves the name 'safe carers'.

This chapter seeks to describe the journey by which we discovered the needs and dilemmas of women who had chosen to maintain contact or a relationship with their partners, who were Schedule 1 offenders. Our personal journey began with the assumption: these women are not traditional 'safe carers' but have the same rights to support and information as other mothers and carers.

Through our work we were significantly challenged and influenced by these women. They have helped us to develop an understanding that it is possible for some women to choose to continue their relationship, in some shape or form, with partners who are Schedule 1 offenders. However, in doing this, they can also remain carers of their children. We have named this 'Living with Risk'.

On a professional level we seek to offer a framework for understanding the conflicts and dilemmas faced by all mothers and carers that moves beyond the point of focusing on the allegations of sexual abuse about their partners. Hooper (1992) urges that the more attention paid to the needs of non-abusing carers at the time of disclosure and beyond, the more those carers will be able to support their own children. This may seem an obvious statement. We will explore how, for some women, assertions of denial initially of an allegation have led to an assumption of collusion and guilt and failure to engage with professionals. The result of this being a long-standing history of social services involvement with families who have become increasingly alienated from the source of support they most need.

As a result of our learning from a group we facilitated, we propose a framework for assessment both for a group setting and for individual work that enables women themselves to move beyond a position of shock to regaining some control and focus on the future.

Finally, we will consider how professional responses, both from individual workers and within the child protection system itself, can be significant in influencing a positive outcome for these women.

Our experience and conclusions for this article have been largely drawn from our work in the Kaleidoscope Project. This project was set up in 1995 as a Salford Area Child Protection Committee initiative. The remit of the project was to develop services based on identified need for children and their families where sexual abuse was an issue (i.e., suspected or proved). As social workers with nine and ten years experience at the time in the field of child protection, we were seconded from our respective employers to 'be' the project. The views subsequently expressed in this chapter reflect those of the authors and not necessarily those of the NSPCC or Salford Community and Social Services Directorate, our respective employers.

As reflected in the process of discovering the wide-ranging needs of mothers of sexually abused children, we initially identified the need for a safe carers group. From this, the need arose for a different group for women who had chosen to remain with their partners (see Appendix 1).

> *For mothers, the discovery that their child has been sexually abused is an assault on their fulfilment of their role as mothers – a fundamentally important role in western societies. This assault has a damaging effect on their self-esteem and identity and, therefore, affects their cognitive and emotional functioning. This...must be borne in mind when assessing mothers' responses within the context of initial assessments of risk to children and when pursuing statutory procedures such as case conferences.*
>
> (Walton, 1996)

Our Theoretical Framework

The philosophy that is enshrined within the current child care legislation is that workers engaged in child protection should work in 'partnership' with the parents. This philosophy should be neatly integrated with the statutory duty to protect children from harm. The tension that exists in achieving practice that meets both these needs, is there in all situations of abuse.

Where the abuse of the child is sexual, the burden to relieve this tension lies fundamentally and most crucially with the non-abusing carer, usually the mother. It has been well established and documented by a variety of sources that, at the point of disclosure, the mothers of children who have

been sexually abused experience major cognitive and emotional dissonance. (Timmons-Mitchell, Chandler-Holtz and Semple 1997, Salter 1988.)

It is usually at this point, where the abuse is intra-familial, that the statutory agencies, in their drive to ensure that the children are protected, enter the fray. The 'safest' immediate intervention which is most commonly sought, demands that the non-abusing carer believes and supports the child and in so doing, ends the relationship with the abusive partner. This then fulfils the worker, departmental and societal views on the role of a mother, whilst also minimising any deeper concepts that may be held of mother collusion. (Joyce, 1997.) Where the non-abusing carer meets these expectations, there is a perfect fit between the need to work in partnership and the need to protect the child.

In their article, Stand by your Man (*Social Work Today*, 1989) Bourton and Burnham consider the process of social work intervention and the conditions that affect the response of the mother to that intervention. (See Appendix 3.) It is always a legitimate question to ask, 'Who is responsible for the abuse?' However, enshrined within is the question that often follows, 'Who will the non-abusing carer choose – their partner or their child?' There are inevitably assumptions by professionals about the women, based on their choice. Bourton and Burnham suggest that women who have low self-esteem, are poorly nurtured themselves, experience financial and environmental stress and/or are socially isolated, are inevitably more likely to have a greater need for the support their partners provide.

Research into abusers would also indicate that it is often families in this position that increase child vulnerability and attract potential offenders. (Finkelhor and Baron, 1986.) The likelihood is that in being asked to choose, many women opt to continue their relationship with their partner in some way, either overtly or covertly. During the course of our work, we have commonly heard professionals attach negative labels to these women. The women have been described as collusive of the abuse, in denial, unfit mothers, minimising of the effects of the abuse, etc. Some of these professionals were asked, during a training session, to complete the exercise in Appendix 4. Their responses to the exercise mirrored those given by the women in the group when asked to recall their feelings in relation to their partners following disclosure of abuse.

When professionals fail to recognise the feelings of the women and the context within which they are asked to make a choice, the negative assumptions about the 'sort' of mothers they are, appears to follow. The perceived hostile responses of professionals to women in this position often serve to strengthen the relationship between the women and their partners, where the women feel needed. Where the woman is in conflict with the professionals, this meets the needs of the male partner. He is able to re-frame this confusing time for the woman as being a positive choice for him. The responses of workers to the women commonly led to the children's names being placed on the child protection register as well as initiation of care proceedings. This action supported the concept of these carers as unsafe, and further entrenched the position of warring sides.

At the point at which we sought a group as a means of working more positively with the women, we could find no reference to a similar group existing elsewhere. So it was that we formulated our own philosophy based on the assumption that our starting point should be in establishing what we agreed on, rather than what we viewed differently. Women have a right to choose their partners, the question therefore becomes, 'How can they make sense of and manage the risk this presents?' The emphasis of the group was therefore based on the principles of a women's support group.

Even though the women were not defined as traditional 'safe carers', they were not the principal risk. We identified that there remained outstanding needs for information and support, which could inform their decision-making on a practical basis. In running the group, this became a task of balancing aspects of nurturing and caring with the challenging of assumptions.

Our Learning
For social workers

If we can accept that the value base we have is fundamental in shaping our practice, we also need to accept that the consequences of this are not always positive for the people with whom we work. In working with women whose choice conflicts with the traditional notion of a 'good mother', our own assumptions are challenged. Throughout the group, our belief remained that, if the 'risk' presented by the continuing relationship between the women and their partners could be managed safely for the children, then this was the best outcome for them in the longer term.

Experience has shown that, if women feel pressurised into ending their relationships, the outcomes for the children are rarely satisfactory and many continue the relationship, but in a clandestine way. The initial task for workers therefore is to be clear about their own values and judgements about women who make this decision, and develop strategies for themselves that prevent these negatively impacting on a carer.

The women who attended the group all said that they knew within the first five minutes of meeting their social worker that they were considered 'bad' parents. This then got in the way of establishing any positive working relationship. The pattern that most commonly developed was a 'fight' to maintain the positions taken in those first five minutes. For us, the starting point had to be that women were asked to make choices, at a time when they were under great stress. This choice need not mean that the children cannot be made safe. All the women we have worked with have been clear that we share the desire for their children to be safe. The most significant confusion lay in workers failing to define with the women what the risk was, or where the differing responsibilities lay for managing that risk. The use of the child protection and court system only served to reinforce the position of fight rather than adding clarity to the plan.

The task for the worker, therefore, becomes one of establishing what is understood of the risk at each stage and considering the options available to support its effective management. This inevitably separates out different responsibilities for different strategies. For example, at the start of the process, it may be that relatively little is known about an offender's individual cycle of abuse, relationships within the family, etc., so it may be that the only safe option is for the alleged offender to leave the household. The responsibility to do this should lie primarily with the offender, rather than asking the woman to tell him to go. An agreement may then be formed about how the relationship is to be maintained for the woman in a way that is safe for the child, e.g. any contact can occur away from the family home. Social services may support this by providing a nursery place, childminder, etc.

As the process moves on, the task of the worker is to provide the information and support that the woman needs, to make and develop an informed, longer-term, decision about the risk, in much the same way as workers themselves will need to do. It may be, therefore, that a programme of work will look at understanding the cycle of offending, defining sexual abuse, and considering the effects on the victim. (See Appendix 5).

Our experience has been that, in providing the information and exploring the issues in a general way, the women were quick to make the connections with their own situations and re-evaluate their position. Having achieved this, the task changes to considering practical, emotional and cognitive ways that the woman can manage the risk. Alongside this, there has to be an acknowledgement of the enormity of the task and an identification both of what the woman can and cannot be

responsible for, and what support may be available, both in the immediate and longer term. For example, it may be acknowledged that, in continuing a relationship, the child may need someone outside the family who is established as an alternative safe adult as well as their mum.

For some of the women, a major change occurred when they were able to let go of the need to be responsible for changing their partner's behaviour. Their role then changed to expecting to be informed and involved in any ongoing treatment programmes. This led to two of the women becoming more challenging of their partners, which changed the power base within the relationship. For one of those women, the choices she explored involved redefining for herself what form she felt any continuing relationship would take to be safe for the children. This led to a move from an assumption that it meant seven days a week, to two to three days a week.

The final, and additional, task for the worker is to assess whether the suggested management of the risk proposed by the woman is safe for the children. If it isn't, where this process has been followed, it should be relatively easy to be clear about why not.

Overall, the worker needs to ensure that they work at the pace of the woman and slow down the demands they make on her to make final choices about her future. Alongside this, we should avoid making assumptions about the women themselves or their capacity to change.

For the women

Despite varied experiences of statutory responses, all the women expressed initial feelings of anger and frustration at how they perceived the way they had been 'treated'. The most predominant viewpoint was the feeling of being labelled a bad parent on the basis of someone else's actions. This view then formed the basis of their 'fight', i.e., to prove they were not bad parents. As with the workers, the women too needed to clarify this standpoint for themselves.

This process proved to be very straightforward for the women. All the women accepted and agreed that putting the children's safety and well-being first was the most important thing. Equally, all the women agreed on some level that continuing a relationship with this man posed some risk, and even if women were saying they felt sure he wouldn't re-offend within the family now, the women acknowledged they were often kept awake at night worrying about, 'what if?'.

Once the risk to all family members had been named, the women were able to acknowledge that they were willing to accept this level of risk and move to developing ways of managing this risk. It is worth mentioning that as we have worked subsequently with women on an individual basis, the principle of establishing whether or not there is shared agreement as to naming the risk still holds true. Even in situations where involvement results in being unable to agree on there being a risk, the process of exploring this can enable women to gain some insight and information into why protective action was necessary.

We initially thought that the process of defining the risk would form the bulk of the sessions. However, we had reached a point by the third session where the women were asking for more information and clarification in order to develop ways of managing their households. Alongside these discussions continued the process of building up the self-esteem and identity of the women as a key component in equipping them with the confidence to challenge their partners with any risks they perceived. For many of the women part of the process of understanding their future role came in being able to acknowledge that their relationship with their partners will never be equal. They were able to explore, through understanding the cycle of abuse and its process, the level of limited significance that they would have with their partners in preventing his re-offending.

The conclusion for many was that they were dependent on the honesty of their partners and the focus then became one of developing rules for safe caring within their own situations, based on the assumptions that they would be unlikely to know prior to their partner's re-offending. The enormity of trying to manage this risk was realised when the women began to think about their daily routine. For example, the simple task of bathing the children could mean the sounds may, for their partner, trigger distorted thinking without being involved in the bathing itself. The emerging theme in answering some of these dilemmas became, 'How do I manage the children as though he isn't there?'

A further key discussion that occurred in developing ways of managing the risks centred around what the women felt they were and were not responsible for. Central to the issue of responsibility for the women, was accepting that both they and their children will require a high degree of support that is independent from those of their partners. Many of the women's only source of social, emotional and, sometimes, financial support prior to the group was their partner and his family. Additionally, the needs of their children over and above day-to-day care became evident. This developed into an understanding of the victim's perspective. The women discussed how they might answer the questions of their children both now and in the future. Within this was a realisation that their children might not now see them as someone they could talk to, so attention was paid to whom could be alternative safe allies, for example, aunts, cousins, people at school, etc.

As you can see, the discussion began broadly and became more and more relevant and personal as the women raised further questions as a result of discussing each issue as it arose. The advantage of the group was that the women themselves were motivated to seek their own answers. Our task as the group progressed became to provide relevant information and a framework to the questions raised the week before.

We subsequently attempted to run another group a year later. Whilst we had sufficient referrals, the women themselves were reluctant to commit themselves to the group process. Each told us, 'we are not like that; our situation is different'. This caused us to adapt the group framework to individual sessions. (See Appendix 5 in thinking through whether group versus individual work is relevant for each woman's situation.) The individual work served the same purpose as the group.

We have generally concluded that individual work suits women who have been involved with statutory systems for a comparatively shorter time and have therefore not become focused solely on fighting the system. For women who have invested time and energy into 'the fight', a group was useful. The most influential function of the group was for the women to meet others in similar situations and know they are 'not the only one'. A spin-off was in hearing their own defences both built up and equally knocked down by other women, rather than workers. This reflected a particular level of openness and honesty.

About their partners

The women rightly discussed that they are not responsible for their partners' actions, either in the past or in the future. An essential part of keeping the children safe, therefore, involved their partners also acknowledging that there was a problem, and taking responsibility for this. In all situations where this had happened, the partners had received some form of treatment. We would be less optimistic about a safe outcome for families where no treatment had been undertaken. This of course raises the issue of how responsibility for and the management of offending behaviour can be learned by men who have never been convicted of a sexual offence or whose offence was so long ago that treatment programmes did not exist (i.e., pre-1990s).

For organisations

Wherever social workers 'intervene' with families, they start with a view about why they are there and what the best outcome could be. Achieving these outcomes can be relatively straightforward, as, where a child is sexually abused by a stranger and the family believe and are sensitive to the needs of the family members. Here, the worker's view of the needs is most likely to be mirrored by the family's view and everybody is agreed about what needs to happen.

Alternatively, the perception of the risk may not be immediately shared, for example, a woman whose partner has offended outside the home may view her own children to be perfectly safe. In all situations, workers have a range of systems available to them for structuring their work with families, both formal and informal. The most formal of these are the child protection and court systems. Of the women who attended the group, all were involved in either or both the child protection and court systems. None of the women had linked the use of the formal system with the risk their partner's offending presented. For the women the system served to reinforce their belief that they were perceived as bad parents. We suspect that this is true of most women's experience in this situation. There appears to be a disparity between the point at which, and purpose for, initiating these systems. This may be as much determined by team cultures as organisational policies and statutory thresholds.

The task for the worker within their organisation is to ensure that they make explicit for themselves and others how the system relates to their management of the perceived risk. The starting point, as already stated, is in defining the risk. As suggested previously, we are working with women who are often at their most vulnerable. Therefore, it is logical that the volume of new information and the time and energy required to make sense of it will take longer for these women. The information will need to be presented in a variety of ways. If the formal systems are used in the early stages, it is important to accommodate the time scales of change needed for the women, within those imposed by the system. This includes the rate change is achieved.

All of the systems a worker may use require a level of assessment. Although workers are familiar with assessing parenting, this is not a useful format where the primary concern is the sexually abusive behaviour of a partner. Through the group we have developed a framework for assessment that can be used either on an individual or group basis (see Appendix 6).

Needless to say, the task is a daunting one. It is crucial therefore to utilise the expertise that exists within and between agencies. The women all felt that they benefited from having a separate identified worker for them. This raises the issue of co-working. For individual workers, the benefit of co-workers is that it promotes clarity of task, shared roles and responsibilities and enhances the planning process. For managers, the advantage is that it ensures worker support.

Contact

Inevitably, in the course of the work done with the women, the issue of partners having contact with the children, both at present and in the future, has been raised.

In many situations, it is right that local authorities pursue maintaining relationships where children are not living with their birth parents. For children who have been sexually abused, this guiding principle may need some refining. Our understanding of the process of offending, together with knowledge of the effects of abuse on the victim, can lead us to make some assumptions at the initial stages of assessment and investigation (Jones and Parkinson, 1995.):

- The development of the relationship between the perpetrator and the victim is based on a distortion of thinking and action.

- Within that relationship there will be blurred role boundaries.

- There will be long-standing cognitive manipulation of the victim.

- The victim will lack conviction that what happened was wrong and/or was not their fault.

- The relationship between the victim and their mother is also likely to have been distorted by the actions of the perpetrator.

- The victim will believe in the domination and power of the perpetrator.

- The mother will not have had time to unpack the overwhelming and conflicting range of emotions for herself, let alone those of her child.

Importantly, any consideration of the child's own wishes and feelings, in relation to contact, also needs to be viewed in the context, not only of their age and understanding, but also all of the above. The implication of the cognitive and emotional distortions that occur is that physical separation does not immediately change distorted thinking or emotional damage for the victim. The likelihood is that supervised contact cannot combat these distortions. Particularly when most of them exist only in the heads of the perpetrator and the victim. The opportunity for these to be exploited further is open to the perpetrator during contact. The implications are that, in the first instance, contact between the victim and the perpetrator should be suspended. The assessment work that follows should then be based on four areas of work with the key question being, 'Is the contact desirable if it is free of abuse?' (Jones and Parkinson, 1995):

- Individual work with the victim. This work should address both the effects of the abuse for the victim, validate their feelings and counteract the distortions.

- Individual work with the mother (the content of this chapter and Appendix 5).

- Work with the victim and the mother together. This work should promote the strengthening of their relationship.

- Individual and group work with the perpetrator

The task for renewal of contact is to provide evidence that the risk of physical, emotional and psychological harm to the child is sufficiently reduced. This is in opposition to the wrong assumption that normal parent-child interaction can continue as long as an abusive incident does not occur. The primary onus to provide this evidence must be in the work with the perpetrator. The victim and mother must have time and opportunity to recover from the trauma at some fundamental levels. The task in working with the women is to provide them with the information that allows them to make sense of the assumptions, noted in one to seven of Appendix 5, and relate this to their own situation.

Domestic Violence

Our work is grounded on the understanding that violence in the home, whether direct or indirect, is abusive to children. Strong links exist between domestic violence and the physical, emotional and sexual abuse of children (Hester, Pearson and Harwin, 1998). Focusing solely on one aspect of abuse will not give a true picture. We are encouraged by survivors of violence to name the problem more readily and assume it is more prevalent than we may initially want to believe. By minimising both the propensity and impact on all members of the family subject to violence, our interventions may be at best inappropriate and at worst, place additional pressure on families.

There are strong parallels for women whose partners are violent and/or sexually abusive. Both issues are complex and may remain unspoken for some time by all members of the family. Some of the reasons for this have been explored earlier. Uncovering the whole picture involves unpacking complex layers of secrets and distorted messages.

Women living in situations of violence may be immobilised through shock or fear.

Remaining in a violent relationship does not mean that the care and protection of the children is not a primary concern. As with male perpetrators of sexual abuse, pressure to leave by professionals places the onus of responsibility for the violence on the woman. If a woman is not able to leave, she faces the possibility of being labelled a bad parent and as colluding with the violence. Thus begins the 'fight' with professionals at a time when information and time to assimilate this is most needed. Women in violent relationships may be acutely aware that leaving does not mean the violence will cease. Thus they may be constantly weighing up the safety issues on a day to day basis. Women will be employing complex strategies to avoid violence in the home. The woman's own mental ill-health, alcohol and drug misuse can be as a result of ongoing violence.

In parallel with the rationale for our approach to women whose partners may be sex offenders, women need to know they are not being judged by workers for the actions of their partners. It we can agree that the children's protection is a shared and primary concern, it is more likely that a creative solution can be found. In order for this to begin we need to believe women are not helpless victims.

What About Male Carers?

Throughout the chapter, we refer to the issues directly in relation to the needs of women as carers. This is primarily because our experience has been that the perpetrators are male. In cases where allegations are directed at the women, the abuse had, in our experience, also involved the male partner. In this situation, the children could not remain safely within the family. We have yet to come across a situation where the roles are reversed, that is, the perpetrator is female and her safe male partner is choosing to maintain their relationship, whilst also having the primary care of the children.

However, there is no reason why the work plan we have developed could not be used in this situation.

It is important to recognise that there may be some additional elements that would need to be addressed. We know comparatively little about the offending patterns, treatment programmes, or their outcomes in relation to female sex offenders. It may be less straightforward therefore to provide information based on a body of knowledge that the male partner can connect to his own experience. Where the perpetrator is a woman, an extra set of hurdles must be overcome, both emotionally and cognitively, not only by the partner and children, but also by workers and organisations. Society as a whole is only slowly adjusting to the role of men as primary carers. This may need further exploration in a programme of work with a man. It may also be important to spend more time considering the outside, long term support that is available to the man, as again this may be more limited and less accessible. As with women we have worked with, the same dilemmas for the man, of balancing their needs within the relationship with those of the children, will be based on defining and managing the risk.

Conclusion

One of the greatest challenges, and rewards, in social work lies in the process of working through antagonism and suspicion to find some common ground. This, in turn, allows for some of the barriers to be broken down sufficiently for the opportunity for change to begin. The most fundamental message that we learnt in carrying out this work is that the antagonism and suspicion lay as significantly with the workers as the women. Likewise, it was as important for us to be open to the need to be challenged and move at the pace set by the women as opposed to that of the organisation.

The most staggering revelation lay in the willingness of these women to co-operate and trust us, despite their long-standing clashes with social services. Valuing and supporting the women in working through the emotional, practical and cognitive dilemmas they are grappling with, does not conflict with the primary need to protect the children. In the course of completing this work we were able to convince the most adamant of doubters of the benefits of working in partnership and evolving a plan that addresses common understandings. Here are some of their comments:

> When I first agreed to come to the group I was full of anger, not only at my partner, but also with the authorities.

> I would build a brick wall in my mind so no-one could see in. I would chip bits off my partner's offence to make myself feel better.

> The child is never to blame, nor am I.
> (Quotes from 'Living with Risk' group).

References

Bourton, A., and Burnham, L. (1989). Stand By Your Man. *Social Work Today*.

Finkelhor, D., and Baron, L. (1986). High Risk Children. In *A Sourcebook on Child Sexual Abuse*. Sage Publications.

Hester, M., Pearson, C., and Harwin, N. (1998). *Making an Impact: Children and Domestic Violence*. Barnardos, NSPCC and University of Bristol.

Hooper, C. (1992). *Mothers Surviving Child Sexual Abuse*. London: Routledge.

Hooper, C., and Humphries, C. (1998). Women Whose Children Have Been Sexually Abused: Reflections on a Debate. *British Journal of Social Workers*, 28.

Humphries, C. (1992). Disclosure of Child Sexual Assault: Implications for Mothers. *Australian Social Work*, 45(3).

Jones, E., and Parkinson, P. (1995). Child Sexual Abuse, Access and the Wishes and Feelings of the Child. *International Journal of Law and the Family*, Vol. 9(1).

Joyce, P.A. (1997). Mothers of Sexually Abused Children and the Concept of Collusion: A Literature Review. *Journal of Child Sexual Abuse*, Vol. 6(2).

Peake, A., and Fletcher, M. (1997). *Strong Mothers: A Resource for Mothers and Carers of Children who have been Sexually Assaulted*. Lyme Regis: Russell House.

Salter, A.C. (1988). *Child Sex Offenders and Victims – A Practical Guide Treating*. Sage Publications.

Timmons-Mitchell, J., Chandler-Holtz, D., and Semple, W.E. (1997), Post-Traumatic Stress Disorder Symptoms in Child Sexual Abuse Victims and their Mothers. *Journal of Child Sexual Abuse*, Vol. 6(4).

Walton, P. (1996). *Partnership with Mothers in the Wake of Child Sexual Abuse*. Social Monograph, University of East Anglia.

Appendix 1

Process of Developing Living with Risk Group

Summer 1995 'Safe Carers' group.	One woman referred who had not separated from her partner.
	Discovery of other women in similar situations – all known to SSD for many years.
Summer 1997 further 'Safe Carers' group.	Spring 1996. Decision to run 'Living with Risk' group.
	Planning phase: – crèche facilities – budget – provided by ACPC – venue – not associated with SSD – considering our own values and beliefs – outline of initial two sessions – referral information – setting up consultation
Plans for further group to be run with women from previous groups co-facilitating.	Referral phase: 1 – aims – criteria – publicity via SSD – five women referred
Links with network of 'safe carers' in the North West.	initial pre-group interview: – to match needs of women with aims – to introduce a 'familiar face' – to plan for any worries or fears – to agree criteria
Expectations of the women for the group (See Appendix 2).	Facilitating the group – 12 weeks, Nov 96 – Feb 97.
	Post-group: – Individual feedback – Reunion after one month – Formal evaluation sought by the women – Own evaluation and report to ACPC
	Planning and referral process begun to run group End 1997. Only two women referred.
	Decision to adapt group programme to meet individual needs of these women.

Appendix 2

What I Want the Group to Cover

- Why are my children on the Child Protection Register?
- How does the child protection system work?
- What does high/low risk mean for me?
- What risk do I have responsibility for?
- What is sexual abuse?
- How can I have a say?

- How can I know…?
- What can I do?
- How can I work out what I want?
- What does this mean for my child(ren)?
- How do I learn to trust again?
- What support is available?
- Some fun.

Appendix 3

Who is Responsible for the Abuse?

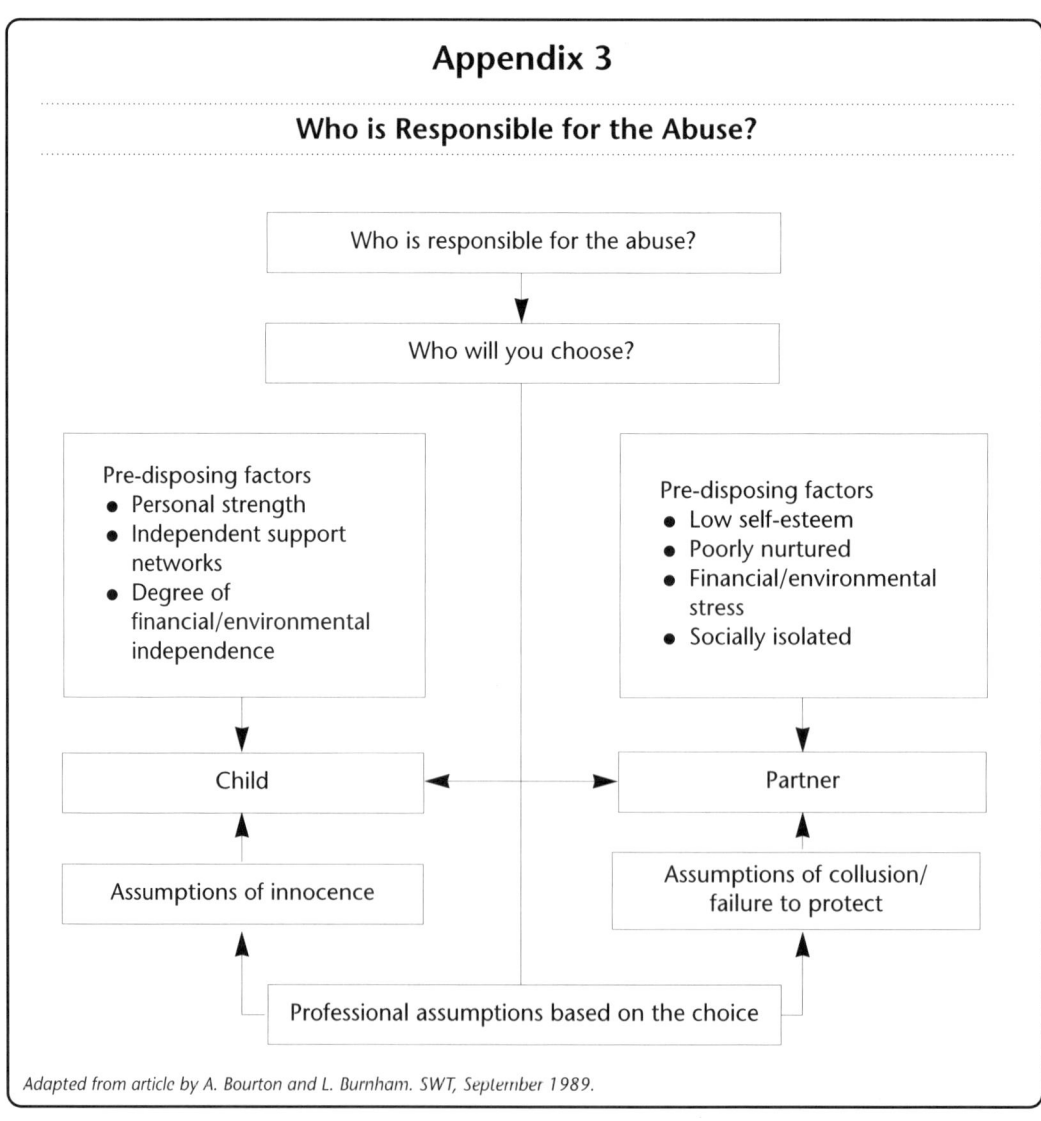

Adapted from article by A. Bourton and L. Burnham. SWT, September 1989.

Appendix 4

Think about a colleague at work that you admire.

Write down three things that you most admire about them.

Today, when you get to work, you are informed that an allegation of sexual abuse has been made by a child against your colleague, and they have been suspended from duty.

Go forward three months. Your colleague has resigned. They have contacted you at work asking you to contact them.

Write down three things that worry you most.

Appendix 5

A Work Plan with Woman Partners Living with Risk

(to be adapted for group and individual programmes)

1. What is sexual abuse?
2. Information about cycle of offending.
3. Responsibility and treatment issues.
4. The effects of child sexual abuse on a child.
5. Why children don't tell – child's perspective.
6. Issues for siblings.
7. The effects of 'knowing' on the mum.
8. The experience of the system.
9. The child's needs, long and short term.
10. Why/How/What/When to explain to non-abused siblings.
11. Issues of responsibility – what you can and can't do.
12. Future relationship with partner.
13. Future contact with children.
14. Safe caring.
15. Living without the social worker.

Appendix 6

Agreement-making Process for Assessment

- Why are you assessing? (e.g., for court, child protection conference, etc.)
- What are the concerns? (e.g., other issues instead of or in addition to injuries)
- How do you establish what the concerns are with the family?
- What sort of assessment will be done? (e.g., needs assessment, risk assessment, or any combination)
- What multi-disciplinary support is available?
- What are the expectations of workers, managers, colleagues, family members and other professionals in the assessment?
- How will workers constantly check out with families that they understand and agree about all aspects of the work?

Setting up assessment (to allow families to succeed)

- What independent support systems need to be in place for all family members?
- What practical considerations need to be made? (e.g, transport costs, ways of confirming arrangements, etc.)
- How will workers facilitate the opportunity for this family to show their strengths as well as addressing the concerns? What stress factors need to be managed and how will these be taken into consideration?

Undertaking the assessment

- Who is part of the assessment? What is being assessed? How will this be managed?
- How will workers encompass the wishes and feelings of the children?
- How will workers support this family in maintaining their self-worth throughout the assessment process?
- What systems for constantly informing and feeding back to the family are in place?
- What ways can workers note change in families that are independent of the fundamental changes around the initial concern? (e.g., parents taking more active roles in the assessment process, with schools, other aspects of their lives that are positive. Parents voicing their disagreement with aspects of the assessment in constructive ways.)
- How can these changes be recognised by the families themselves?

Concluding the assessment

- What longer-term needs have not been addressed in the assessment process? How can support systems be set up to prevent families from re-entering the system at a future stage?
- How can the parents be facilitated in explaining events to the children? In what ways can workers support children? Who else is available to do this? What longer-term support do the children need?

SECTION THREE
Health

12   Speech and Language

Rosemary Bazley

Speech and language therapists work with parents throughout the course of assessment and therapy. In this chapter details of this parental involvement are described. Specialist terms used within the text are explained at the end of the chapter.

The Aims

The main aim of working with parents in speech and language therapy is to improve the child's communication skills, which is the overall aim of the therapeutic process. Initially, parents need to be involved as information providers as part of the assessment and, in the longer term, diagnostic procedure. Parents know more about their children than anyone else. They are able to provide information in two main areas; developmental history and the child's communication and behaviour at home, which may be very different from that observed in the clinic room or school. Information gained from parents is an essential prerequisite for therapy planning.

Parents are the child's main interactive partners. As parents form this central part of the child's communicative environment, they can also alter this environment as part of the therapeutic process.

At a more specific level, it should be obvious that no child is going to progress well in acquiring skills as complex as those involved in speech and language, from forty-five minutes per week with a therapist. Particularly when these are the very skills that the child has had difficulty in acquiring in the first place! It is therefore essential that therapy activities are repeated outside the session and this task often falls to the parents. In addition to these specifically

structured one to one activities, the parent is well placed to carry over the speech and language structures taught in therapy and promote their use in everyday situations.

One aim of working with parents is to reduce their anxiety levels. Although this can be seen as a valuable aim in its own right it can also have benefits for the child who is part of a family dynamic.

Another aim of working through parents can be to ensure that the child's potential for communication is reached through supporting the parents. For example, if the parents are coming to terms with the news that their child has a significant special need, the therapist can support them through the grieving process to a place of acceptance where they are willing to receive appropriate help for the child.

The Evidence

Some research has been undertaken into who most effectively carries out speech and language therapy intervention. These studies compare the results from therapists or specialist teachers with those of parents and others. The following information is taken from the literature review by Law *et al.* (1998). Although professionals were more effective than parents in cases of speech delay, the results were comparable in the area of spoken language delay and parents following professional advice were more effective than 'direct intervention' in the area of understanding of language. It should be noted, however, that the difference in this last area was taken from only two studies. In summary, Law *et al.*, comment that

> *The data support the adoption of indirect models of intervention relative to the more traditional direct*

models for all language difficulties, though not for speech delays.   (Law *et al.*, 1998, p 50)

The Professional Guidelines

The Royal College of Speech and Language Therapists has produced clinical guidelines. These are a first attempt by the professional body to improve the equity and quality of the provision of services by analysing the evidence for best practice and making explicit the standards of care.

As an example, the College Guidelines which mention parents in the section relating to pre-school children with speech and language disorders, are quoted here:

- Assessment must include observation of the child's communication with the parent or carer and contain information about the child's communication in a range of other situations, e.g., with siblings, peers and both familiar and unfamiliar adults.

- Assessment will include looking at the need, appropriateness, type, timing and frequency of intervention, which will be established in consultation with the parent or carer, child and other professionals. It should include assessment of the child's need, and their readiness and ability to change over time.

- Assessment must include discussion and reporting of findings with parents or carers and other professionals.

- Parents and carers should be informed of the assessment results in a manner which facilitates understanding, discussion and joint decision-making.

- A written management plan detailing aims and objectives, roles and responsibilities within therapy, expectation, duration, and contact procedures should be drawn up with parents, carers and relevant others and recorded in the case notes.

- Following assessment, therapists must inform, in writing, the parent or carer,

referrer, child's general practitioner and other appropriate professionals, of the assessment results and management plan.

- The speech and language therapist has a statutory responsibility to participate in the identification and assessment of special educational needs for pre-school children. This must include a detailed description of the child's communication difficulties, in terms of their learning requirements, along with a judgement regarding communication potential and communication needs. The content should be discussed with the parent or carer before submission and should be written in a style suitable for the lay person.

- The therapist has responsibility for directing the intervention, whether carried out directly or indirectly (e.g., via parents or carers, nursery staff, assistants etc.)

- The agreement between the therapist and the parent, carer and other professionals should outline the location of the contact, the frequency of contact, the nature of the contact and the respective responsibilities.

- Intervention must work towards enabling the child's communication skills to develop within their functional communication setting and will involve education and supporting the parent or carer and others significant to the child's care.

- Discharge will be at the discretion of the therapist providing the service in full consultation with the parent or carer and others involved in the child's care and education.

- A discharge report summarising details of therapy, outcomes and reason for discharge will be sent out within one month of discharge to the parent or carer and other relevant parties. In some cases it may be helpful to alert the nursery school of potential difficulty in language related learning.

- The process for re-referral or future access to therapy must be made clear to the parent or carer and other appropriate parties (Royal College of Speech and Language Therapists 1998).

Parents are central to the therapeutic process, from assessment to discharge in speech and language therapy. They are involved in planning and decision-making, as well as carrying out aspects of the therapy.

Specific Approaches

Working with and through parents is the central part of a number of therapeutic approaches. Some examples of these are outlined here:

- Parental-based Intervention (Gibbard 1977). A programme for use with language delayed children through parent groups. Language objectives are set for parents to follow and achieve, aiming to foster children's language development through the context of daily activities.

- The Hanen Early Language Parent Programme (Fryer, A. 1994). A programme to equip parents to be able to facilitate their child's communication development by interacting in the most effective way they can. The parent course includes use of video and feedback to help parents adjust their interaction. It has been developed for parents of language impaired children, particularly pre-school children.

- WILSTAAR (Ward Infant Language Screening Test Assessment Acceleration Remediation) (Ward 1999). An early intervention programme in which children are screened for potential language difficulties by the health visitor at the eight month hearing test. Those failing the screen are assessed by speech and language therapists at home. Those

found to be at risk for a language problem are seen for a few (e.g. four) home visits where advice on promoting language development is given.

- Preventive Therapy (Irwin 1988). A programme in which parents remove pressures on their child's speech during a period of non-fluency to prevent a stammer developing or becoming established.

Settings

Speech and language therapists work with parents across a range of different settings:

Clinic or health centre

In this setting the speech and language therapist has as much contact with the parent as the child. The child's attendance depends on the parent bringing the child to clinic. In some areas attendance is very poor and a high proportion of cases are discharged for non-attendance. Some years ago when I worked in a health centre in one such area a colleague and I undertook a small scale project. Ten randomly selected referrals were offered a home visit as their first appointment with the speech and language therapist and their attendance record was compared with that of ten randomly selected control referrals who were offered routine clinic appointments as their first contact with the speech and language therapist. By the time all twenty cases had passed through the system to the point of discharge, significantly less children in the home visit group had been discharged for non-attendance than the control group. It was concluded that the initial home visit established a different relationship between parent and therapist, resulting in a better attendance record.

Parents are a vital source of the information needed to plan therapy, and this can be particularly true when the child does not demonstrate their true level of communication or is unco-operative in the clinic setting. Parents play a vital role in clinic based therapy, especially with pre-schoolers, in carrying out therapy activities between sessions. Unfortunately, it is common for there to be a lengthy waiting list for regular therapy in this setting, which can cause difficulties in the relationship between parents and therapist. It is extremely difficult to assess a child and tell parents that their child does have a communication difficulty requiring intervention, but that there will be a wait of so many months. It is perhaps even harder to review a child's progress and tell the parents that their child still has a problem, but that they must continue to wait for therapy. During this waiting time parents are always advised of general ways to help their child.

Mainstream school

Speech and language therapists often support children with speech and language difficulties in mainstream schools. They visit the school to assess the child, liaise with staff and provide a programme to be carried out in school, by staff who are trained and supported in doing this. As their child gets older parents become less involved with their child's speech and language, but therapists endeavour to keep parents involved in the process by inviting them to assessments, talking to them on the telephone and sending them copies of speech and language therapy reports and programmes.

Family centres

Speech and language therapists work with communication impaired children in family centres run by social services. They work closely with the staff and parents. The parents are supported by the staff in carrying out programmes provided by the therapist. The speech and language therapy programme will often form part of a wider programme of work including such areas as parenting skills. Families attending these centres are often dealing with a number of issues, and the child's communication must be viewed within this wider picture and addressed accordingly.

Child development centres

These centres are run by the Health Service and offer a wide range of services to families of children with developmental difficulties. The children often have complex medical conditions and the child development centre team are often involved in the diagnosis of the exact nature of the child's difficulties. Children are sometimes assessed by the speech and language therapist as part of a team assessment with a physiotherapist and occupational therapist. They may be attending numerous appointments with a variety of different professionals. These factors must be taken into account when planning and implementing therapy, for example by organising physiotherapy and speech and language therapy appointments for the same morning, to reduce the number of trips the parents have to make.

Language units and special schools

In these settings the speech and language therapists work as part of the school team, providing programmes for other staff members to carry out. The therapists have to make arrangements to maintain contact with parents in a similar way to that described for mainstream schools, but the children may live some distance from the school. It is common for speech and language therapists to attend parents evenings to be available to talk to parents. Therapists also attend statement review meetings if possible.

Home visits

In addition to one-off home visits carried out for a specific purpose to children receiving speech and language therapy at school or in clinic, some courses of therapy are carried out entirely through home visits. This domiciliary therapy is usually provided for pre-school children with significant difficulties who do not respond well in clinic.

Working in the home is very different to working in any other setting. The balance of the relationship between the parent and therapist is altered and the parent is on their own territory. It can be harder for the therapist to control the session and achieve their aim. Obviously there are times when it is in the best interests of the therapeutic process for the therapist to be flexible. Domiciliary therapy is sometimes undertaken in conjunction with a Portage programme, with the therapist and Portage worker making joint visits and planning communication objectives and activities together.

Knowledge

In order to provide a good quality service to children and their parents, speech and language therapists need to have a sound knowledge of normal development, communication disorders and therapeutic approaches. This enables them to detect disorders, diagnose them accurately and select appropriate approaches to treatment. It allows the therapist to inform parents as to the nature and severity of the child's difficulties, answer their questions and explain the rationale behind the course of therapy undertaken.

If using the parent-based therapy approaches, the therapist needs to have a good knowledge of the approach. Some of these are specialist approaches, such as Hanen (Fryer 1994) and Wilstaar (Ward 1999).

Speech and language therapists also draw on knowledge specific to working with parents. This may in part have been taught, much is also gained from the experience of working with parents and learning what does and does not work in different situations. This knowledge covers a broad

range of topics, such as how to explain approaches and particular activities, when to give written information, when to demonstrate activities and ways of encouraging good attendance.

Speech and language therapists working with children and parents where English is not the first language have to know how to access relevant services and information. Therapists need to know how to contact interpreters, to facilitate communication with parents if their English is limited, and to assist in the assessment of children's speech and language skills in the home language. Speech and language therapists must know how to obtain information regarding language development in the language in question, and cultural information so that this can be taken into account when working with the family.

Another area of knowledge which is important in working with parents is psychology. Relevant aspects of psychology are taught to speech and language therapists during training and used during therapy.

Speech and language therapists also need to have a knowledge of general information regarding related services and procedures. For example, it may be necessary to refer children to educational psychology or child and family therapy to achieve the long term aims of therapy. The speech and language therapist may be the person with whom the parent chooses to raise issues concerning feeding, sleeping and behaviour, and the therapist needs to know how to put parents in touch with the help they need. This can have a beneficial effect on the home situation, which may facilitate the therapeutic process. In addition, providing this general, practical support can improve the quality of the relationship between the parent and therapist, and the better that relationship the easier working together becomes. Other types of information that therapists need to make available to parents is the availability of Makaton training, contact details for the local AFASIC group (Association For All Speech Impaired Children, a national network of parent support groups), local toy libraries, libraries and play groups.

The last area of knowledge that speech and language therapists need in working with parents is that of the English language. Therapists necessarily use a great deal of jargon when thinking, reading and discussing with colleagues about speech and language disorders. They must, however, be aware that much of what they say and write is jargon and often impossible for parents to understand. They must know either how to express what they want to say without the use of jargon or know how to explain the terms used so that they make sense to the parents, and other professionals!

Skills

Speech and language therapists working with parents need a wide range of skills. They need to establish a good relationship with the parents. They require the skill of being able to relate to, and interact with, people of different ages, backgrounds and lifestyles. Part of this is accepting people as they are and respecting them, rather than being judgemental.

Speech and language therapists need to be confident and confidence-inspiring. From the outset, parents are looking towards the therapist for answers and are trusting them to help their child. Parents become more confident in the therapist's abilities as they see demonstrations of competence, such as picking up on concerns the parents raise and establishing a rapport with the child.

An important part of working with parents is being approachable. If the parents do not feel that the therapist is approachable, they may not inform them of vital information or ask about activities or advice they have not understood.

The speech and language therapist needs to be flexible in their work with parents, as in all direct work with children. Parents bring to each session their own agenda, feelings, experiences and concerns. I have been on a home visit the very day a mother has heard she is being evicted; obviously in such circumstances it is difficult to focus on speech and language therapy! However, flexibility must be tempered by some single mindedness in sticking to the plan and achieving the aims of the session if possible. If the therapist is sidetracked too easily or too often the parent will begin to wonder whether there are any objectives and what is the purpose of the session.

Therapists also need good listening skills, so that they can gain all the information stated or implied in what the parent says. One issue that therapists can pick up on through careful listening is that of parents' priorities. During discussions with parents it is possible to ascertain where their child's communication problem lies in their list of priorities, and what their priority is within their child's communication problem. Parents are often contending with a range of problems in addition to their child's communication. This was once starkly put to me by a parent in a family centre. 'Your kid's talking is the last thing you worry about if you haven't got any money'. Although when talking to parents about their child's speech and language they may be focusing on other issues such as housing, relationships, finance or addiction. It is essential to take this into account and modify the parents' role in therapy accordingly.

For some parents, the commonest aspects which take priority regarding their child are behaviour, sleep patterns and eating problems with the child's communication being least important to them. Also, a parents' concern about the child's communication difficulties may be given a different priority at different times. Speech and language therapists need to be careful and sensitive communicators, choosing their words carefully and judging when the time is right to broach particular subjects.

Therapists working with parents need to have excellent time management skills. Parents should not be kept waiting or feel rushed. Working with parents can be extremely time consuming. To make efficient use of this time, therapists should plan the objectives of the session carefully and strive to achieve them. They also need to develop skills in the area of explaining and demonstrating activities and to tailor the written advice given to the individual parent, being sensitive to any difficulties the parent may have with literacy.

The Author's Current Practice
Introductions

I currently work at a nursery school catering for children with a wide range of special needs, from speech (pronunciation) problems to severe learning disabilities. The majority of children receive speech and language therapy input before entering nursery. For those who have not previously been referred, the teachers will ask the parents' permission to refer them for assessment. No child is seen whilst in the nursery without the parents' permission.

The first contact with parents of children entering the school is normally an informal introduction. At this brief meeting, I explain to the parents that I will be in their child's class on a specific day each week, carry out an assessment and leave a programme for the staff to carry out in class. I explain that the child will have additional one-to-one input with a therapist or assistant available should their child require it. This is normally put into place after the first term when the child will have settled into the school.

Parents are routinely invited into school once per term, but they are welcome to come in at any time. I point out where the speech and language therapy room is. I explain that if they want to ask or tell me anything, messages for me in the child's home book will always be passed on by the teaching staff and that I will use the home book to communicate with them on occasions. I also try to help the parents to overcome any fears or worries and give them an opportunity to ask questions.

I ask the parents what speech and language therapy input the child has had, and where. I then explain that I will get the file/case notes so that I can see what has been done. I explain that the parents will no longer need to take the child to clinic because it will all be done at nursery.

Appointments

Parents are invited to the termly appointment via a standard appointment card. These are sent two weeks in advance, to allow parents time to make arrangements. I plan the main points of what I wish to ask or tell them beforehand. I have found it better to see only two or three children's parents in a day, as the sessions go better and the quality is improved. The parents often have significant issues to discuss, such as diagnosis, prognosis, or future school placements.

At the beginning of the session I welcome them and offer them a tea or coffee. I feel this sets a relaxed atmosphere in which they will feel free to talk. It conveys the idea that I have time to talk to them and to listen.

I was trained at college in the importance of seating. I do not sit behind a desk, as this can form a barrier. If both parents have come, I sit them next to each other with my chair opposite. If only one parent is present, I sit opposite but at a slight angle as this is less threatening/confrontational. The most important issue about chairs is size. I try to ensure that we all have adult sized chairs, as this is comfortable for a lengthy conversation and signals equality between us. If enough adult chairs are not available, I would give the parents the adult sized chairs and sit on the child sized table or even child sized chair. I would never give parents child sized chairs if I had an adult sized chair. I have experienced this as a parent and it may have contributed to me forgetting several things I wanted to ask the professional concerned.

A record is made in the case notes, of what is said during the session, by all parties. It can be difficult to recall all the topics covered and ideas expressed if it is left until the end of the session, or later in the day for any reason. Make notes at the **end** of each topic covered as these breaks for recording give the parents a breathing and thinking space without stilting the discussion itself. Always explain to the parents that what has been said needs to be clearly recorded.

If it is my first appointment with parents, I explain in more detail the way speech and language therapy operates in the nursery. I explain the main approaches that will be used with their child, usually the Derbyshire Language Scheme (Masidlover 1994) and sometimes The Makaton Vocabulary (Makaton, 1996. See also Glossary). At each stage I check with the parents whether particular aspects of the assessment, therapy or statementing procedure have been explained to them and that they fully understand.

I always give parents a brief resumé of the main points of any advice given which should prevent parents going home thinking, 'I know she told us to do three things, and I can remember two of them, but what was the third?' If giving specific therapy activities, I both talk them through and write them out in detail. For most activities, it is necessary to demonstrate them, as the activities could be worthless or even discouraging to the child if not carried out correctly. I give all parents suggestions and general advice, and only give specific activities to those who respond positively to the offer of a home programme.

I do not generally include the child in the session. This is because the child will often demand the parents' attention and distract them from the discussion, there are issues which are best discussed out of the child's hearing, and it can be extremely disruptive to the child's nursery day to see their parents. On occasions I will carry out an assessment or therapy task with the child in front of the parents. This is normally to reassure parents that the child is co-operating and responding well in therapy sessions, particularly when this has not been the case in the past. It may also be to demonstrate a specific difficulty the child is having, particularly in understanding.

Some parents report that the child 'understands everything you say', giving examples such as 'go upstairs and get your pyjamas'. The child may be gaining information from the daily routine and, if he knows where his pyjamas are kept, need only understand the one word 'pyjamas' to carry out this seemingly simple six-word request. After explaining this to the parents it can sometimes be helpful to demonstrate how many words in a sentence the child can actually understand, without clues from context or routine. Normally, when I am explaining the child's assessment results or therapy activities without the child present, I show parents the assessments used and the therapy equipment and explain what has been done.

I explain to the parents the range of their child's difficulties and the order in which therapy will focus on each one. This relates to the order of priority in which I view aspects of speech and language. If the child enters nursery with no understanding of spoken language, then assessment and therapy will focus on pre-language skills. These include such skills as responding to speech-action rhymes and signalling when they want an activity repeated. This will continue to the point where the child is ready to begin working on communication through speech, symbol, sign or a combination thereof.

My priority at this point is to encourage communication between the child and adults in the environment through whichever means they find easiest. This is often a new idea to parents who have previously focused on wanting their child to talk. For many children with whom I work, a sign or symbol programme is a means to develop spoken language, for others it can open a communication channel which will benefit the family and often help the child's behaviour.

A Makaton sign or symbol programme is never introduced without the parent's permission. There is a base of research evidence showing that signing does not delay the development of spoken language, but in fact facilitates it. I tell parents this when discussing the introduction of signing (Grove and Walker 1990). My main priority is the development of the understanding of spoken language. Children cannot meaningfully use words and sentences they do not understand. Again, parents may have been concerned that the child was not talking but may not have considered the area of understanding of language.

My next priority is the words, sentences and grammar the child is able to use and then pronunciation (or speech). Sometimes these last two priorities have to be reversed because the child's speech sound difficulties are preventing them developing in the area of spoken language.

The child's pragmatic skills, that is the use of language, are also monitored as well as vocabulary. Intervention in these areas is necessary if they do not keep pace with other aspects of language. If at any time the child has a feeding problem or becomes dysfluent, these automatically become top priority.

I share these priorities with parents so that they are aware of all the aspects of speech and language that are considered, and they have an overview of the path that therapy is likely to take.

Home visits

I make home visits if the parent does not or cannot attend appointments at the nursery or if there is a specific reason for wishing to see a child at home, for example if they communicate very differently there from at school. As the teachers from the nursery spend one day each week visiting the children in their groups at home, I often arrange to go with the teacher to discuss issues with the parents or observe the child. These 'one off' home visits are very different to domiciliary therapy where all the speech and language therapy the child receives is via regular home visits.

Case meetings

Wherever possible, I attend case meetings about children whose main difficulty is with communication. These are most often informal four-way meetings between the parents, the teacher, the educational psychologist and myself on the occasion of a visit or assessment by the educational psychologist. At all case meetings it is important to smile at and speak to the parents on entering the room, to make contact and assure them that you are the same friendly and approachable person.

Normally I will have spoken to the educational psychologist before the meeting, and, through regular liaison, will usually know the teacher's views, so I do not get any surprises during the meeting. These meetings are usually about educational statements and future placement. I am more likely to get surprises from the parents who have changed their minds about the school they would like their child to attend. When reporting information during the course of the meeting, it is important to check back with the parents that they are happy with what you are saying, by asking 'Is that how you find him at home?', 'Would you agree with that?' This may also be necessary when someone else has contributed, to give the parents an opportunity to comment.

Parent courses

I run a Makaton workshop each autumn term for parents of children using Makaton at nursery. These days form a different experience of working with parents as I am transformed from therapist to adult educator and their role from parents to course participants. These training days are relaxed and fun. They provide the parents with the opportunity to meet and talk as well as learning something which will benefit their child. Although it is an extra commitment, I have found it constructive and helpful for both the parents and myself.

The courses are run during nursery days and the nursery provides all-day child care for the children concerned. This enables some parents to attend who would not otherwise be able to due to child care difficulties. They are run at the nursery or nearby, so that the venue is accessible to parents. Account is taken of parents' need to collect older siblings from school. Parents' attendance on the course is a huge factor in the success of a Makaton programme with a child. This course enables the parents to sign to the child at home to aid their understanding, and to understand the signs the child uses. With this approach also being used in nursery, the child can learn signs used consistently around him and feel confident that his attempts at signs will be understood. These days are often a welcome change for children who may be quite lively, and even disruptive, as their confidence grows.

Case Studies

The following cases are included to provide further insight into working with parents in speech and language therapy.

Paul

Paul's mother became concerned about his behaviour and interaction from a young age. She raised these concerns with the health visitor and Paul was referred to a paediatrician and a speech and language therapist. There were initial concerns about Paul's hearing which was, however, found to be good, and autism, which decreased as he became more interactive. The first intervention I undertook was a course of Non-directive Therapy (Tierney and Cogher 1994) to increase his interaction with others and his initiation to communication. He was initially unco-operative with any adult-directed activity but, after the course of play and communication therapy, it became apparent that he was interested in picture material and books, and happy to engage in looking at these with the therapist. It was then possible to undertake an assessment of

his understanding using picture material. This showed that he had a significant delay in the area of understanding which then became the focus of intervention.

During the above period, Paul's mother varied in her view of his difficulties. She was at different times anxious, accepting, pessimistic, optimistic, frustrated, guilty, questioning, motivated and confused. This situation was not helped by the fact that she was receiving different advice from different sources and not receiving some of the answers she asked for because none was available, for example, regarding cause. During this time I explained I was always available to discuss any question or concern. I attempted to answer her questions and when I could not, I explained why. I tried to focus her on the present, demonstrating Paul's current skills and giving feedback on his progress. Gradually, over time, Paul's mother focused on carrying out activities and he made good progress.

James

James was the only child of a single mother. He had significant behavioural problems on entering nursery, including aggression towards staff. His mother was facing similar problems at home. Gradually he conformed to the consistent boundaries in the nursery. At this stage it became apparent that he had no understanding of any single spoken words. Makaton signing was introduced and James was able to recognise many signs on first showing. He was able to learn to understand spoken words through the use of the corresponding sign. James' mother supported the use of the Makaton programme wholeheartedly. She attended nursery regularly to be shown new signs and attended a Makaton workshop at the earliest opportunity. James used signs to communicate with adults and children, then began using words and sentences. He was diagnosed as having a severe language disorder and continued to benefit from the use of signing to teach new aspects of language. His behavioural difficulties having been resolved, he went on to attend a language unit.

Colin

Colin was attending nursery for a severe speech sound disorder. His mother was extremely anxious and sought a specialist opinion. She also engaged a private therapist in addition to the therapy he was receiving at nursery. Colin undertook his speech exercises at nursery and at home most days, and he made good progress. At the point where his speech was within the acceptable range for his age, and the frequency of his programme at nursery was being reduced, he became dysfluent. I undertook a programme of indirect therapy with the parents (Irwin 1988). Again Colin's mother sought a specialist opinion and undertook a course of indirect therapy at a specialist centre (Rustin, Botteriall and Kelman 1999).

Throughout the time that Colin was dysfluent, his mother was extremely anxious about it. At times she could not bear to hear him talk and she worried constantly about whether the dysfluency would become a permanent stammer and what the future would hold for Colin. At this stage her priorities changed and she said she would rather go back to having the speech problem than the dysfluency. Most Mondays would see a lengthy session discussing Colin's dysfluency over the previous week and weekend. His mother's anxiety was so severe that it was necessary to provide the time for these sessions and in the longer term it was necessary for her to receive professional counselling. Colin's dysfluency was resolved, but his mother then became concerned about his grammar. She was told that direct intervention was not recommended, as it might disrupt his fluency and she accepted a period of review. Happily, Colin's remaining grammatical difficulties were resolved.

Sarah

Sarah came to nursery from a mainstream nursery where she had become withdrawn as no-one could understand her due to her severe speech disorder. She had previously received therapy in a health centre with carry-over at home. She had become resistant to the activities and her mother was 'just trying to correct her speech in conversation'. I decided to give them a break from activities at home and advised her mother not to correct Sarah's speech in conversation, as she was unable to change her pronunciation of words at this stage and this was a negative experience for her.

I spent time with Sarah in class initially and both her teacher and I adopted a non-threatening approach of joining her in activities, commenting, encouraging and, if we were unable to understand her, saying 'You're telling me about the…' I undertook a thorough assessment of all aspects of Sarah's speech productions, imitation and discrimination. At this stage I gave no feedback on the accuracy of her attempts, praising her for making the attempt. I designed a carefully graded programme where she would be able to achieve success and began gently providing feedback on how her attempt varied from the target. I invited Sarah's mother in and went through a series of assessment and therapy tasks so that she could see the precise nature and level of Sarah's difficulties.

By the end of the summer term I was able to give a home programme to be carried out over the summer holidays. I supported her mother through the statementing process, which resulted in Sarah entering a language unit where she has continued to make good progress.

Conclusions and the Future

Parents play a major role in speech and language therapy. This role involves providing information and supporting and participating in the therapy process. Increasingly, attention is turning to indirect approaches in which parents carry out the therapy activities with the support of the therapist. The research to date has found indirect approaches to be effective with language problems. These results were from middle income families (Royal College of Speech and Language Therapists 1998). Further research is needed to identify the characteristics of parents most likely to succeed in carrying out indirect therapy (Law *et al*. 1998). They also question whether the level of co-operation and compliance in the studies supporting indirect therapy matches those in every day practice, and this requires further investigation. They suggest that some parents will be unable or unwilling to take on the level of commitment required by these approaches, and suggest that ways of working will need to be found for families where this is the case.

They make further suggestions regarding future involvement of parents in the communication development of their children. One is that parental concern could be incorporated as part of a screening procedure for speech and language problems. Others are that parents could be empowered through distribution of information to all parents, the setting up of drop-in clinics responding to parental need and primary prevention activities such as parent-child interaction programmes.

Whatever the future may hold, it will continue to be a fact that parents play a vital role in the development of children's communication skills and speech and language therapists must work closely with parents to achieve each child's potential in the area of communication.

References

Fryer, A. (1994). The Hanen Early Language Parent Programme. In Law J. (Ed.). *Before School: A Handbook to Approaches to Intervention with Pre-school Language Impaired Children*, pp 1–18. London: Afasic.

Gibbard, D. (1994). Parental-based Intervention with Pre-school Language-delayed Children. *Eur J Disord Commun*, 29(2): 131–150.

Grove, N., and Walker, M. (1990). The Makaton Vocabulary: Using Manual Signs and Graphic Symbols to Develop Inter-personal Communication. *AAC Augmentative and Alternative Communication*, p 15–18. Baltimore: Williams and Wilkins.

Irwin, A. (1998). *Statementing in Young Children*. Wellingborough: Thorsons.

Law, J., Boyle, J., Harris, F., Harkness, A., and Nye, C. (1998). Screening for Speech and Language Delay: A Systematic Review of the Literature. *Health Technol Assessment*, 2(9).

Makaton Vocabulary Development Project (1996). *The Makaton Vocabulary.*

Masidlover, M. (1994). The Derbyshire Language Scheme. In Law, J. (Ed.). *Before School: A Handbook to Approaches to Intervention with Pre-School Language Impaired Children*, pp 19–33. London: Afasic.

Royal College of Speech and Language Therapists (1998). *Clinical Guidelines by Consensus for Speech and Language Therapists*. Royal College of Speech and Language Therapists.

Rustin L., Botterill, W., and Kelman, E. (1996). *Assessment and Therapy for Young Dysfluent Children: Family Inter-action*. London: Whurr.

Tieney, K., and Cogher, L. (1994). Non-directive Therapy. In Law, J. (Ed.). *Before School: A Handbook to Approaches to Intervention with Pre-school Language-impaired Children*, pp 62–76. London: Afasic.

Ward, S. (1999). An Investigation into the Effectiveness of an Early Intervention Method for Delayed Language Development in Young Children. *International Journal of Language and Communication Disorders*, Vol. 34; 3: 243–264.

13　A Paediatrician's Perspective

Cathy Hill

Introduction

All children depend on parents for their physical and emotional health and capable parents are the best advocates for a child. The paediatrician, trained to recognise and treat illness and disability, can only help the child if they have a good working relationship with the parent. This relationship will at times be difficult. Even the most pleasant and rational parent will not remain calm if their child is sick. Dealing with caring and effective parents in a stressful situation is not always easy but dealing with abusive parents presents very different challenges. Non-accidental injury, non-organic failure to thrive, and behavioural problems are a common feature of paediatric practice. 'Munchhausen Syndrome by proxy' (McClure *et al.* 1996) a very medical model of child abuse is now well recognised. These situations can be very challenging, frequently there is not the 'diagnostic' certainty we would like and one has to tread a difficult line between supporting a family in distress and colluding with an abusive parent.

In this chapter I would like to draw from my personal practice to illustrate some of the ways this important working relationship with parents can be cultured or indeed jeopardised. Like others I am constantly learning and in an age where 'joined up thinking' and inter-agency working are key, I believe we have much to learn from one another.

What is a Parent?

Reproductive technology and social change have generated new concepts of parenting. Children conceived from anonymous donor sperm and ova, surrogacy and gay couples as parents challenge our definitions. Fewer children in the UK now live with two biological parents in a nuclear family. Good parenting requires more than a genetic relationship and biological parents are often inadequate, as evidenced by the 50,000 children in England and Wales looked after by the local authority (House of Commons Health Committee, 1998).

Many children experience periods of 'parenting' in a foster care or residential care environment. In a country that boasts the highest teenage pregnancy rate in Europe (Office for National Statistics, 1999) many parents are still technically children themselves. For the child the parent is the responsible individual, usually adult, who is the child's prime carer and advocate.

How Do Parents View Their Doctors?

Doctors inhabit a fearful world of disease and few adults will admit to pleasure at the thought of a medical consultation. Some adults are sufficiently anxious that they suffer 'white coat hypertension' with a measurable increase in their blood pressure during a consultation. Where the consultation is related to acute illness, accident or disability in their child, any feelings are inevitably exacerbated, particularly if the child is suffering or in distress. How the parents view the doctor will of course depend on their past experience with health professionals, their own sense of control (Figure 1), the situation they find themselves in and of course the manner and communication skills of the doctor.

Figure 1. – Locus of control

External control: 'I have no power'
Internal control: 'I am in charge'
Powerful other: 'You the doctor are
                    in charge'

The 'locus of control model' recognises three perspectives which parents may adopt with respect to their children.

Parents with External Locus of Control: 'I Have No Power'

Parents who are helpless in the face of their helpers may also be passive and helpless in the face of their child's problem. This is particularly difficult if the child has a chronic illness or disability.

Case study

Edward was a boy of 14 with cystic fibrosis. He was diagnosed in infancy and had always lived with his healthy parents and younger brother. His father worked for the local council offices and his mother was a housewife. He always came to clinic accompanied by his mother and sibling although staff felt that the relationship between Edward and his mother was cold. It was increasingly clear that he was not complying with his treatment and his health was deteriorating to such an extent that he needed to come into hospital. When this was broached, Edward's mother sobbed uncontrollably and was unable to comfort Edward. Attempts to comfort them were met with anger from the mother and silence from the teenage lad. Despite this they returned to the hospital for treatment but refused to see me. I respected this but was concerned that I had tapped into an important obstacle to Edward's well being that needed to be further explored. Edward's mood in hospital

was increasingly withdrawn and un-communicative. Over many sessions with the hospital psychologist it emerged that Edward's parents had been told at diagnosis that his life expectancy was around 14 years. This had become fact for them and was never openly discussed. His mother was gradually able to come to terms with the fact that she had experienced feelings of rejection towards Edward and had invested all her affection in her well son. She had become passive to Edward's fate and this, compounded by depression, had set up a cycle of inevitable decline in Edward's mental state and health.

Key messages

- Passive parents may be depressed.
- Passivity doesn't necessarily mean compliance.
- Causes of passivity and depression may be rooted in misunderstandings about the nature of the child's problem.
- Never assume that the parent shares your understanding of a problem.

Parent with Internal Locus of Control: 'I Am In Charge'

The adversarial patient presents an obvious and immediate challenge to our traditional professional role and the assumption that we have the knowledge and ability to help. In the practice of adult medicine the patient who 'knows best' and refuses advice may be frustrating but is ultimately at liberty to refuse consent to treatment. Where the patient is a child the controlling parent presents a dilemma. A degree of control is, of course, normal, indeed desirable. Whatever our professional competence, the effective parent knows their child better than anyone else. Indeed, a parent with no sense of control, as illustrated by the last case study, is a poor advocate for the child. The practitioner must recognise the difficult boundary between a parent's need to have some control to deal with a difficult situation and the parent whose control is to the detriment of the child.

Case study

Baby Caroline was diagnosed in the womb as having a rare form of muscular disorder. At birth the situation was worse than had been expected and her muscles were so weak that she required assisted ventilation. Her parents were very closely involved with her care in the neo-natal unit and rarely left her incubator. Initially they were co-operative with the nursing staff. Over time they became very critical of Caroline's care and started to impose rules about what staff could and couldn't do for the baby. These rules were not always in the infant's best interests. Furthermore, they tended to monopolise staff time.

Gradually staff began to refuse to care for the baby. The problem was tackled by the medical and nursing team agreeing a unified approach. The number of staff caring for the infant were restricted to a few and arrangements were made to ensure optimum hand-over of information from identifiable staff both verbally and orally. The parents were invited to scheduled progress meeting and encouraged to collect together their questions, concerns or grievances for these sessions which were always attended by the senior nurse and consultant. At these meetings ground rules of care for the infant were re-negotiated and recorded as a 'care plan' countersigned by the parents. They remained difficult to work with but staff felt much more secure in their handling of the situation.

Key messages

- Dealing with adversarial parents can feel very threatening and undermine feelings of professional competence.
- Good communication is essential where a team of staff share responsibility for a child, particularly if parents are felt to be manipulative.

- Parents may be adversarial and difficult for a good reason. Acknowledging the stress of their situation and allowing them to participate as part of the team may help to reduce their fears.
- Negotiating clear ground rules of what is expected of parents is important in this specialist situation.
- While staff felt the parents were behaving unreasonably, the parents were unfamiliar with the situation and needed explicit guidelines to allow them some control.

The Powerful Other: 'You the Doctor Are in Control'

In a busy clinic the 'yes' parent can seem like a godsend. They can, however, be a liability. Good practice must be a process of shared information and decision-making between the professional team and the carer who knows the child best. There can be nothing more frustrating than the parent who unquestioningly follows instructions even when the child is clearly not benefiting. With the advent of parent held medical records and increasing home care of children, parents feel more empowered and happily this scenario is less common.

Case study

Joanne was a child of seven years who had a long-standing problem with daytime wetting. She had attended a local enuretic clinic for many years and no underlying cause for the problem had been found. Despite conventional approaches and meticulous compliance she was showing no sign of improvement. She was admitted to a special unit for intensive observation and therapy. The family arrived with the stated expectation that this was the last therapeutic option. They brought with them several years of fastidiously maintained diaries detailing Joanne's progress. These diaries had been encouraged by the enuretic clinic as a useful monitoring tool. Further inquiry revealed that the threshold for documenting an 'accident' was inappropriately low. Mother and child had become locked into a cycle of observation and documentation for the benefit of the clinic doctor that was detrimental to Joanne's self-esteem and had set up a cycle of failure. It was not clear initially whether this reflected an obsession on the part of the mother. However, she was more than happy to relinquish the diaries. By de-stressing the situation and redefining the problem, the wetting problem slowly resolved itself.

Key messages

- Our advice may be carried out over-zealously and we need to recognise where this may be to the detriment of the child.

- Invest time in finding out how your advice has been implemented in practice and what this means for the parent and child.

- Always give advice on the understanding that you need feedback and the parent and child are part of the team.

- Beware the parent who always agrees with you as they may be flattering your professional ego and will not follow advice.

Understanding the Parents' Perspective

Each of us has a set of expressed or unexpressed beliefs about individual health behaviour that governs whether we follow advice. The roles we adopt in our interactions with parents will influence outcomes but in paediatric practice the parent's view of their child's problem is critical. The health belief model (Figure 2) allows some insight into why families respond differently to their doctors and indeed their illnesses. I recognise

---

Figure 2. – Health Belief Model

1. Motivation for change.
2. Perceived vulnerability.
3. Perceived seriousness.
4. Solutions; cost benefit assessment of required response.
5. Cues to action.

---

all of these situations from practice and inevitably, as 'professionals', we feel more or less comfortable with each and indeed generate our own patterns of behaviour or 'professional approach'.

Motivation for change

Many of my encounters with parents involves giving professional advice. Assuming this is well communicated and understandable to the parent, a number of factors will determine whether the advice is followed. If the advice involves changing an established behaviour the parent must feel motivated to make the change. A typical example would be the smoking parent of an asthmatic child. The medical advice is clear. Smoking damages children's lungs and is likely to make the asthma worse. The parent should stop smoking.

However, if that parent is a single unsupported mother with limited social contact, cigarettes may be her only 'selfish' pleasure in the day. Whilst the smoking may indeed exacerbate her child's asthma and damage her own health it may represent an important prop. A judgmental dogmatic approach will induce guilt, reinforce feelings of failure and be unlikely to cause a behaviour change. A positive approach, which recognises the factors impeding change and sets achievable goals, is more likely to achieve some success and maintain a helpful working relationship.

Perceived vulnerability

Most of us have an inappropriate perception of what is risky to our health, and this perception is particularly vulnerable to media and external influences. For example, thousands of parents rushed out to buy new cot mattresses after media reports which associated certain constituents of mattresses and sudden infant death syndrome. Fewer parents stopped smoking, which is established to have a much clearer association with cot deaths. Equally, statistics seem to become meaningless when compared to personal experience. We are all familiar with this as practitioners. No matter how evidence based and effective a treatment is known to be, if we have witnessed an adverse reaction, we are much less likely to use it again. The same is true for parents. A parent whose first child's onset of epilepsy followed their first immunisations may refuse immunisation to future children. Due to prior experience they perceive unrealistic vulnerability and are unable to look at the risks rationally. It is important to understand parents' perceptions of risk and obvious areas to explore are past experience, experience in the extended family, or their knowledge of folklore or media stories.

Perceived seriousness

I am constantly surprised by how different families view the same situation. One family's crisis is another's weekly visit to the local accident and emergency department. Like any behaviour the extremes are always more difficult to manage. Extreme anxiety and over interpretation of non-serious problems is unhealthy for the child, who misses school for minor ills and learns a pattern of hypochondria. The causes may be related to perceived vulnerability, the parent may be expressing their own anxieties and distress about a quite separate issue or they may be well-meaning but unable to

discriminate about when to seek help. However, more worrying are parents who do not recognise their children's problems. In this case a distinction needs to be made between an inherently high anxiety threshold, neglect and limited understanding. All types of parents need support and education and an exploration of the factors behind the behaviour.

Solutions: cost-benefit assessment of required response

Health scares significantly influence vaccination uptake rates. For example, the recent suggestion of a link between MMR vaccine and autism resulted in a drop in the vaccine uptake levels which is likely to allow a future measles epidemic. The most rational parents can find it difficult to assess cost-risk benefit with respect to their child. Perceived seriousness and vulnerability influence decision-making and corrupt logical risk analysis. Clear facts, time to decide and an honest view can help parents.

Cues to action

Internal and external cues may provoke a change in health behaviour. Unfortunately these often rely on another's misfortune. For example, the family who finally lock their medicine cabinet after their child takes a serious dose of iron tablets. Or the family who become evangelists for the wearing of cycle helmets after their child sustains a serious head injury. It is difficult to know how to use these cues sensitively to encourage healthy behaviour. The 'told you so' approach does little to promote a working relationship. 'How can I help you to stop this happening again?' is generally more helpful.

The Practitioner's Perspective

Most doctors are attracted to their profession by a genuine desire to help people. Much of our working life is spent communicating with families, colleagues and increasingly working in multi-disciplinary teams. Communication skills are recognised to be a vital part of medical training. There is good evidence that most diagnoses can be made on the basis of a good medical history (Hampton *et al.*, 1975). with no recourse to physical examination or expensive investigations. Communication is the most powerful diagnostic tool. Furthermore, poor communication is a liability and patients are more likely to complain about poor communication than technical aspects of care (Hickson *et al.*, 1994). Why then do doctors sometimes have a reputation for poor communication?

Empathy

Good communication requires a degree of empathy. Doctors refer to their 'clinical practice'. 'Clinical' is associated with a cold, detached approach. It is perhaps this very conflict between becoming emotionally involved with a family and maintaining a professional distance that creates a tension. All practitioners resolve this in their own way. I vividly remember sick children from my early years of practice where my personal level of involvement left me emotionally drained. The skilled and experienced practitioner finds that delicate balance between empathy and the ability to make rational decisions. Much of this balance is learnt through experience. However, mutual support of colleagues and a culture where stress is acknowledged as a fact of the job rather than a failing of the colleague, is important.

Time

Another constraint on good working relationships is the pressure of time. I often hear, 'I am sorry to disturb you, you must be very busy'. However, even in a busy clinic it is possible to give quality attention. Simple measures such as always reading notes before a family enters the room, avoiding interruptions and setting a clear agenda at the outset are helpful. If there is not enough time it is best to acknowledge this and arrange a further meeting or 'phone call rather than trying to rush the consultation. Limited time encourages closed questioning such as 'Last time I saw Helen her fits were less frequent than they are now?'

Open questioning, as 'How are things?', allows parents to voice their concerns. For example the family's principle worry may be the child's deteriorating school performance. A period of listening without interruption improves satisfaction and indeed efficiency of the consultation (Beckman and Frankel, 1984). It avoids the 'just before I go doctor' syndrome where the parent asks the question really concerning them at the threshold.

Language

Doctors learn thousands of new words during their medical training. The terminology of medicine becomes second nature and allows the practitioner to distance themselves from the distress of ill-health and human suffering. It also alienates and dehumanises the patient. Children need terminology tailored to their understanding. I overheard a colleague announce to a bemused four-year-old; 'Now Tom, I would like to examine your testicles'. The child did not understand this terminology and was most surprised when she advanced on his genitalia. This does not inspire confidence in parents.

It is important to involve the child in any discussions. Children need to contribute their own view and parents usually appreciate this, particularly where the child has a disability. Disabled families are used to the public assumption that the child cannot communicate and expect more from professionals. If I am meeting a disabled child for the first time the first thing I ascertain is their level of understanding and means of communication. Thereafter I aim to include them as commensurate to their abilities.

Language can, of course, be a real barrier for a working relationship where parents are first generation immigrants with a poor command of English. Translators are important but need to be encouraged not to interpret but translate literally as heard (Lloyd and Bar, 1996). I frequently hear a five-minute response from a parent condensed to a five-second translation. It may be the translator is well-meaning and is trying to clarify an unclear account or save time. It may be that the subject matter is embarrassing. Be sure that both your client and your translator are confident to discuss the matter before you engage their services. They may wish to have a chance to discuss the situation informally before you engage in a more formal fact finding discussion. If your client has a major language barrier they may have felt isolated up to this point and value conversation in their mother tongue. It is most important at the outset to explain the ground rules to your translator. Tell them exactly what you would like of them including time scales. Limiting the amount of conversations translated to small amounts may avoid the risk of them engaging in independent discussion.

Supplementing the Spoken Word with Written Information

It is well documented that patients recall less than 50 per cent of medical consultations when they leave the room. There are a number of effective ways of improving communication. Simple techniques such as the provision of written information, availability to answer questions at a later date and asking the parents to recount what they have understood are all useful tools. Most treatment requires understanding and compliance from both the child and parents. Making this explicit in the form of a written treatment plan is often helpful.

Difficult Situations

1. Breaking bad news

As diagnosticians, the doctor's role is sometimes to bear bad tidings. The experience of receiving the news of a serious diagnosis is usually remembered with clarity by parents for many years to come (Kings Fund, 1987).

How the news is given may influence the working relationship and the family's attitude towards the problem. Inevitably the experience of learning that a child has a serious problem will involve all the feelings of grief, anger, resentment, guilt, denial, sadness. Some of these negative feelings may be transferred to the professionals who need to bear them with sensitivity and insight.

There is no guaranteed right way of breaking bad news to parents, but there are some tried and tested principles which may help.

How to break bad news

The setting: Privacy, comfort, freedom from interruptions and time are rarely guaranteed in medical practice. These are imperative and ideally the setting should allow parents uninterrupted privacy afterwards.

People: Only key professionals should be present, ideally, those already known to the parents. Voyeurism is unwelcome. Students should only be present if the family already knows them as part of the team and this is felt to be part of the necessary learning experience. Everyone should be introduced and the parent's permission sought for the presence of students preferably before they are invited in. Where the ongoing care of the child is to be managed by a team of people, the moment of diagnosis is not the appropriate time for new introductions, these can follow later.

Timing: This should be convenient to the family, ensuring important adults can be present but avoiding unnecessary delay. Parents often recount the mounting anxiety of an appointment with the consultant, which they knew must be serious as their partner had been summoned. Consideration for the child and siblings must be a priority. Whether the child is present is a matter of personal practice. Most doctors would prefer to see parents alone first, allow them to have some time to absorb the information and then break the news to the child later with the parent's present. There is a risk that parents, particularly where the diagnosis is terminal, may wish to maintain a veil of secrecy. This should be avoided at all costs. However, parents know their child better than anyone and may be the best judge of how the child should receive the information and what they are likely to understand and be fearful of. An agreement between the parents and professional that any questions the child asks will be answered openly and honestly is also important.

What to tell

It is always important to find out what the parents know and understand already. This should not take too long as anxiety may mount, and usually the parents are expecting news from the doctor and would rather the point was reached promptly. Prevarication should be avoided. The diagnosis should be given concisely. Use of medical terminology is important but only supported by clear explanations. It is easier for the parents if the news is given incrementally allowing time for questions along the way. One question may then automatically lead to the next piece of news and allow an idea of how much information the parents can cope with at one sitting.

Follow-up

Some parents remember irrelevant incidental details of the consultation with clarity but need many sessions of follow-up discussion to reinforce their understanding of the diagnosis.

If possible they should be given literature or information to take away with them allowing them to assimilate and seek information at their own pace. Arrangements should be made for someone who has been present to answer further questions in the short term. A follow-up session should be arranged to which the parents should be encouraged to bring written questions.

2. Maintaining a relationship

Where children have a chronic illness or disability a long-term working relationship with parents becomes important. Like any relationship this will have ups and downs. Familiarity with a family usually makes a working relationship easier and more rewarding although can mean that we lose our professional objectivity. After a stressful episode parents may turn negative feelings towards professionals. Complaints about our practice are increasingly prevalent and often come from the least predictable quarters. Where there is an established relationship a complaint can feel very personal indeed and maintaining a working relationship can be challenging. It is important to acknowledge this and seek a supportive view from a colleague. A second opinion or informal discussion with a colleague may shed light on an intractable situation and allow a working relationship to resume with new confidence. Where confidence has been irreversibly lost, it is far better to acknowledge this and if possible transfer care to a colleague. The variety of human nature means that even the most accomplished communicator will occasionally fail to maintain a rapport with a family.

3. Maintaining a working relationship with parents and growing adolescents

As a child grows to independence through adolescence, the practitioner must balance their working relationship with the parents and the young person. The process of independence is gradual for most and extremely varied in its timing. I have known some perfectly sensible young adults with chronic illness continue to attend clinics accompanied by a parent until well into their twenties. As much as some parents can have difficulties letting their children grow to independence, it is not unusual for paediatricians to be reluctant to relinquish the care of their adolescents to adult physician colleagues.

For parents of children with chronic illnesses there is often a tendency to infantilise the child, encouraging dependency and making the transition to adulthood more problematic than usual. Equally, adolescents with acute medical problems may regress to a more childish state. In all situations it is important to maintain a respect both for the growing autonomy and independence of the young person and the parents' reasonable wish to be informed and involved. In most functional families, children and young people are encouraged to take part in incremental experiences of independence, practising more challenging tasks until they are prepared to fly solo. Thus the walk to the local shops progresses to a trip to town on the bus, which progresses to a weekend away with friends.

Unfortunately, in the past, many public services, including health, did not formally recognise the need for this progression. Transition care and planning is now valued and in health the need for tailored services to adolescents is recognised.

Adolescent services can develop expertise in easing this transition for the adolescent and parents by providing a structure within which to work and pacing the independence process.

As the relationship between the practitioner and the young person matures, parents may feel very anxious about being excluded from discussions. Use of tools such as medical records held by the young person can help. These can be used to record agreed decisions and objectives that the young person is happy to share with their parents. This allows some autonomy and confidentiality, but also enables parents to maintain some involvement, as the adolescent becomes fully responsible for their own treatment.

Conclusion

The paediatrician's first responsibility is towards the child whose rights and interests are always paramount. The parent may promote or undermine those best interests but while they retain responsibility we can only help the child in partnership with the parent. This complex triangular relationship demands patience and understanding. Like all challenges, successful management brings satisfaction. There can be no greater reward than working effectively to ensure that those children and their parents receive the best support possible.

References

Beckman, H.B. and Frankel, R.M. (1984). The Effect of Physician Behaviour on the Collection of Data. *Ann Intern Med*, 101: 692–696.

Buckman, R., (1992). *How to Break Bad News*. John Hopkins University Press.

Hampton, J.R., Harrison, M.J.G., Mitchell, J.R.A., Pritchard, J.S. and Seymour, C. (1975). *Relative Contribution of History Taking, Physical Examination and Laboratory Investigation to Diagnosis and Management of Medical Outpatients*, 2: 486–517.

Hickson, G.B., Clayton, E.W. and Entman, S.S. (1994). Obstetricians Prior Malpractice Experience and Satisfaction With Care. *JAMA*, 272: 1583–1587.

Hinchcliffe, D. (1998). Children Looked After By the Local Authorities Second Report, Vol. I and II. House of Commons Health Committee.

Kings Fund (1987). *Shared Concern: Breaking the News to Parents That Their Child has a Disability*.

Lloyd, M. and Bor, R. (1996). *Communication Skills for Medicine*. Churchill Livingstone.

Maddison, J.C. (1998). Psychological Issues. In Hill, C.M. (1998). *Practical Guidelines for Cystic Fibrosis*. London: Churchill Livingstone

McClure, R.J., Davis, P..M., Meadow, S.R. and Sibert, J.R. (1996). Epidemiology of Munchausen Syndrome by Proxy, Non-accidental Poisoning and Non-accidental Suffocation. *Arch Dis Child*, 75(1): 57–61.

Office for National Statistics (1999). *Social Trends* 29. London: The Stationery Office.

Tate, P. (1997). Different Types of Patients. In *The Doctor's Communication Handbook*. Medical Press.

14   Palliative Care

Pat Mood

Introduction

Parents have different needs from palliative care depending on their role: a child may be dying; a partner may be dying; or they themselves may be facing imminent death. The support they need as parents in helping children cope with the event is distinct from that which they need for themselves as individuals facing the same event. This chapter is about working with parents when they or another close adult is facing death or bereavement. Although much of what is said generally is applicable when a child is dying, there are additional issues which are not dealt with here.

The Setting

Death and loss are facts of life that we all have to face at some time, yet, with most deaths occurring in old age and in hospital, post-modern Britain has become insulated from a familiarity with death. It is argued that death is so far removed from everyday life that there is no longer a shared philosophy and ritual for coping (Walter, 1994). As a consequence, when someone young or in mid-life is discovered to have a terminal illness there can be a sense of outrage and disbelief. In fact, a significant minority (22 per cent in 1987) of those who die each year are under 65 (Seale, 1993). Half of all deaths in the UK are anticipated and it is this group of people who may be considered to need palliative care (N.C.H.S.P.C.S., 1995).

Palliative care begins with the knowledge that an illness is no longer curable. Its focus is on providing the relief of physical symptoms, and offering psychological, social and spiritual support and the best possible quality of life for the person who is ill, their family and carers. Care is patient and family centred, responding to changing needs wherever the patient is. Its knowledge base derives from people living with and dying from cancer, but the social and psychological needs remain similar whatever the diagnosis.

Being a parent involved in palliative care will imply having dual, if not multiple, responsibilities either as the person who is ill or as their parent, partner, carer or adult child.

Aims

The core aim of working with parents in palliative care is to use knowledge and skills to promote their confidence and competence.

Parents access palliative care for a range of reasons which may include seeking help in preparing and supporting their children. They may be intent on pain control or benefits advice and resent as intrusive any suggestions about their role as parents. Support and advice must be offered with tact, sensitivity and respect for individual autonomy. Becoming the 'expert', the only person who can deal with the situation, will de-skill parents and encourage dependency.

Support for parents can be achieved by a variety of methods: providing information, working with families to facilitate communication and adjustment to new situations, helping parents to access resources they need in order to cope effectively.

Priorities

Priority has to be given to those who are most vulnerable because of their situation. These will be parents, especially single parents, who are dying and those who for various reasons are overwhelmed by their caring responsibilities or grief and have depleted energy to give children the support they need.

Knowledge

When a parent is dying there are major implications for the person who is ill, the family unit and others close to the family. While the shock of diagnosis may be immediate, subsequent events may take place over a period of weeks, months or years, throwing the family into an ongoing crisis of adaptation to each new change and threat. Problems will have practical, psychological, spiritual, and emotional dimensions.

Individual Perspective

The parent who is terminally ill is immediately confronted by the loss of themselves and all they love. Shock, disbelief, anger and fear are common emotions as the world appears to be suddenly out of control. There may be questions that dare not be asked, such as, 'How long?' or 'How will the family manage without me?'. Individual reactions can vary from optimism and determination to fight, denial and resistance to talking, through to helplessness and wanting to give up. Partners experience as much emotional distress as do those who are ill. After the death they often recall the time of diagnosis as being the beginning of their bereavement. Shock, fear, depression and pre-occupation with thoughts of dying are common, but frequently concealed, reactions. (Gotay 1984, Hays *et al*. 1994, Sales 1991.)

After the initial shock, a period of adjustment or 'living with the illness'

(Buckman, 1993) may afford some opportunity for getting on with life, if only in a limited way. There may be unexpected gains of greater intimacy and stronger marital bonds as people learn to value precious time together and to share a courage and humour of which they had not previously been aware. (Parkes, 1993, Sales, 1991, Weisman and Worden, 1986.)

It can also be a time of worrying uncertainty and for 'the little deaths' that precede death itself. Loss of job, income, a sense of future, good looks, health and vigour, sexuality, and control over one's body often give rise to emotional distress, a lack of self worth and practical and relationship difficulties. Adjusting to the role of 'sick person' and 'carer' may create further tensions. Thoughts of their partner dying, facts about the seriousness of the condition and feelings of sadness and fatigue are frequently concealed from the person who is ill, often at great cost to all the family, including the children.

As going out and entertaining at home becomes difficult, social contacts shrink. During the final period of life many experience help from extended family to be less than they would wish (Seale, 1994).

Family Perspective

The disruption of everyday life and removal of the future they had expected to share will have immediate and long-term consequences for the family.

The precise impact will depend on a number of factors (Herz, 1980).

The Timing of the Illness in the Family Life-cycle

Parents face all sorts of developmental challenges such as a new baby, adolescence, older children preparing to leave, and dependent elderly parents. These impose additional demands that leave them with fewer reserves to respond to another crisis.

Bill and Janet's daughter was due to give birth to their first grandchild and their son was about to join the army when Janet's cancer was found to have spread to her brain. The energy that they were preparing to invest in the new baby and launching their son was used up elsewhere.

The Nature of the Illness

By its nature terminal disease will be distressing but some illnesses are especially traumatic, for example a brief illness occupying only a few weeks of rapid decline with too little time to absorb what is happening, or symptoms and treatment which appear horrific.

Helen was five years old when her father had a brain tumour. During six weeks of treatment in hospital she had not been able to visit him. When he returned home she did not recognise him. He was bald, huge from steroid treatment and in a wheelchair. She remained fearful of being with him on her own.

The Family Position of a Dying Person

The death of anyone in the family is devastating, but the loss of each role will bring its own problems.

John's terminal illness at 36 meant the loss of the major income, and further financial hardship when his wife gave up her job to care for him. Insurance premiums could not be paid and the family eventually lost their home. His children lost their 'fun-maker' and, more importantly, a loved parent. His parents lost the gifted son who must not die.

The impact of the illness and death of a grandparent should not be underestimated. Their role as child-minder, confidant and someone who is 'always there when things go wrong' can be central to a family's coping. The terminal illness of a child is likely to be the greatest outrage, both untimely and robbing parents of their stake in the future.

The Openness of the Family System

A pattern of open communication and flexibility gives a greater potential for coping with the demands of a terminal illness. Rigidity of roles and communication patterns will restrict the ability to adapt.

Mike and his wife, Sue, had a close and relaxed relationship with both sets of parents. When he suddenly became ill and was diagnosed with cancer the news was shared with them. Mike's wish to remain at home was achieved by the parents organising themselves to help with his care yet still leaving Sue, Mike and their children time to be on their own.

Communication in even the most cohesive family is likely to be threatened in the process of one of its members dying. 'Frightened people distance themselves from one another and may find themselves isolated just when they most need support and intimacy' (Monroe, 1993, p 192). People sense the situation to be overwhelming and may vacillate between feeling frustrated that they do not fully understand and fearful of being told something worse. Unfamiliar hospital routines, jargon and treatment regimes can add to the problem. As doctors and nurses tend to communicate with individuals rather than families, information is not uniformly dispersed (Krant and Johnson, 1978). The result may be that individual parents become isolated from each other in their fear and their desire to protect each other.

This is particularly evident in communication with children about illness. If the prospect of a close family member dying is difficult to accept for oneself, it becomes doubly difficult to think of a child losing a loved and needed parent or grandparent. A young father struggling to keep his own distress at bay so as to care for his ill wife, to keep his business going and to get the children off to school will find it easier to argue that they seem OK, have asked no questions and are better not knowing their mother will die until they have to.

Children are keen observers. They learn that something serious is happening from changes in family routine, tense and worried looks, overheard conversations at home and school and from the appearance of the parent who is ill. They frequently respond by maintaining the silence and worrying on their own.

> Becky's mother had been ill with breast cancer for over two years when her condition deteriorated rapidly. Becky had to be warned that she would probably die that day. In the ensuing conversation she said she had been told only that mummy was ill. She often worried and wanted to ask her parents more, but she 'looked at their faces and decided not to'.

Parents may be unaware that, far from protecting their children, the children are protecting them. This is vividly illustrated in a study of children with leukaemia in a US hospital (Bluebond-Langner, 1978). Although they knew they were dying they behaved as if they had a future to protect the adults around them and to maintain social order. Parents may underestimate both their children's capacity for understanding and the impact the illness has on their feelings, thoughts and relationships (Breyer *et al.*, 1993). To be effective supporters of parents in palliative care it is important to know what children understand and how they feel.

Children's Developmental Understanding of Death

Learning about death develops through childhood. Some research indicates children as young as two or three are able to understand death as a permanent and altered state, while other opinions are that this level of understanding is not generally present under five (Furman, cited in Raphael, 1984, Grollman, 1990, Dyregov, 1991).

Over half of five-year-olds and almost all children of eight and over understand that death is a permanent state, has a cause and happens to everyone. (Lansdown and Benjamin, 1985.) The degree of understanding depends on age, experience, and how that experience has been used. Exposure to death

through the media and in the world around presents opportunities to learn, but the role of parents in using such opportunities is crucial. Unfortunately, opportunities for learning may occur when parents are least able to make use of them because of their own distress (Irizzary, 1992).

Acquiring a concept of heaven can be difficult, especially when parents offer apparently contradictory explanations ('Granddad is in the sky/in the ground'). The mother of daughters aged six and nine could not bear to tell them that their daddy's body had been cremated, so vaguely implied that he had been left at the church. They began to have nightmares, which were found to be related to their fears about him returning to the house at night for something to eat. Children under ten think in concrete terms. They frequently have gruesome thoughts of ghosts and bodies being eaten by worms.

Children up to the age of ten can also be disturbed by 'magical thinking' about death (Sheldon, 1997).

> Ben's parents explained gently and fully that his mother was dying. He coped well initially after her death but his father became worried when Ben began refusing to attend school. The problem was that he got headaches when he had to read aloud. Ben's mother had died when her breast cancer spread to her brain. He was asked whether he thought he too would die. He produced a photograph of the family in a holiday competition, his mother and sister holding a card showing the number 32 which was her age when she died. Ben and his father's number was 12. Ben felt sure this meant that he would die when he was 12, and that the headaches were the first sign of it happening.

Increased intellectual understanding and the experience of the death of someone close brings an awareness that the world is not a safe place, and that they and others will die.

By adolescence there is an ability to think about death in more abstract and complex terms. The developmental tasks of this stage can make the experience of the death of someone close particularly difficult (Gray, 1989).

It is therefore important that parents learn about children's understanding, and that they are given advice, support and help in breaking bad news to them.

How Children Grieve

An understanding of how children grieve will help parents to give appropriate support to their children.

From infancy children react to separation from an attachment figure with protest and distress (Bowlby, 1969,1973, 1981) and there is ample evidence from research and practice experience that their feelings in grief are powerful (Worden, 1996, Silverman and Nickman, 1996, Pennells and Smith, 1995). There are some indications that without appropriate support in their grief they may develop serious problems in later life (Brown and Harris, 1978, Black, 1978). This has been questioned as being based on studies of pathology rather than of coping and adaptation. A study of parentally bereaved children in the general population found 19 per cent 'highly distressed' as scored on behaviour and anxiety after the first year, and that the surviving parents' coping was influential (Silverman and Worden, 1993).

Children have similar feelings to those of grieving adults but they usually experience them in different ways and over a longer period of time. Shooter (1998), describes the process of emotions as 'more like a washing machine' with anger, guilt, confusion, happiness and despair occurring in a haphazard way. Children are more likely to act out their feelings in aggressive or clinging behaviour. Like adults they may have difficulties with concentration, sleeping and eating but they have less control over their environment and are more vulnerable to others' lack of understanding of their situation. David, a normally quiet teenager, struggled to cope with the death of his father but when his 19 year-old brother died accidentally eight months later he behaved uncharacteristically at school, giggling and distracting those around him. The school's response was to send letters to his mother threatening exclusion.

When someone in the close family dies the remaining adults will themselves be grieving. Many bereaved children feel the pressure to act in a certain way so as not to create problems for their surviving parents (Silverman and Worden, 1993). Even when they are not urged to be more grown up, children often assume the role of parental protector and try to hide their feelings. Adam was described by his mother as being 'eleven going on forty-two' soon after the death of his father.

There are many secondary losses for children after a death, especially that of a parent. The surviving parent may appear unavailable because of their own grief, there may be a reduced income, with less money for holidays, treats and even necessities; the safe daily routine is lost.

Children are continuing to develop cognitively and emotionally and their loss will need to be 'revisited' as they reflect on what their relationship with the deceased would have been over a period of time. This may happen particularly at times of change and development when a deceased parent or grandparent would have had an important part to play.

A major contribution to the study of bereavement has been made by Klass *et al.* (1996). Their findings challenge the long held assumption that grief has an ending, or resolution, after which the bereaved move on leaving the dead in the past. Across a range of studies, including those in other cultures and times, the deceased are found to still have an important role in the ongoing lives of the survivors. Studies of parentally bereaved children confirm the significance for them of maintaining an ongoing relationship with their deceased parent. This takes the form of locating them (in heaven), experiencing them (through feeling watched over), reaching out to the deceased (visiting the grave, talking to a picture), thinking of and remembering the deceased as a conscious process, and keeping special mementoes (Silverman and Nickman, 1996). Parents under pressure to 'move on' may need reassurance that their coping and that of their children is normal.

Practical and Legal Knowledge

Having access to information about the benefit system, legal matters, practical help and services is vital in providing an adequate source of support for parents in palliative care. Financial hardship adds greatly to the burden of dying and bereavement. Some parents do not know about the financial benefits and practical services that would improve their quality of life MORI, (1992); Kelly, (1993). Practical help from organisations such as Crossroads, Marie Curie nurses and social services can supplement care given by the family, enabling them to continue as normally as possible while helping the person who is ill to feel less of a burden. Assistance from Cancer Relief Macmillan Fund and other charitable sources can give much needed help with heating and lighting costs, paying for a washing machine or a last holiday together.

Dying parents, particularly if they are single parents, will want to make the best provision for their children. Help and advice in making a will, arranging for a house tenancy to be transferred, information about making care and residence arrangements may be needed. Some parents, concerned that medical treatment may be prolonged unnecessarily and may create more distress for children, may wish to make a living will.

What Skills are Required?

Flexibility in working with individuals, couples, families and groups is needed. While the family as a whole is the focus of care there will often be differing degrees of awareness and a perceived need to protect others from the depth of some feelings. Skills in working with families to encourage

openness with individuals and sub-groups of the family are important.

Experiences in palliative care tend to isolate people. Skills in group work with patients, carers and those in bereavement can put parents in touch with a potentially helpful source of information, mutual support and reassurance.

At the point when someone is referred for palliative care there may be months, weeks or only hours in which to work. Being able both to plan long-term and work effectively in a crisis are necessary skills.

Breaking news of an impending death is one of the most difficult tasks a parent has to face. Skills may be needed to assist them in planning, choosing words and images that are simple, and avoiding confusing euphemisms. Although bad news is best given by a parent or someone with whom a child feels safe, there may be times when this is not possible. The worker will need skills in maintaining safety and giving information which is clear, sensitive, age-appropriate and in a manner that allows further questions.

Sensitivity to and respect for religious beliefs and cultural identities are required skills in this and every aspect of working with parents in palliative care.

Working with other disciplines involved in the overall care of the person who is ill is an important skill. Doctors, nurses, social workers, aromatherapist, day care teams, home care staff, chaplain and volunteers are all potentially involved in the care of one person.

Developing professional trust, good lines of communication and working jointly with other team members and external agencies maximise the skills offered to parents and support for the worker (Firth and Anderson, 1994).

Being flexible in other ways such as offering the service indirectly, through other professionals and other means (leaflets, book-loan) will help parents who for various reasons find these more acceptable.

Communicating through drawing and play may be more effective than words alone when working with children.

What is Important?

Intervention should be offered with the aim of promoting parents' competence and confidence in their role. In the strange and frightening situation when they or someone close is dying they may feel emotionally and physically exhausted and uncertain of the family's ability to survive. Their confidence will be further diminished by gloomy accounts of how things might go wrong and indications that only expert intervention will suffice. A more helpful approach is to offer a partnership, acknowledging the importance of their role and unique understanding of their children and supplementing it with what has been learned from experience gained from working with children in this situation.

> Angela had recently told seven-year-old Tim that his daddy was dying. Information from the worker helped Angela identify Tim's odd behaviour in removing chocolate biscuits from the supermarket trolley and returning them to the shelf as a concern that the family was about to lose its income. Tim had been told that daddy's work paid for the house and food. With the worker's help, Angela explained to Tim how they would be able to manage in the future.

Establishing trust and safety is an important foundation to any work with parents. This means agreeing, in advance of any direct work with children, what can safely be talked about and what cannot. Talking about what is happening now, rather than what will happen in the future, is a useful way of demonstrating that it is both safe and helpful to talk about a serious illness and how it is affecting everyone. Two useful publications for this purpose are *My Book About* (St Christopher's Hospice, 1989) for young children and *When Someone Has A Very Serious Illness* (Heegard, 1991). Both encourage children to write and draw, helping to show what they already know.

It is always important to recognise the family's need to maintain an appropriate degree of hope.

Helping Parents to Focus on Children's Needs and Perspectives

Before the death

The timing of news is important. Learning that someone will die may cause a child to expect the event at any time. Prolonged fear and distress can be avoided by information about how soon it will happen and reassurance that they will be warned when the time is near.

Knowing how children may react will prepare parents for a range of responses including weeping, protesting, going off to play and frank curiosity.

Reminders about the importance of routine will enable parents to create safe structures for their children. Consistency and reliability in who is there at bedtimes, ensuring regular mealtimes and continued attendance at school can be comforting to children and reassuring that their world is not falling apart. Encouraging parents to inform the school can provide for ongoing support.

Reassurance about the normality of feelings of irritability, anger, sadness and the need to let off steam and to have fun will help parents allow for these in themselves and their children.

Support in finding ways of expressing thoughts, feelings and memories of shared history can help the person who is dying to create a continuing link that will help children after the death. These can take the form of journals, videos, tapes, letters or memory boxes of photographs and other mementoes. Useful as these are, the work involved may be too painful and parents should not feel pressured to complete this work.

Around the time of death

Warning that death is close means deciding whether children should be present. Ideally, children should decide this for themselves. Parents will need reassurance that, far from being a damaging experience, it can help children to be involved and to face reality instead of some horror of their imagining (Dyregov, 1996). Information about what the dying person looks like and a warning about any equipment that may be in the room will be helpful.

Immediately after death

All that was said about the time of death still applies. Parents need continuing reassurance that reactions may vary widely from one child to another in terms of their wish to be present, their outward expression of grief etc. In a family where a loved grandmother died all five grandchildren (aged 18 months to 13 years) stayed at the hospice all day. A twelve year old too upset to go into the room chose to sit with an aunt while her seven year old sister popped in to see her grandmother many times before and after she died.

The funeral

The importance for children of attending the funeral is widely acknowledged by professionals (Worden, 1996; Dyregov, 1996). It may need to be explained sensitively and with respect for their views, to parents who are distressed and wish to protect children from painful experiences. Other important ways of making the ritual of the funeral a meaningful one for children include being involved in the planning, and putting a photograph, toy or message in the coffin.

In bereavement

In the turbulence of their own feelings of loss and grief parents will have limited resources for supporting their children. It is too easily assumed that children provide a motive for perseverance in bereavement without considering the emotional cost of this responsibility. Parents may need support in their own grieving in addition to help in understanding their children's distress. They

will also need reassurance that they are 'good enough' and that they will survive.

To remain effective in palliative care a worker needs sound professional supervision, good team leadership and staff support. In some settings their existence may be no more than a pious hope and the worker may have to find the means of making up for the deficiency. It will be time well spent.

What Have You Done and Why?

Information and support to parents may be offered through other professionals who have initial contact with parents such as doctors and nurses.

Leaflets are also available for parents describing how children are affected when someone is very ill and in bereavement, suggesting what they can do to help and offering support.

The worker can offer help in breaking bad news, advice about the affect on children of visiting someone who is dying, advice in practical and legal issues, and ongoing support in coping with the conflicts and challenges of terminal illness. Some people often initially find the written word helpful. A range of provisions for differing circumstances, such as individual counselling for bereaved adults, and choice, including opting for not having any, may be offered. Many parents will need support in their own grieving and in managing their task as parents.

Small group work can be a valuable source of mutual understanding and support. For some parents, 'the only place where I can say exactly what I feel and know that I will be understood', as a bereaved husband and father of teenage boys and a three year old girl said. Groups can promote problem solving. Members compare notes and access a wealth of information that is more acceptable because it is offered by someone in a similar situation. A father of girls aged seven and eight was worried that they might not remember the wonderful person their mother had been. The warm and positive response from someone whose mother had died when she was seven provided all the reassurance he needed. Information from a counsellor would have been sterile in comparison. The group helps members rehearse social skills and develop confidence.

There is also individual, family and group work for bereaved children. Parents may access any of these for their children if they feel it might help. Terms of confidentiality are agreed in advance of any work on the basis of it being helpful for children to talk to someone outside their situation. Like those for adults, groups for children are an effective means of discovering that the feelings they have are normal and shared by others and that they are not alone. The style should be informal and flexible with a range of activities including: art work – discussion – letting off steam and drama – sharing memories of the parent who has died – learning about feelings – discussing changes with which they have to adjust, such as insensitive or deliberately spiteful remarks made by others, concerns for their surviving parents, coping with nightmares, having less money, and identifying strengths for the future. Parents are invited to the final session where children and leaders demonstrate what the group has been doing.

Case study (1) Breaking Bad News

Adam (11) and Kerry (8). Their father had a brain tumour and was dying at home. A referral to the hospice was made four days before he died. He was too ill to communicate. His wife, Jane, aware that his death was imminent, asked for help in breaking the news to the children.

The first task was to find out what the children already knew and to involve Jane as much as possible. They had been told that dad was ill but little more. His deterioration had been rapid over the last month. Jane felt too upset to tell them herself but she helped in

planning how they were to be told and wanted to be present to support them. She chose her in-laws' home as a safe environment.

Jane and 'gran' sat with the children on their knees while the social worker broke the news the following morning. After their immediate distress Adam and Kerry asked whether there was any possibility that the doctors might be wrong. They were told that although everyone hoped he would not die and had tried to make him well it now seemed certain that he would die in the next few days. With the support from the social worker, Jane was able to take part in answering the children's questions and in planning what they wanted to do next ('to return home to see dad'). The social worker left whilst the family were comforting each other, their father died three days later.

Through this work Jane maintained her central parenting role with the children. The children said they were glad they had warning of dad's death. It gave them time to prepare and to give him extra hugs. Jane used support in bereavement to reassure herself about the normality of her own and the children's reactions. Adam and Kerry grieved in different ways which initially surprised her, but she had been told that this might be the case.

Case study (2) Long Term Support for Dying Parent

Meg was a mother of four children aged between twelve and eighteen. Her marriage had ended six years earlier and she devoted most of her energy to providing a stable and happy home for them. When she was diagnosed with terminal cancer she was devastated, feeling that not only her life but all she held dear was threatened. In assessing her needs it became clear that there would be four priorities for the work: helping her fight her illness, minimising the practical difficulties, reflecting on the family's needs, and support in dealing with previous losses in her life which now resurfaced.

Support in fighting her illness comprised, at her request, weekly sessions for counselling and relaxation, when she would visualise the cancer being eliminated by her immune system. She also needed to talk about symptoms, treatment and ways of dealing with her fear.

The practical difficulties were mostly income-related, as she had been forced to give up work. Benefit advice was backed by referral to a specialist advice worker and charitable help sought to meet bills and to provide a family holiday. As time went on help in meal preparation, laundry and shopping was needed and referrals were made to Crossroads and social services. It was important to Meg that family life continued as normally as possible through her illness. Through discussion she recognised the children's need for information and acted accordingly. Meg introduced the children to the worker and there were some subsequent meetings with them and other family members, including her ex-husband. On the whole she preferred to use the worker's support for reflecting on issues relating to the children and then to deal with them herself. Topics for discussion were their coping with her illness, her encouragement for them in getting on with their lives, as in going to university, having boyfriends and planning for when she died. Work with Meg continued for two years until her death and with some of her family afterwards. It involved close liaison with other members of the team and contact with social services, Crossroads, the district nurse, her GP, priest, friends, school and university to ensure the provision of support which she needed for herself and her family.

Case study (3) Ongoing Bereavement Work

David's death at the age of 43 after an illness lasting just three months left his wife, Sally, and their only daughter, Claire shocked and alone. Sally had attempted to prepare Claire for the event but Claire, who was fifteen, refused to discuss it. Sally become increasingly concerned for Claire as she was avoiding spending time with her mother, choosing instead to go to the homes of school friends in the evenings.

Work with Sally focused on the many strands of her grieving: her deep sense of loss, her fear for the present and hopelessness for the future, the changes in her social network which seemed to reinforce her isolation, her concern for her daughter's well-being and her loss of confidence as a parent. Sally had regular individual counselling, the content of each session being led by what was uppermost for her. Its aim has been to maintain her coping and strengthen her confidence.

Initially, she occasionally telephoned between sessions to talk about a recent episode of Claire's behaviour, replaying an argument or rehearsing a course of action. She has also taken part in a hospice-based group for bereaved partners. Through the group she has been able to meet other parents and learn that they all have similar experiences. In particular she has been reassured to discover that an open sharing of feelings between parents and children of whatever age in bereavement is more the exception than the rule.

With increased confidence, Sally has become more assertive about doing what she wants to do with her life. Claire, seeing her mother as more robust, is becoming better able and willing to relive memories of her dad in conversation. There are still bad times for Sally but surviving each one increases her coping and reassures her that she will come through.

Conclusion

In the relatively short history of modern palliative care, knowledge and skills have been acquired by careful listening to those parents, and other members of families, who are experiencing illness, death and bereavement. Research and practice experience have validated these observations, enabling the development of services which are both responsive to identified need and soundly based. Hospices and specialist palliative care units do not claim sole rights over their knowledge and skills. Only a minority need or will receive their care directly. Many more will benefit if those who meet them in other contexts have an understanding of what has been learned by palliative care professionals. It is vitally important that professionals in the field are encouraged to practise in the community at large, the understanding gained by the specialist few.

References

Black, D. (1978). The Bereaved Child. In *Journal of Psychological Psychiatry*, 19: pp 287–292.

Bluebond-Langner, M. (1978). *The Private Worlds of Dying Children.* Princeton University Press.

Bowlby, J. (1969). *Attachment and Loss. Vol. 1. Attachment.* Hogarth.

Bowlby, J. (1973). *Attachment and Loss. Vol. 2. Separation: Anxiety and Anger.* Hogarth.

Bowlby, J. (1981). *Attachment and Loss. Vol. 3. Sadness and Depression.* Hogarth.

Breyer, J., Kunin, H., Kalish, L.A., and Patenaude, A.F. (1993). The Adjustment of Siblings of Paediatric Cancer Patients: A Sibling and Parent Perspective. In *Psycho-oncology*, 2: pp 201–208.

Brown, G., and Harris, T. (1978). *Social Origins of Depression: A Study of Psychiatric Disorder in Women.* Tavistock.

Buckman, R. (1993). Communication in Palliative Care: A Practical Guide. In Doyle, D., Hanks, G., and Macdonald, N. (Eds.). *Oxford Textbook of Palliative Medicine.* Oxford University Press.

Dyregov, A. (1991). *Grief in Children: A Handbook for Adults.* Jessica Kingsley.

Dyregov, A. (1996). Children's Participation in Rituals. In *Bereavement Care*, 15: pp 2–5.

Firth, P., and Anderson, P. (1994). Teamwork With Families Facing Bereavement. In *European Journal of Palliative Care*, 1: pp 157–161.

Gotay, C. (1984). The Experience of Cancer During Early and Advanced Stages: The View of Patients and Their Mates. In *Social Science and Medicine*, 18: pp 605–613.

Gray, R. (1989). Adolescents Experiencing the Death of a Parent. In *Bereavement Care*, 8: pp 17–19.

Grollman, E.A. (1990). *Talking About Death.* Beacon Press.

Hays, J., Kasl, S.V., and Jacobs, S. (1994). The Course of Psychological Distress Following Threatened and Actual Conjugal Bereavement. In *Psychological Medicine*, 24: pp 917–927.

Heegard, M. (1991). *When Someone Has a Very Serious Illness.* Woodland.

Department of Social Work, St Christopher's Hospice (1989). *My Book About.* St Christopher's Hospice.

Herz, F. (1980). The Impact of Death and Serious Illness on the Family Life-cycle. In Carter, E.A., and McGoldrick, M. (Eds.). *The Family Life-cycle: A Framework for Family Therapy.* Gardener Press.

Irizarry, C. (1992). Spirituality and the Child: A Grandparent's Death. In *Australian Journal of Psychosocial Oncology*, 10: pp 39–58.

Kelly, M.H. (1993). The Needs of Carers of the Terminally Ill. In *Palliative Care Today*.

Klass, D., Silverman, P.R., and Nickman, S.L. (1996). *Continuing Bonds: New Understandings of Grief.* Taylor and Francis.

Krant, M., and Johnson, L. (1978). Family Perceptions of Family Functioning in Late Stage Cancer. In *International Journal of Psychiatry*, 8: pp 203–216.

Lansdown, R., and Benjamin, G. (1985). The Development of the Concept of Death in Children aged 5 to 9. In *Child Health Development*, 11: pp 13–20.

Monroe, B. (1993). Psychosocial Dimension of Palliation. In Saunders, C., and Sykes, N. (Eds.). *The Management of Terminal Malignant Disease.* Edward Arnold.

MORI (1992). Survey on the Social Impact of Cancer. Cancer Relief Macmillan Fund.

National Council for Hospice and Specialist Palliative Care Services (1995). *Specialist Palliative Care: A Statement of Definitions*, Occasional Paper No.8.

Parkes, C.M. (1993). Bereavement as a Psychosocial Transition: Processes of Adaptation to Change. In *Handbook of Bereavement: Theory, Research and Intervention.* Stroebe.

Pennells, M., and Smith, S.C. (Eds.) (1995). *The Forgotten Mourners: Guidelines for Working With Bereaved Children.* Jessica Kingsley.

Raphael, B. (1984). *The Anatomy of Bereavement.* Routledge.

Sales, E. (1991). Psychosocial Impact of the Phase of Cancer on the Family: An Updated Review. In *Journal of Psychosocial Oncology*, 9: pp 1–18.

Seale, C. (1993). Demographic Change and, the Care of the Dying (1969–1987). In Dickenson, D., and Johnson, M. (Eds.). *Death, Dying and Bereavement.* Sage.

Seale, C. (1994). Caring for People Who Die: The Experience of Family and Friends. In Seale, C. and Cartwright, A. (Eds.). *The Year Before Death.* Avebury.

Sheldon, F. (1997). *Psychosocial Palliative Care: Good Practice in the Care of the Dying and Bereaved.* Stanley Thornes.

Shooter, M. (1998). *Children and Bereavement.* National Association of Bereavement Services Conference, Bristol.

Silverman, P.R., and Nickman, S.L. (1996). Children's Construction of Their Dead Parents. In Klass, D., Silverman, P.R. and Nickman, S.L. (Eds.). *Continuing Bonds: New Understandings of Grief.* Taylor and Francis.

Silverman, P., and Worden, J.W. (1993). Children's Reactions to the Death of a Parent. In Stroebe, M.S., Stroebe, W., and Hansson, R.O. (Eds.). *Handbook of Bereavement: Theory, Research and Intervention.* University of Cambridge Press.

Walter, T. (1994). *The Revival of Death.* Routledge.

Weisman, A.D., and Worden, J.W. (1986). The Emotional Impact of Recurrent Cancer. In *Journal of Psychosocial Oncology,* 3: pp 5–16.

Worden, J.W. (1996). *Children and Grief: When a Parent Dies.* Guildford Press.

15   Working with Parents in Child Mental Health

Rosie Nichol Harper and Lisa Lewer

Why Do We Need Child Mental Health Services?

Unless as a society we can overcome our discomfort with the very notion that we are all mental beings and that our mental health and that of our children is a fragile and precious commodity…the evidence clearly shows that the consequences for all our futures will be very worrying indeed.

(Mental Health Foundation, 1999)

This report quotes UK figures of one in five children currently having some form of mental health problem, and about one in ten children needing professional help. An HMSO report put this figure higher for teenagers

At any point between 10–20 per cent of teenagers have worries or problems severe enough to need help in overcoming them.

(Department of Health, 1995)

This information helps us to realise the scale of the problems, with 'mental health' being notoriously difficult to define. A useful starting point is:

Mental health is not the mere absence of mental illness. It is about having psychological resources, a sufficient sense of self-worth, self-esteem and self-confidence to make the right choices, to cope with adversity, to make the best of one's potential. The acquisition of such resources depends on the physical integrity of the brain and the quality of early formative experiences.

(Cooklin, 1999)

Mental health problems in children do not present themselves in tidy packages. Once developmentally appropriate functioning, and relationships with family or friends are affected then a type of mental health problem may have developed.

Meeting the mental health needs of children, young people and their families focuses on behavioural and emotional disturbances but also encompasses physical symptoms, developmental delay, environmental and social factors and family interactions. As one child psychiatrist says,

Widespread ignorance of the nature of child psychiatry is not simply due to lack of information. It is evidence also of a wish to make invisible the mental pain of young people and their parents.

(Kraemer, 1999)

Who is Involved?

The most important point to make is that any child from any family may develop difficulties, and there are no social or class boundaries to abnormal grief reactions, to severe epilepsy, or bedwetting. There are parental cultural differences between perceptions of what causes a persistent tummy-ache leading to a child missing school, but there may also be bullying or harassment of that child, who alone in a class, family or community, develops 'symptoms'. It is as interesting to reflect on why some children seem to have protective factors preventing mental health difficulties, like resilience, as to speculate why the particular combination of personality, temperament, biological and genetic make up, gender position in the family and community, and social environment leads to the development of a mental health problem. Similarly, children of all ages are vulnerable to mental health problems, although some of the disorders present in the adult population, such as schizophrenia, only develop in adolescence, or, rarely, in late childhood.

Secondly, the vast majority of mental health preventative work is done by non-specialised people seeing children on a daily basis. Parents, friends, siblings, grandparents, neighbours all play a part in passing on advice, acknowledging feelings and noticing changes. Teachers, playgroup leaders, health visitors, school nurses and GPs also bring their own life skills as well as a professional perspective when asked for advice or an opinion.

Therefore, by the time a referral to a child mental health service is made, there has already been a great deal of effort put in to try to understand and help a family. Finding out what has already been tried, can be a key to finding 'the family's unique way of co-operating' (de Shazer 1984).

Thirdly, each child mental health team is unique. The widely differing provisions across the UK has developed as much in response to different professional groups abilities to obtain funding to extend the particular areas or styles of working, as to local needs.

As a minimum, health trusts employ one or more consultant child and adolescent psychiatrists who will have undergone general adult psychiatric training, before specialising in work with children and young people. There will usually be other, less experienced doctors, training in this specialisation and any combination of the other professionals in this field. These include:

- child psychologists
- child psycho-therapists
- art therapists
- music therapists
- occupational therapists
- nurses with backgrounds in mental health or children's nursing
- family therapists
- social workers
- drama therapists
- play therapists
- teachers in in-patient units
- and others with less formalised titles

Each team member brings their own theoretical views, practice methods and additional training to provide a vast combination of different skills and methods.

This diversity and richness may, however, appear confusing to other professionals, let alone parents who can often remain bewildered by the titles and work methods. It is hoped that as teams diversify and expand to meet current unmet need, that some priority will be given to a wider educative role, ensuring effective liaison with primary health, education, social service staff and particularly with parents. If in doubt about what a particular member of the team does, parents should ask, ask and ask again!

Where Does Involvement Take Place?

Each team operates on a different basis depending on historical location, and differing theoretical views. Most teams operate on an out-patient only basis, although some have access to some beds, or have a designated in-patient unit in a hospital. This may include parents staying in the unit. Some teams are based wholly in the community, using GP surgeries, schools and the family's homes as their primary meeting places. Many have the flexibility to include a variety of settings.

There are various reasons for the majority of teams being based in a 'clinic' – primarily, teams need to work and plan together. Many more families can be seen if the travelling is done by the families rather than the staff. In some instances, the commitment for a child or parent to change is tested by the commitment and courage needed to attend an initially unknown institution. In many instances, it is important to the children and their parents that they are coming somewhere different, where they can test out different ways of interacting, or have some private and confidential space without fear that they will bump into the workers, people they know or indeed other family members. However, if it is known that the family are not able to overcome their concerns about the building where the team is housed, an alternative venue should be offered.

When Should There Be Involvement?

Generally speaking, the right time for a referral and intervention is when it is right for the child or young person and their parents. It can often be very frustrating to watch a situation worsening before your eyes, but in most cases, unless the parents can recognise the need for change, change is unlikely to occur.

Most teams will welcome a query or expression of concern by another professional. They can offer consultation to that professional, whose own work may enable the desired change to occur, or for the parents to recognise that further help is needed. There will be instances where a crisis precipitates referral, for example a suicide attempt made by a teenager will result in a psychiatric assessment, which may then lead to ongoing involvement.

What's in a Name?

The idea of children having mental health problems is still relatively new. The first ever child guidance clinic opened in 1927 in Spitalfields, East London. The title is still one that most parents recognise today. This has a powerful impact on their expectations of the help they may receive. With the focus firmly on child guidance, there is a danger that parents believe their problem child can be fixed and returned to them without any input from themselves. Despite the decision of most clinics to change their title to 'child and family consultation service,' or 'child and family mental health', or 'child psychiatry', many influential professionals such as GPs, health visitors or teachers still talk about child guidance with its overtones of receiving pearls of wisdom and the use of a magic wand. It must be deeply disappointing to parents when these illusions are rapidly shattered.

Similarly, the use of the word 'clinic' with its feet firmly in the medical world, has huge implications for parents. Most people are familiar with attending a doctor's clinic or hospital out-patient clinic and expect to see a doctor and receive answers to questions on any such visit. Far fewer people are familiar with attending a psychiatric clinic, whatever the setting, and are usually much more anxious about what form that visit might take. If therefore they rely on films or television to inform them, they expect to meet a doctor who will see them on a couch and quiz them about their childhood in an obscure manner, before prescribing powerful drugs or lengthy individual therapy which may be more damaging than the original difficulty. Woody Allen has a lot to answer for! These cultural images or stereotypes are extremely powerful and in turn, form part of the many parents' view of mental illness which is predominantly one of ignorance and fear of 'madness'.

Clinics are for those who are ill, and suddenly 'mental health' is translated into 'mental illness'. Therefore, most parents have an intuitive, but inaccurate and often frightening view of what referral to such a service might mean for them and their family simply from the associations with its title. Acknowledging these ideas and concerns, both by an enlightened referrer, and during initial contact with the service, makes a big difference in establishing a successful partnership 'contract' with parents in order to help bring about changes.

A helpful analogy is that of dental health. Most people agree that regular preventative work by a dentist to maintain dental health is preferable to only attending once there is a major problem requiring potentially painful, difficult and expensive work. Most parents find ways of overcoming any concerns they or their children have about seeing a dentist and ensuring that it happens, even if their child is not willing to attend. Substituting the word 'mental' for 'dental' often helps parents link the unknown with a known situation about which they do feel confident, and demystifies the title.

There is also a crucial importance to the language associated with 'the problem'. If a child is referred to as 'the patient' this has implications of reinforcing the parent's view of where the focus of intervention should be. Conversely, if every referral is treated as if it is a 'family' problem, some families will feel criticised and decide not to appear or return, and there is a risk of failing to detect behavioural problems with a biological component. Similarly, parents can be thought of, and treated as if they are 'clients', which now has welfare-laden overtones or a 'customer' with rights and bargaining powers, or as 'partners' in a collaborative process of bringing about change by thinking and acting in different ways. Language, as always, defines or obscures meaning, and needs careful use from the outset of any intervention. Perhaps the most obvious example is whether the workers choose to discuss a child and their family's 'problems' instead of looking at 'solutions' the family already use.

How Change is Achieved

An entire library could be filled with books and journals about how to achieve change within a child mental health setting. As a specialisation which has always been rooted in multi-disciplinary practice, the contribution of different perspectives and viewpoints has been valued and expanded, and workers have generally become expert at incorporating ideas from each other to create a 'personal toolbox' of methods, theories and techniques.

Therefore we have not attempted to make this chapter a 'what to do' checklist, despite our own tendencies to look for them in textbooks. We have highlighted our own personal view as to important factors – 'food for thought' – and expanded a few of these ideas specific to working with parents.

Assessment

This normally takes the form of at least two workers meeting the child and parents, to take a detailed history of the 'problem', and how this is defined by the various family members, as well as a family and child's

history. It may be viewed as a luxury that two workers are involved in an assessment, but both for practical reasons – being able to talk to the parents and child separately – and to have two different viewpoints to formulate ideas and plans, it is preferable. In order to observe interactions and to think creatively about conflicts, two heads are definitely better than one. Additionally, the development of co-working skills can ultimately lead to more efficient and effective interventions.

Diagnosis

The single issue of making a diagnosis probably crystallises different professional viewpoints more than any other. The medical model of ill-health leading to diagnosis, treatment and discharge could be viewed as an over-simplification of the complexity of child mental health issues. However, the refinement of diagnostic distinctions over the past forty years have transformed child and adolescent psychiatric practice. In the fifties there was a single diagnosis of behaviour disorder of childhood, so most children received the same long-term treatment. In contrast the multiple diagnoses in use today give rise to a wide range of treatments. Unfortunately, this model, which many would argue is grossly inadequate to describe adult mental health difficulties, transfers even less easily to child mental health.

In some cases, having a diagnosis implies a problem is sufficiently serious to warrant extra resources, and parents and professionals alike will push for this as a means to an end. For example, the statementing procedure for the education of children with special needs, is often speeded up, or indeed, started if the child has been given a diagnosis and resources are then a legal obligation of the local education authority. Similarly, scarce resources such as child and adolescent in-patient beds can and should only be justified for young people with definable, treatable mental health disorders.

So, it is not surprising that often parents push for a diagnosis. It may be the key to accessing material resources, medication in a few cases, or information and knowledge. It may also be the vindication of years of believing 'something is wrong', and may shift their feelings and reactions to a child's behaviour. As one mother put it "I know I'd feel different towards him if I knew it was a case of 'can't' rather than 'won't." In this case, work focused on helping the mother recognise what she would do differently, if she knew this for certain and doing it anyway.

A diagnosis can often move a sense of blame, either from the child, or from the parents themselves. This may be healthy, but conversely, a desperate search for a diagnosis may be a denial of the parents' role in perpetuating the difficulties. Giving a title to aspects of behaviour can sometimes help a child and parent make sense of the behaviour and react in a different, perhaps more helpful way. However, many parents will also need help to understand that a diagnosis in itself does not solve the day-to-day behaviour and relationship problems, nor that professionals can hand them a 'what-to-do list'. The most important thing, is

to discover what the meaning is of a diagnosis for this child and the parents.

Focusing the Intervention – Where in the System?

Once an assessment of need has been made, the next most important step is to decide where the most effective intervention might be. The growth of systems and attachment theories since the 1950s have dramatically influenced the way in which children's mental health problems have been perceived and treated by professionals. However, prevalent lay perceptions of psychoanalysis in combination with psychodynamic theories are still the most prevalent influence, which, in combination with a cultural shift towards the American stereotype of 'everyone needs therapy', means that many families come hoping that their child can have a course of individual counselling. In some cases this might be highly appropriate, but a useful checklist might be:

Parents	– Does the stated problem have an echo in their own lives? – Are they requesting help to include themselves? – Do they need specialised help in their own rights? (e.g. marital counselling, or referral to adult mental health services.)	*Friends*	– Children's or parent's supporters and advisers are often overlooked. – Are there significant events in the child's friends' lives?
Siblings	– Can their ideas be used? – What are the reasons for their similar / differing reactions? – What is the impact on them of the focus being elsewhere?	*Professionals*	– Are there any involved already?
		Network	– Should more or less be mobilised? – Could consultation to other professionals be more effective than direct work?
Family sub-groups	– Which different combinations of members might be helpful?	*Groupwork*	– Is there a need for this type of intervention with other children / siblings / parent? – Do other agencies already provide groups?
School system	– If the difficulties are primarily in school, how could change occur?	*Supervision*	– Who will provide this for the identified workers?

In some cases, parents will need convincing that they should be part of the intervention. Conversations to help achieve this include:

- *You're with your child for longer periods than anyone else.*

- *The real therapy occurs at home, so it helps if we give you some guidelines.*

- *You're the expert on your child's needs.*

- *Other parents have told us that they've found…really helpful.*

- *Being a parent involves being great at adapting to situations that constantly change. It would be helpful to think about how you could build on those skills for this situation.*

Of course, engaging parents in the process of change may involve solely working with them, with the whole family, parent and child together, or working with parents alongside some individual time for the child. Often it needs to be made explicit that individual work cannot be helpful if it is either covertly or overtly sabotaged by parental non-involvement and that work to address ongoing family conflicts has to either happen before or alongside individual therapy.

Case Example

S is an 11 year old boy referred for problems at school. He lives with his mother and two younger sisters. Father lives elsewhere. Mother is known to have a long history of mental health difficulties – primarily obsessive compulsive disorder symptoms which fluctuate in severity. Various courses of treatment have been so far unable to effect change. At assessment, mother's main concern were the relationship difficulties between herself and S, but thought that S needed space to 'talk about his worries'. The school had confirmed this view.

The workers reflected back to mother that since approaching the GP for help there had been some improvement in the relationship between herself and S. They reinforced mother's strengths and courage in requesting help and being open about her own difficulties. However, they felt that before any major changes could occur, mother needed to address her own difficulties via the adult mental health sector. They would not offer individual time to S at this stage, but would continue to meet with mother and S together to address how they could continue to improve their relationship. S appeared considerably relieved that the 'problem' had been identified as mother's mental health.

There have been a number of volatile and powerful sessions, where feelings have been expressed by both mother and S which sometimes felt as if two teenagers were sparring. A turning point came when one worker expressed how uncomfortable she had felt during one particularly heated exchange, which provided a talking point for S and his mother in between sessions. Nearing the end of the work, mother has been able to acknowledge how important it was to both S and herself, that the focus was firmly and explicitly placed on the need to address both her psychological difficulties and interactions between herself and S in a non-blaming manner.

The workers have reflected that this piece of work could not have been achieved by a single worker alone, as there was an element of risk-taking, and because of the need to contain and then think about the powerful feelings evoked in each session. Equally, relatively quick access to the adult mental health service was critical which involved much inter-professional liaison and persuasion.

Collaboration and Consultation

Often the best use of specialist workers is by joint working with non-specialists, or by using their different perspectives to help think about the existing professional interactions with a family. This has the knock-on benefits of increasing a non-specialist's confidence in being able to translate existing skills into new areas, keeps specialists in touch with the reality of primary care, and helps the process of de-mystifying child mental health.

The collaboration need not be with a single family unit, for example, post natal depression groups jointly facilitated by a health visitor and child mental health worker can have an indirect but important effect on the mental health of a large number of infants and their parents. This is also an example of preventative work in practice.

Confidentiality and 'The Need to Know' – Stigmatisation Versus Liaison?

Children experiencing difficulties often cannot confine these to a single context. Therefore, a number of people outside the family may become involved either because a parent asks their advice, or because the child's behaviour affects others, who might then encourage a parent to seek help. Particularly as a full assessment prior to any intervention may require obtaining information from sources outside the family, it is often difficult to justify why there should not be a general 'tit for tat' information sharing.

The law regarding medical confidentiality, although relaxed in terms of a patient's rights to see their own records, remains firmly against disclosing any information without a patient's consent. In the case of young people under sixteen consent lies with their parents. Even when consent is given, it remains a professional judgement as to how much information should be shared on the 'need to know' principle. Of course, in situations where behaviour management techniques have been suggested, it would be counter-productive not to enlist the support of the child's school in reinforcing the principles. However, where the work is of a more individual nature, or indeed family therapy, it can become extremely difficult to justify giving details of individual sessions. Requests for such information are usually made with the best intentions of 'being

supportive', but disclosure may undermine the importance of a child or family using a therapeutic setting as a safe place to vent feelings or try out new ideas, and of course may undermine the family's respect and trust for the workers.

There seems to be the danger that if workers are seen to 'stall' such requests for information, that this perpetuates myths and stereotypical ideas of therapists being unapproachable. These reinforced ideas then may jeopardise future work, as other families who might benefit from the service receive distorted views, which in turn further stigmatises mental health work.

It is a particular challenge when resources are scant, to prioritise enough time and energy to tackle effective liaison. It has to happen in a way that does not breach a child's right to confidentiality, but helps parents and professionals alike to gain a greater understanding to empower them to help in the process of change. Parents and particularly children often find it helpful to rehearse what they will tell others about their meetings with mental health workers. At least raising the issue with them reminds them to think about the impact of that information on others.

There is the additional issue of a child's right to privacy and confidentiality which arises through a professional seeing a child individually or for group work. It often evokes incredibly powerful feelings of jealousy and concern in parents. Parents who run the risk of becoming intrusive with their child, if adequate preparation and ongoing time with parents to address these feelings is not given. It is generally considered better for this to be done by a different worker, so as to have clearer boundaries. It also provides greater objectivity, greater creativity of ideas and reduces the risk of unhelpful feelings towards the therapist being picked up by the child. Both child and parent need separate space to explore their feelings without needing to protect the other. In complicated situations, there may need to be separate times for consultation for all the significant adults in a child's life to ensure that the benefits of the work are not undermined by parental concerns of a practical or more emotional nature.

Parenting Work – Whose Needs are Paramount?

Despite common sense and experience telling them otherwise, many parents believe that there is a blueprint for perfect parents. Media and other cultural images obviously play a part but the proliferation of parenting courses, books, magazines and other 'how-to' guides imply to many that, if they only learned new techniques, they could get it right. While of course this is not the intention or message of parenting groups, most parents seeking help overlook the most obvious point – that everyone has been at the receiving end of being parented, and that this massively shapes our feelings and ideas about being a parent. Most adults coming into contact with small children for any period of time experience the surprise of singing the words of long forgotten lullabies or using angry words which might have sprung from the lips of their own parent.

There are some adults who are aware of the damage caused by having been ill-treated as a child, who are determined not to make the same mistakes, and can explore this openly. For others, however, any enquiry about their own childhood results in a much less definite, vague or bland response, or even anger at the question. For parents already self-blaming and anxious, enquiring about their experience of being parented may reinforce their view that they are the cause of the difficulties. However, even when a behavioural or solution-focused problem-solving approach is indicated, certain assumptions are made. These may be inaccurate unless the minimum information is obtained, and explanation given as to the necessity. There is likely to be little progress made when talking to parents about 'rewarding the behaviour you wish to

encourage' and 'praising the child' if they perceive that they never received either as children. A useful question is often 'How would this (difficulty) have been dealt with in the family where you were brought up?' This opens up the opportunity to discuss the parents' upbringing in a non-judgmental way and firmly establishes a valid reason for enquiring about the past. There is also a need to check on extended family history of any mental health problem, and the possibility of post natal depression. These will both impact on early attachment and the parent's perception of how they relate to their child.

Although many professionals can feel demoralised when faced with an example of family patterns being carried through generations, recent findings suggest:

> ...that it is not necessarily what happened in a parents own childhood, but what they made of that experience which influences whether or not they can provide a secure base for their own children. This has implications for therapy. It suggests that to help parents to achieve a coherent picture of their past may enable them to provide a better parenting experience for their own children.
>
> (Byng-Hall, 1997)

Using carefully constructed family trees or genograms (family tree diagrams with further information about the lives of individuals and the relationships between them) can often help parents to recognise family patterns, notice the importance of the position of each person within each group, and make sense of some of the complex and powerful expectations and values passed down through generations.

Equally useful tools are diagrams of current support networks (sometimes called ecomaps) which may, or may not, overlap with a genogram.

Both methods become most helpful when, rather than being a tool for professionals to understand a family, they become a way of really helping the child or parent(s) make sense of their own position – to achieve the coherent picture of their past, and present.

Case Examples

Ms R sought help when her six year old daughter's behaviour became so aggressive and defiant that she had considered requesting foster care. She was in close contact with a health visitor and an education outreach worker but behavioural strategies did not seem to be having much effect and she was becoming demoralised about her daughter's ability to change and her own ability to stay in charge. She attended a parenting group for 12 weeks, and became an active, committed and thoughtful member. As a result of this new confidence, Ms R started to report major improvements in her daughter's behaviour. This followed Ms R's decision to have access to her own medical files and to understand why she had been hospitalised as an eight year old child.

J, aged nine, had been referred for assessment of his attention deficit and hyperactive behaviour. His father, Mr S, was often observed to relate to J in an inconsistent and overly critical way. The staff group found him hostile and unco-operative and very pessimistic about the likelihood of change. During a meeting with Mr S to share information about J's new medication, Mr S stated "I'm fed up with being told I'm doing things wrong." It emerged that his own childhood was spent with harsh, uncaring parents from whom he had desperately tried to elicit praise. Acknowledging the pain of his own experiences enabled him to recognise that he needed to practice praising J and to accept the intensive work needed as part of this process.

In both these examples the main focus of intervention shifted to working with parents in order to bring about change. In Mr S's case it was suggested that longer term follow up might need to include work in his own right, through adult mental health, to address the very deep seated emotions he experienced, as this is beyond the remit of child mental health.

The Use of Analogy

Many family therapy techniques have contributed to workers 'toolboxes' – but using analogies is a simple one often already employed by parents and professionals alike in everyday language.

In emotionally laden situations, being able to see the difficulties from a different perspective, can free families to think more objectively and creatively.

Particular examples are:

a) A supermarket analogy helps parents to see that the range of different skills needed are like products stacked on a shelf. The role of therapists is to help guide them to a particular area of the shop, explain and maybe test the different products, but leave the ultimate choice to them. Even more specifically, parents recognise that if, for example, you choose the perfect biscuit, it would become very boring if you ate it every day. They feel more comfortable with the idea of 'buying' several different packets of 'biscuits' than recognising that they have 'developed a range of appropriate skills'. Families often become keen to develop this analogy to suit their particular eating habits!

b) A hanging mobile – useful to have in the room, and ideally one with similar shaped pieces hanging at different levels. When thinking about change, the mobile becomes a useful analogy for a family to demonstrate how the slightest shift or change to one piece, automatically involves the remaining pieces having to move to accommodate this change. It demonstrates beautifully how an apparently insignificant change, 'a puff of wind', can dramatically alter the whole picture.

c) Similarly, talking about how kaleidoscopes change the picture by small changes can be useful.

The mobile has the advantage of being instantly visible.

Modelling

As for us all when situations prove difficult to change, the way we behave and what we do feels 'risky', and it is much easier and feels safer to start with what we know.

Having a worker explicitly model a different way of interacting allows parents momentarily to step outside their 'parent role' to identify new ways of managing their child and to take the risk of trying on a new role for themselves while staff support them and help them to adapt it to suit their own circumstances.

As always, the 'doing' rather than 'talking about doing', can have a huge impact and demonstrates that a worker has truly 'got alongside' a family.

Conclusion

Working within the field of child mental health can be challenging both personally and professionally, partly because of the way it is perceived as a difficult specialism, and partly because it raises questions about the role of parents in the development and continuation of mental health problems in young people. All of us have been parented, if not been parents ourselves and inevitably there are times when some family situations strike chords within us all. Effective supervision and team working are important factors in ensuring that these feelings are understood and remain within their context, and do not undermine the positive impact of interventions with families.

This holds true for other referring professionals who may have struggled to help a family seemingly for ever, before a referral to a specialist resource brings about a miraculous change. Usually the referral process itself causes a family to dig deep into their reserves of strength, creativity and resilience, triggering change. On-going liaison between professionals helps clarify expectations, maintain appropriate boundaries, and reduce confusion and competitiveness.

The mental health of children is everyone's business, not the responsibility of any single agency. It must be based on a partnership of all relevant agencies, including education, health, social services, juvenile justice, youth service and the wider community. As in the opening quote, this 'fragile and precious commodity' needs all the careful handling and understanding it can get.

References

Byng-Hall, J. (1997). *Rewriting Family Scripts – Improvisations and Systems Change.* The Guildford Press.

Cooklin, R. (1999). Comment. *Young Minds*, 38: p 11.

Dept. of Health (1995). *Mental Illness – Can Children and Young People Have Mental Health Problems?* HMSO.

de Shazer, S. (1984). The Death of Resistance. *Family Process*, 23: p 79–83.

Kraemer, S. (1999). Who Needs Child and Adolescent Psychiatrists? *Clinical Child Psychology and Psychiatry*, 4: pp 121–127.

Mental Health Foundation (1999). *The Big Picture: Promoting Children and Young People's Mental Health.* MHF.

Rutter, M., and Hesor, R. (1985). *Child and Adolescent Psychiatry*, 2nd Edition. Blackwell Scientific.

SECTION FOUR
Education

16   A Teacher's Perspective

John Stevens

What Are We Trying to Achieve?

A 'head of year' working in secondary education has an automatic tendency to think of working with parents as being related to dealing with the problems experienced by their children. This may well be the most time consuming part of the job, but it will not involve all pupils. During three terms with my present year group some 60 pupils out of a total of 125 have required individual parental contact as a result of some concern. These concerns range from family worries and health to major behaviour problems. The majority of pupils are thankfully on the favourable side of a continuum reaching from those well-adjusted individuals who give little concern, to those whose lives are a sequence of major problems.

The overall aims in education appear to be relatively simple. We are firstly trying to maximise the academic potential of the individual related to their innate ability, but we also have the responsibility to develop social qualities, which will help the young person cope with life after school. Sadly the modern imposition of standards in education sometimes promotes the first aim to the detriment of the second. This can raise the expectations of parents, not always in a realistic manner, and create difficulties between home and school. Routine, whole group issues provide the overall framework for much of the contact between pastoral heads and parents. These include:

- work (school reports, merit certificates, marking)
- behaviour and attitudes (detentions)
- uniform and equipment (planners, ties and jumpers)
- attendance and punctuality (notes, holidays, authorisation)
- health (school nurse, vaccinations)
- special events (visits, extra-curricular activities)

Routine contact with parents of secondary pupils begins with the choosing of a school by parents at the beginning of year 6, which then progresses to the induction process at the end of the year. The aims here are a mutual 'getting to know you' process which clearly benefits the new pupil by increasing confidence in the transfer process, but also opens up important avenues of communication between home and school. The setting up of effective communication routes can be tricky. There is a progression of responsibility from the tutor who has daily contact with a pupil, through the head of year who takes responsibility for the whole year group, to the head teacher. The challenge for the head of year is to set up a situation where parents have confidence about who to contact, and tutors are given enough authority without being overloaded. The year head should then be able to deal with almost all serious issues, using the head teacher where support at the highest level is required.

Many of the problems faced by a year head in a school will of course relate to the normal issues listed above. Some of these will be trivial and involve a single issue, but in the worst cases many or possibly all of the issues will be involved. Year heads have many difficult decisions to make on how and when to involve parents. Parents will also make the first contact in many cases and this can create a need to make judgements on how serious the situation really is before proceeding. Some parents will approach the school on minor issues such as best friends having a temporary disagreement, while others will do their best to avoid contact with the school even when the situation becomes really serious. Perhaps the worst case of all is when parents are being unco-operative and the behaviour of their child is affecting the education and well-being of others. The outcome of this can be a damage limitation exercise in which the needs of the individual child can become secondary to the needs of others.

While the primary aim of a pastoral head must be to work with parents for the benefit of the child, there is a fairly common situation where we try to succeed with a young person in spite of problems initiated by parents and/or family. Cases like this readily spring to mind, such as pupil 'M' who came into the school from a family with limited academic success, poor attendance, and a history of poor communication between home and school. In the first year of secondary education 'M' was a bad attender with an attitude problem. Now 'M' is doing 'A' level exams and hopes to become a doctor. The mother never did establish a good working relationship with the school, despite a huge effort, but convincing the daughter that she had talent, giving her self respect, and being there when she needed support was enough to make the change. Success doesn't always follow that easily, and may not be so readily measurable.

Working with parents can be very frustrating due to entrenched attitudes and a failure to accept or understand the considered advice of professionals. In the case of pupil 'W' problems were expected due to the previous diagnosis of a personality disorder which required medication to keep it in check. During the first term however, 'W' settled in very well despite frequent calls from her mother telling us how bad her behaviour was at home. The school made every effort to support the family, even to the extent of trying to help them get rehoused. Despite this, relationships between home and school deteriorated, when following a meticulous reassessment of the personality disorder, 'W' was found to have been misdiagnosed in the first case and no longer in need of medication. The school supported these findings, but the parents refused to accept the situation and demanded special consideration in school for 'W'. While the school recognised some special needs for 'W' related to low ability and poor social skills, parental demands were unreasonable, and the school operating by normal standards refused to accept them. The parents have since taken 'W' out of school and refuse to send the child back. What was becoming another success has been jeopardised by parental attitudes.

The Skills and Qualities of the Professional

One of the biggest demands on a pastoral head in schools is the regular, frequent, and often unexpected need to change roles within the job. Within a matter of minutes it may be necessary to investigate an incident, decide on guilt, issue punishment, give support, and then perhaps contact parents of both offender and victim, before recording the essential details of the whole matter. The well worn expression 'you don't have to be crazy to work here: but it helps' often springs to mind. The real trick however, is to be very flexible and fairly tough.

Listening is an essential skill for dealing with both parents and their children. This can be easy for a good teacher dealing with a responsive pupil who is well used to giving information in the classroom. Listening to a parent can be much more demanding however. You have to realise that you are probably discussing the most important person in their life, about whom they hold very strong views and have powerful emotions. Hearing their side of the story, no matter how biased and unrealistic it may be is a vital part of coming to an understanding with them. We even managed to do this with the mother of pupil 'W' until her entrenched position made it impossible for us to give way any more without going against established values and procedures within the school.

Together with listening go the patience and negotiation of counselling skills. Knowledge of basic counselling is extremely useful, and once acquired will be frequently reinforced by contact with other professionals who are working in the same way. Taking a problem solving approach with parents can be effective for two reasons. Firstly because the problem with a child may well have developed from situations at home, and secondly because most parents will naturally want to help. J often came to school not in school uniform. The mother was asked to come to school to meet J's tutor who explained the problem. J's other clothes were unsuitable for school, and it created the wrong impression for others, and she was breaking school rules. J's mother explained that her washing machine had broken and she had to wash all the children's clothes by hand. The tutor helped the mother to make a case to social services for a replacement machine. It was agreed that after half term J would always be in uniform and until then no action would be taken about non-compliance with rules. J, her mother and the school kept their promises.

Decision making is another essential skill for working with parents. Action taken over problems should satisfy the policies and values of the school and as far as possible be acceptable to parents. Decisions are sometimes taken in situations where there is a conflict between the need for time to listen, and the need to act quickly. They will always need to be justified, and communicated effectively to the persons involved, which will include parents.

Linked to the skills of counselling and decision-making is the ability to mediate. Pupils are always falling out with other pupils and with teachers, but it is also surprisingly common for parents to fall out with each other. In a recent case the mothers of pupils 'TK' and 'BR' decided that each pupil was a bad influence on the other. Both the pupils are actually pleasant and hard working in school, and are also usually the best of friends and work together well. We now have a difficult task satisfying the demands of each mother whilst trying to improve the situation for the sake of two nice pupils. Many pupils experience relationship problems with parents, often as a result of problems with the parent's own relationship. Sitting in a meeting with two parents who are going through a very messy divorce can be an experience that requires the greatest tact and diplomacy. In one of the worst cases, mother and stepfather threw pupil 'R' out of home at the age of 12. Years of mediation by social services, school, and child and family guidance have failed to change the situation. The future now looks very bleak for 'R'. In this case there was no opportunity to work with the parents.

The final quality discussed here is determination: never give up! How many of us have got to a point with our 'clients' where we have tried everything we know, sought advice from everyone else we thought might be able to help, and still have not made any progress with the situation. A few years ago I came across an article in a newspaper written by a senior social worker about his own schooldays which had been very difficult. Who the person was is not important but what he said has stayed with me ever since. This person portrayed himself as a major problem at school, and every teacher except one had given up on him. This one teacher kept trying, and eventually lit a spark, which made the boy see sense, and changed his life. The plea from this person was to keep trying no matter how frustrating the situation is when working with young people and their parents. This may only be possible however, if lines of communication remain open.

What is Important?

Knowledge

This is important in a number of ways to give a sound basis for taking decisions and acting on them. Firstly, know your rights as a professional, and those of the parents and young people with whom you are dealing. Secondly, take great care over dealing with young people until you know something of the home situation. In a recent case pupil 'X' started coming to school regularly out of uniform. Fortunately a few weeks before this the parents had contacted the school to say that mother was going into hospital and that the father would be running the home on his own, as well as holding down a full-time job. This very simple case illustrates clearly how knowledge of the home situation totally changed the action required. Instead of being spoken to harshly and punished for wearing trainers and multicoloured shirts to school he was offered support and understanding while his mother recovered. Previous schools, external agencies, friends, and the family itself are all useful in providing background information. There may, however, be issues of confidentiality, which will have to be handled with discretion.

Contact with parents

This has previously been mentioned as an important part of the routine business in schools, but is vital to the effective handling of most pupil problems. It is very important to show parents that they are respected and valued especially if staff are not well known to them. Some years ago we organised a vocational course which involved a number of pupils who were not particularly well motivated and whose parents were rarely, if ever, seen in school. To encourage these parents to come into school we issued personal invitations on specially designed cards and provided substantial refreshments. Every parent either attended the meeting or made an appointment to visit the school at a later date. On another occasion I was guilty of the dreadful crime of sending home a note to a parent written with a red marking pen. The explosive telephone call received from the father within a few minutes of the child reaching home showed clearly the effect of

disrespect on a parent, even when none is intended. I have never written to a parent in red ink since!

Consistency

Many of the problems involving young people today arise as a result of conflicting standards within the home or generally in society. Consistency therefore needs to be an important principle in actions within a school, and in the joint action of school and parents. Pupil 'O' could well have been the most serious problem in the new entry this year, but his single parent mother has developed an excellent working relationship with the school and incidents are down to a quarter of what they were in his first term. Two other pupils, whose parents are clearly at odds with each other although for different reasons, continue to be a major source of concern. In one case the parents have long since split and live separate lives with different attitudes, and in the other the parents simply have very different personalities which lead them to treat their child in different ways.

Trust

We live in world full of suspicion and after working for a time with parents from impoverished backgrounds it becomes apparent that there is even less trust in some of these families. Making progress with problems in some families can therefore be heavily dependent on first building trust. The first contact between the school and the mother of pupil 'O' was a decidedly icy affair. You could almost hear her thinking 'who is this man? And what gives him the right to make such comments about my child?' Several meetings and phone calls later and the situation had changed completely, allowing the positive working relationship already mentioned to develop.

Getting to know parents

This obviously helps a great deal in developing trust, and ensuring that parents feel valued. Taking a genuine interest in the family and not just the problems of the child can be a key to success. Simple friendly enquiry's such as 'How are you?', 'How is the new baby?', 'Has your husband recovered from his illness?', can help break the ice. Perhaps meeting the parents in comfortable surroundings without the presence of the child can be very helpful. Conversations can be more open and problems shared more freely. Giving time willingly also makes people feel valued. Meetings should feel unhurried, and if they have to be brought to a sudden conclusion a good reason for this should be made clear. Setting up a review meeting sometime in the future will be a familiar principle to social workers. It works in education as well, partly by letting the pupil know that the problem isn't going to be forgotten, but also by giving extra value to the parental contribution. The appointment should be made at the original meeting if possible to make sure the review happens, and was not just a matter of empty words, which would be totally counterproductive.

Lines of communication

Normal communication such as a telephone call, letter, or e-mail is often taken for granted in the workplace. The vital nature of communication with parents becomes very apparent when it is not there. Two recent problems have really highlighted this. In the first case pupil 'T' argued with teachers and then ran out of school. 'T' s parents are very responsive but do not have a telephone, which makes contact really difficult and leaves the school in an awkward legal position. We could notify the police when 'T' runs off, but up until now he has always gone straight home, and doing this could be seen as a waste of resources. Negotiation with the parents has produced a promise to get a telephone. It will be very interesting to see

what effect this has on the behaviour of pupil 'T'. The second case is that of pupil 'B' who has the potential to behave badly, and plays truant. Again there is no telephone contact and in this case parents refuse to answer letters from school. Our only course of action here is through external agencies such as education welfare who can make home visits. We anticipate a lot more problems with pupil 'B' unless better communications with the home can be established.

The local authority has introduced an 'Inclusion Project', previously known as 'Towards no Exclusions' with the aim being to maintain all pupils at school.

The project entails working with the young person to find strategies for improved behaviour such as anger management. Before the young person participates in the project, the parents are invited to the school for discussion and to obtain their written permission. Throughout the project the parents are involved by making suggestions, agreeing to help with tasks and in coming into school regularly to be involved in decisions.

Sharing feelings

Being told that your child has sworn at a teacher or thumped another child must be a stressful experience for many parents. Making parents aware that you understand how they feel should ease this situation. Sharing a moist eye with a worried mother or father is a familiar experience to many of us, and is probably a good thing provided that professional integrity is maintained. Experienced professionals should have a wealth of relevant experiences that could be shared to make parents more comfortable about the problems of their own child.

Building on the positive

Many of the problems experienced by young people are related to poor self-esteem. They need to be given the confidence necessary to take control of their own lives. Parents will also respond better if they are given something positive to focus on rather than being subjected to nothing but a list of problems. There is nearly always something good you can say about the most difficult of pupils. Perhaps that they are good at sport or simply loyal to their friends.

This is one area where not giving up can be so important. If a young person has experienced failure for most of their life it will not be easy to convince them that they are capable of success. It may take some time and a great deal of patience.

Biting the bullet

Taking the final drastic step will sometimes be the trigger for focusing minds and lead to real improvements. In education, that step is often exclusion from school, a process that at the moment is being actively discouraged by the Government. When pupil 'O' was finally excluded after months of trying to avoid it, the seriousness of the situation, together with the good relationship between home and school, produced beneficial effects which have lasted to the present. Exclusion might well be a total waste of time if pupil and parents treat it as a holiday from school. The problem then is to find an alternative idea that will convey the seriousness of the situation. Biting the bullet is never easy!

Sharing information

This has obvious importance when other people are working with the same young person. Classroom teachers, for example, will need to know of issues that may lead to flashpoints or embarrassment. Colleagues may well also be prompted to give back information and ideas, which may help the person with the main responsibility. Careful judgements obviously have to be made on who needs to know what. In a recent case, pupil 'Z' had her head shaved by her mother and suffered great embarrassment as a result.

The mother was unable to control her children's nits and had resorted to shaving her children's heads as a way of resolving the situation. Staff therefore needed to know why 'Z' was allowed to wear a hat in school and given special consideration to avoid mixing with pupils apart from her own friends. What they did not need to know were the other details of the home situation revealed at the subsequent child protection conference.

Forgiving

Anyone who works with people who find it difficult to manage their lives will suffer some form of abuse from time to time. Hopefully, this will normally be a simple verbal disagreement. This is where the qualities of toughness and patience come in, and the worker will have to forgive in order to get back to a position of trust where progress can be made. There is no point in taking an aggressive stance to 'get back' at the person involved. Be assertive and make your point if you have to, but do make an attempt to improve relationships and get back to solving the real problem. After working in schools for years it is easy to spot the teachers who bear grudges. They are the ones who pupils really dislike and mistrust, often suffering the most complaints from parents and pupils.

Recording

Paperwork is often seen as a curse of modern working practices but it is an essential part of working with parents and their children. When parents contact the school or attend a meeting it can be a significant event in their lives. It is sometimes amazing just how accurately a parent will recall facts from a meeting which occurred months before. The worker, however, is at a serious disadvantage having dealt with dozens of parents since that meeting. Have you ever noticed how your doctor has to be reminded of why you attended the surgery just a few weeks before?

The answer to this is recording the main points of the situation, probably the significant points of the problem and certainly the action that needs to be taken. A behaviour-monitoring card for difficult pupils has proved an invaluable aid at school. Most incidents require no more than a two-line entry comprising the following: date – nature of the incident – staff involved – action taken. A simple computer database would serve the same purpose. The only slight problem associated with this idea is a delay on filing. Overall it saves work, and possible embarrassment!

Looking back through the points listed above it is very striking how interrelated many of the issues are. This greatly emphasises the need for those who work with children and their parents to be flexible and sympathetic in their approach. Success depends on the skilled use of many of the points above. There are other factors that substantially reduce the chance of success and can be very difficult to overcome.

Reasons for Failure

It is perhaps inevitable that some attempts to work with parents for the benefit of children will end in failure, at least in the short term. Success and failure are also very difficult to quantify, but my impression from meeting young people years after they leave school is that some of the values that teachers try to impress on them do make a positive difference to their lives as they mature into adults. This is another reason for never giving up. Hopefully, if we try to understand the reasons for failure we will have a better chance of success. So what are the reasons for failure?

Firstly, there is the influence of their peers on young people. Thinking back to our own teenage years quickly reminds most of us that the people we most wanted to impress were our own friends, not our parents. Nothing much has changed except that increase of media hype has probably increased the pressure on young people to follow their peers. The combined effect of parents and teacher will have great difficulty succeeding over the influence of strong peer pressure. Pupil 'B' who truants openly admits to doing so because he has a very streetwise friend in the year above who does it. He sees his friendship as being much more important than getting into trouble and ending up with a visit from the education welfare officer.

The second reason for failure is partly a symptom of the government's policy of forcing more pupils from special education into mainstream schools, a policy, which one suspects, has more to do with economics than benefits for pupils, parents, or teachers. Teachers are professional educators, some of whom have become fairly skilled social scientists and psychologists. They are not experts in these fields however, and all too often find themselves out of their depth, especially when dealing with issues such as mental health problems in both pupils and parents. This situation is made substantially worse by a chronic lack of external support particularly with psychiatric problems. Child and family guidance appears to be the only clearly defined avenue open to give support with mental health in children, and even then referral is more easily done through parents and the family doctor rather than directly from school.

Other reasons for difficulties in working with parents relate to their previous experiences of authority, which have left them with deep-rooted mistrust or apprehension. It is quite common to come across parents who openly admit to being very nervous about meeting teachers because of their own bad experiences at school. Others have experienced difficulties with other agencies such as the police, and have an unrealistic view that all professionals should be viewed with suspicion.

There is also a very worrying tendency today for parents and their children to have high expectations of professional people while not taking adequate responsibility within their own family. The attitude in school can be 'you are the teacher, you sort it out'. This has a habit of backfiring on parents. Pupil 'V' has a very interesting mother who we knew had clashed with schools and other authorities before 'V' joined the school. At the beginning the mother was very keen to come into school and discuss how her child should be handled. Despite her somewhat aggressive manner a good working relationship began to develop, but sadly this seems to have been too late. Pupil 'V' still has a bad attitude in school, but now her mother has serious problems with her out of school and is desperate for help. This is a very common situation today where a child has learned to challenge authority from parents but the parents then lose their own authority and serious problems are inevitable.

Perhaps the most serious reason of all for any failure in working with parents for a teacher is serious breakdown within the home environment. This may be the type of problem that triggers a child protection case, such as physical abuse, sexual abuse, neglect, or domestic violence. In these cases other agencies such as police, social services and health services will automatically be involved and success will depend on a carefully co-ordinated multi-agency approach. Outcomes of this type of issue are extremely varied. Where children are removed from parents, the new carers are usually much easier to work with – but the child has been through a great deal of trauma and however effectively the new carers work with the school, succeeding with the child is still very difficult. The most likely chance of success in cases where the family is split up appears to come when some other member of the family takes on responsibility. Pupil 'C' sadly lost her mother when she died a year ago. Until then 'C' had been a very poor attender, behind with her work, and was developing poor attitudes to authority. She went to live with her older brother and his family, who took on the parenting role. She has become a totally different pupil. She is a joy to teach and rarely misses a lesson.

Conclusion

Working with parents as a teacher can be a very rewarding experience. It can be tough but it is never dull. There are many successes to keep you going, sometimes when least expected. Boundaries are always changing, and unexpected events happen with great regularity.

In working with parents the needs of the child will always be considered, but in working with children the needs of the parents must not be forgotten.

17 Working in Partnership with Parents at The Willows

Mair Dyer, Gerry Emson, Anne Scowen, and Meriel Mann

Introduction

This chapter explains how The Willows staff work with parents and the rationale behind the work. How they evaluate what they do and how they would like to further develop and improve this service.

The Willows is a local authority special school for pre-school children who come from all over Portsmouth and surrounding areas. The children are offered free school transport if they live outside a one-mile radius, as most do. This means that the majority of our parents do not have a daily personal contact with The Willows as often happens with area main stream schools.

In the first part of this chapter Mair Dyer, gives a personal account of being a parent of a child with special needs and tells how she feels she is able to contribute to the work of the school. Gerry Emson's section details a piece of research she undertook when studying for her post-graduate diploma in education. Anne Scowen describes how she is developing outreach work on behalf of the school working with parents in the community. The final part is by Meriel Mann, the deputy head, who tells how the school continually monitors and evaluates their work in order to maintain the Charter Mark/Investors in People standards.

Mair's Experience

When we first knew that our son had special needs we were overwhelmed. What did it mean for him? What did it mean for us? Most of all we were overwhelmed with the amount of different professionals that we saw in a very short space of time, including medical officer, audiologist, educational psychologist, to name a few. All of them saw us in formal clinic settings, and we gave endless hours of history, and repeated lists of missed milestones and delays in our son's development. Everyone wanted a different piece of him and a different focus on the information we gave them. No-one seemed to be looking at the whole picture.

Rhys was then referred to The Willows Nursery. To us this was confirmation that he was now 'in the system' and was identified by his special needs. Cancelling his place at the local playgroup his brother had attended was a very hard thing to have to do. There was no doubt that we were relieved that he would get much needed help for his problems but this was balanced with fear that this was another group of professionals who would judge our parenting skills. We couldn't have been more wrong.

The nursery helped us to take back some of the control in our lives at a time when it felt chaotic. It has a real commitment to families and carers and in providing them with support in all areas where they may need it. There is an understanding and recognition that the difficulties that arise do not confine themselves to school hours! The support or advice may come directly from the school staff themselves or they will find someone else to help if necessary. Nothing has ever been left unattended to because it didn't 'fit'.

The first contact with the nursery was in our own home. This was unbelievable as it made us feel that someone was interested in us as a family. Having a child with special needs is not something that affects just the child but the whole family. That first home visit to tell us about the nursery enabled us to feel that they would be supporting us as a whole unit, and supporting us to help Rhys at home.

We quickly found out this wasn't just a comforting speech for new parents but this was the real practice for Willows. The home visits were a structural part of the school programme with a clear expectation that we would work on targets with Rhys at home. There was an opportunity for all areas of Rhys' life to be worked on, including those which weren't strictly educational, such as toilet training.

The relationship and communication between nursery and home was a complete one – as equals – as any professional relationship can be. We gained confidence in our own skills as parents, were encouraged to meet other parents, to share achievements however small, and to find support from whatever sources were available to us. We also had access to information about our rights and where we could find other services. Overall, our time with Willows nursery has prepared us to approach the 'next steps' with a more positive outlook than we'd ever hoped for and a wealth of friendships and support to take with us.

While our son was attending Willows nursery, the opportunity arose to become a parent governor. This was something I was interested in doing as I saw it as a very positive way to put something back into the school. At the time when we felt that we were on the receiving end of most services and support, however positive, this was very important.

However, I wasn't at all sure what being a governor involved, or whether any of my experiences would be relevant or appropriate to the work of a governing body. I found a quote in a pamphlet about governors that stated the strength of the governing body lies in the collective knowledge, experience and expertise of its members. I realised that while other members may be professionals, I did have expertise and experience in parenting, and in particular parenting a child with special needs.

My obvious interest is that of family / carer support and so I have been able to be involved in Friends of Willows meetings which are run by the deputy head as a vital, informal support group for parents. In addition, a Buddy System for parents has also been developed by the nursery. This grew from issues raised by parents and my own experiences of living away from family support which I could express through my role as a parent governor.

The 'buddy system' recognises the ability and need for parents and carers to support each other. This is so important when you feel that in many areas of your child's life other people are seen as the experts and you may already be blaming yourself for what your child's difficulties may be. It isn't seen as a system in competition with the good relationships with the staff, but a way of complementing them. It allows parents to share the ups and downs of life, to share information about their own experiences of different services, and to provide support at times when the nursery staff may not be around. It is promoted in a sensitive way to all new parents offering to link them with an existing parent, initially just to say hello. The relationships between parents build to meet the needs of the individual parents involved.

Becoming part of the team of governors has been a rewarding experience in many ways. I have learnt more about the way in which the nursery works and how decisions are made. Most importantly, I have been able to give feedback from a first-hand experience of receiving the service and while I am not a representative for other parents and carers I am a representative parent. Ideas that come from parents are listened to carefully and responsively and as such I have felt a valued member of the governing body.

Gerry's Research

Introduction

This section looks at the outcome of a piece of action research, using surveys and interviews with parents and staff. It examines how partnership has been achieved through the Home Based Projects scheme at The Willows Nursery School.

All its results are examined and subsequently applied, so that the scheme might become a model for other establishments to employ and to provide a basis for a policy reflecting the desires and equal status of all partners.

Rationale

During the last thirty years, there has been a gradual acceptance of the sharing of expertise between home and school. Official acknowledgement of the parents clamouring at the doors can be tracked through reports as far back as Plowden (1967). The Willows Nursery School recognises that our accurate but sensitive interpretation of current legislation has a reciprocal effect which can influence the whole system of education. We recognise that a flexible approach to current educational ideology is required to serve best the needs of our pupils and parent partners. To this end, we employ a 'living' curriculum, based on aspects of Portage, High/Scope and TEACCH (see Glossary), all of which rely to some extent on empowering parents. We also review our policies and practices regularly.

The Home Based Projects scheme was initiated in 1992 as a result of a long held desire to forge stronger home/school links, and in the belief that parents are critical to the success of a child's regime, especially when they only attend school part-time. The scheme ran for two years on an initial policy written from a staff viewpoint. It was due for review both according to the school development plan and the head's appraisal targets.

The National Portage Association also produced a code in response to the 1993 Act. Bastiani, (1989, pp 19–26) documented ten rules of home/school relations and also suggested six strategies:

- the critical examination of existing arrangements
- listening to parents
- tapping the grapevine
- engaging in practical activities…of a joint nature
- establishing home-school matters as a priority in the school's 'development plan'
- borrowing from other people's ideas and experience

During this research my main aims were to examine and evaluate the 'home based projects scheme' using these rules and strategies as a yardstick against which to measure our success. The information was used to instigate modifications to present practices and inform a new policy in partnership with parents.

Much has been written about home/school relations in recent years, partly because research which led to changes in legislation has brought the subject to the forefront of people's thinking.

The gradual acceptance that parents are a force for good in education, and that they are important to the processes and success of educational endeavour has been re-enforced by recent government edicts.

The notion of partnership has grown in importance throughout the decade. The Code of Practice for Children with Special Educational Needs which came into force on 1st September 1994 states that parents must have 'information, partnership and access' (section 2.33). We are therefore working at present in a climate in which initiatives towards full partnership are both more highly valued and underpinned by current legislation. The Hampshire (Portsmouth) policy statement notes that:

the management of all services should indicate how partnership with families is being pursued.

Whatever educational legislation is in force, its success is determined by the responses evident in the working practices of schools. These practices can only be deemed successful when their outcomes are monitored and assessed as fully as is practicable.

The Development of Partnerships in Schools

The assumption that partnership and parental autonomy were modern ideas and ideals was disproved by a reference in Sharrock (1980, p 60) to Mulcaster (1532–1611):

> *the schoolmaster…is a counsellor to act along with the parent, if the latter is willing to take advice, I should wish that parents and teachers should not only be acquainted, but on friendly terms with each other.*

Partnerships may operate on many levels and, with a little thoughtful planning, can be engineered to suit the needs of most schools. The school must determine the level of partnership appropriate. It is in both the quality and the quantity of response that schools can achieve the level of interaction that is practicable for them, bearing in mind the official guidelines. Pugh (1981, p 4) discusses the five levels of partnership that Gordon (1969) suggested were possible with parents as:

1. supporters in fundraising
2. learners from teachers
3. teachers of their own children
4. teachers' aides and volunteers
5. policymakers and partners

The 'Mother Child Home Program' in New York encouraged mothers to follow a 'structured curriculum of verbal interactions' (Levenstein, 1971, p 130) modelled by toy demonstrators who called weekly to leave free toys. When the programme was evaluated, Levenstein tells us 'it was clear that demonstration is a two-way street with implications for teachers' (p 131).

Far from being passive recipients, many parents were ready to engage in high levels of partnership as we understand it today.

Two of these programmes, Portage and High/Scope, have had deep effects both internationally and within our own school. Both have a counselling element within their relationships with parents.

Current Thoughts on Partnership

It is clearly important to remember that in out of school interactions, staff, as well as parents, need to feel empowered. Training needs must be addressed so that staff feel confident in what is sometimes unfamiliar territory. Bastiani's (1989, p 100) ideal of partnership is:

> *the devolution of power and shared responsibility where teachers and parents work together, through non-hierarchical relationships in a partnership of equals.*

In our school we hope that we are achieving this aim in a thoughtful yet practical way, living up to our mission statement of being committed to working with parents/carers and other professionals. We would all agree that:

> *Parents are more likely to respond more warmly when they are made to feel as if they have an important, and equal, role in their children's education.*
>
> (Edwards, 1988, p 28)

Ethics

During the course of this study, I looked at the home-based projects scheme from many viewpoints and asked for personal views from both staff and parents. It was most important to do this in a way which encouraged honest answers but treated them with confidentiality.

I sought permission at all stages to use material which might seem to identify individuals, and to negotiate changes or remove any comments found to be insensitive to the thoughts and feelings or professional status or otherwise of my colleagues and parent partners. All answers were encoded to further lessen identification; conversely I acknowledged the ideas of those who would wish for this to be done.

The Research

I used a questionnaire as a basis for focused interviews. Half of the parents were interviewed by telephone and half in their own homes at mutually convenient times. Most telephone interviews tended to be undertaken 'after bedtime' for working parents. Those non-working parents who tended to prefer a personal daytime visit were those who had prior experience of visits, and I interviewed all those who replied to my request to participate.

The research was both quantitative and qualitative and further details may be obtained on request from The Willows.

I used a variety of methods. These included surveys, interviews and group discussion. I also used the same method on different occasions, and looked for alternative viewpoints by seeking the views of staff, parents and past parents, and by seeking evidence and information in books, reports and journals. In this way I hoped to have gained a sufficiently wide spectrum of opinion to limit possibilities of bias and narrowness that would undermine the validity of the research.

The surveys and interviews used a mixture of open and closed questions, thus affording the greatest possible flexibility of response. The quantitative data was useful to test and determine practical management and organisational issues, whilst the qualitative data reflected the thoughts, feelings and aspirations which might generate new initiatives. Use of the former would modify practices and principles of operation, and use of the more unexpected qualitative data would modify policies and point to areas for further research.

All staff and 65 per cent of families participated. One third of replies came from single parent families which reflected the ration on roll, other variables were similarly reflected to represent all shades of opinion. Although past parents preferred two visitors, 60 per cent of present parents and 66 per cent of staff expressed no preference, and this allowed some home visits to be single person so that frequency was increased.

Outcomes

The answers in the research reflected a positive attitude. Home visits might be used to close the gap between some children's co-operation at home and in school and generalising improvements in either direction.

All staff valued and sought participation in the scheme. They were positive about the benefits, and we must accommodate their desire for inclusion. Home visiting days also provided time to facilitate paired and shared placements and transfers. Four 45–60 minute visits seem a normal manageable pattern, and since 82 per cent of staff were prepared to undertake solo visits their initiation would provide valuable flexibility and meet parental desires for more frequent visits. Meriel's suggestion that visits be prioritised by need when necessary would also be easier to manage.

Staff choose equipment in line with the child's interests and language programme, but also use alternatives to promote new skills. The recording form used fulfils requirements, but has been modified to include sections deemed 'missing'. Some 82 per cent of staff sometimes leave a list or chart of activities and since this is something parents also asked for, I devised a new activity chart.

It was clear that a problem existed with regard to resources used, since too many items were borrowed from the speech therapist and the high/scope areas. The problem was resolved by an injection of money to properly resource home visiting boxes. The equipment is regularly reviewed and modified. Current training needs were clearly identified. After the survey, an INSET day was held based on portage techniques such as task analysis.

The question of support was particularly relevant to one staff team where part time working reduced opportunities for all to visit and to share outcomes and occurrences. In consequence, working patterns have been altered to enable a more equitable approach and greater ease of management. Staff generally recognise the need to give mutual support when difficulties and anxieties arise. For health and safety reasons, a mobile phone was purchased so that contact might be maintained with school.

I asked only three open ended questions of all participants and these were intended to elicit both negative and positive views and general comments about the scheme which might influence our policy decisions. Most comments were appreciative and positive. I had expected more criticisms but got very little, so this might suggest that our present mode of operation was good. Equally, some parents may have felt unsure about complaints to 'interested parties'. I responded favourably to all negative statements and revised our policy accordingly, whether the comments were from staff or parents. In particular, the views expressed by past parents resulted in renewed efforts to extend invitations about interest groups and special occasions to them, and visits post transfer were made to ease the feeling of loss. Our head suggested that the results be disseminated to local special schools, and this was done.

I found in general that our methods and structures were sound, but some fine tuning was required to make the service more balanced and equitable, and to ensure accountability. Planning, resources, training and monitoring were modified. We moved forward with a tighter framework that remained flexible enough to respond to individual needs:

- new activity chart/list forms were devised
- new equipment was purchased and inventoried
- training needs were and continue to be addressed
- visits are made to families post transfer
- parent interest groups were planned

I hope that our example will encourage other establishments to embark on home visiting schemes and on evaluation exercises.

As early years practitioners, we initiate the education partnership, and the bonds we forge should promote the best of home/school relationships. In being successful, we create a climate of continuity and responsibility which needs a response from schools at later levels. Sadly, at present neither resources nor expertise are always available when we transfer children, and parents who are full partners at the pre-school stage become disillusioned and disenfranchised at the next. Somehow schools must be given the resources of finance, staff and time in order to redress the balance.

Anne's Work

The Willows offers a very individual service to its families. Our home-based projects service is regarded as an important part of the work we do not only from the child's point of view, but also the parents, and often the wider family unit as a whole.

The aims of home visits are to:

- encourage and develop closer home to school bonds

- work in partnership with parents and carers to provide practical support and listen to concerns

- identify mutual learning targets and opportunities

- agree consistent handling of the child in school and at home

- enable and encourage the enjoyment of parenting

I have a particular interest in working in partnership with parents and could see the vast amount of experience both from staff and parents that we share during individual home visits. Willows' staff team has been encouraged to develop a flexible approach to their work. We realise no two families are the same but can often have similar difficulties. These can be:

- Isolation – children whose behaviour is so challenging it is easier to stay indoors than face looks and comments from others.

- Frustration and often extreme tantrums from a child who has difficulty in communicating their needs.

- Lack of sleep for the parents and often the whole family because of an active toddler who has little concept of routine or just does not need to sleep for any long periods of time.

- Meal times becoming a battle of wills.

- Conflicting advice – families not agreeing on behaviour strategies.

- Parents finding extended family are not ready to recognise there is a problem – confusing advice.

We are already entering a potentially stressful area for parents, but parents/carers say they appreciate the additional support given by staff during our home visits.

In true Willows tradition I wondered could we further improve on the service we are already offering? What can we take out and learn additionally from home visits? Finally, where do we go from here to extend the service if anywhere? I looked at the home-based service as a whole and then asked myself a number of questions:

- Is there a way of regularly assessing home visits without breaking confidentiality?

- What do we talk about for those forty-five minutes?

- Can we use the information for identifying training issues both for staff and parent or carer use?

- Can we identify termly trends in topics for planning future Friends of Willows talks by guest speakers?

- Is there a need for any other service, which we do not already provide?

The first step was to design a form which gave a quick and accessible way of producing the data required for statistics. A form that would not breach confidentiality and would not require staff to spend valuable time plodding through piles of paperwork to gain the relevant pieces of information needed.

There are many topics of discussion which have evolved over the time home visits have been in operation, and whilst some issues are common amongst parents, e.g. behaviour difficulties, issues around mealtimes, there are also many more. I must also stress we do not see ourselves as the experts in these fields. On the contrary, we are generally just the people who know through experience which service can help with a specific issue and point the parent in the right direction, or we may share our experience of a particular problem that has helped in the past with another child presenting similar problems.

It seemed to me that issues could be divided into two separate categories, child based and parent based. The data was taken over a twelve-week period during the spring term, 1998.

The following list shows a sample of child-based issues discussed on home visits over the term.

Areas for Discussion

Behaviour strategies

Often children attending Willows present challenging behaviour. In partnership with parents we explore and find a consistent approach, which will work for everyone including the child. It is not always easy, and regular support for parents is one of the keys to the success we have in this field.

S.A.L.T.

Speech and language therapy is not surprisingly the biggest area of discussion on child based issues with parents, for the reason that the majority of children attending Willows have delayed or disordered language. There are on-site speech therapists who work with the children individually and provide programmes for working with the child in the classroom. The speech therapist will also have regular contact with parents. While on visits staff will also work on the child's language programme in order to model for parents what the child is working on currently at school.

Toilet training

Speaks for itself. Our experience of what worked for past pupils is a good resource for parents to tap into. We also have a positive praise system in place which is highly amusing to see in action in the nursery especially when little Georgie has his first wee on the potty!

I.E.Ps – Individual Education Plans

Teachers will assess and give every child an education plan tailor-made for that individual pupil. This document will also include behaviour strategies, toilet training, and also any interventions around eating and meal times. We endeavour to discuss the education plan with parents and work with them in partnership. Sometimes parent/carers will request homework to do with their child. This can be a variety of tasks from language and literacy skills to an activity for encouraging eye contact or concentration.

Health

Issues are constantly around for Willows parents and staff. Along with the child's particular medical problems there is the ongoing problem of head lice, skin infections, worms to name just a few. The battle never seems to be won.

Sleep problems

Often crop up as an issue for parents. They have been known to turn to us out of desperation. We will often work on the problem with the parents if it is an obvious one. However, if it is a more complex problem we refer them on to another agency for more specific help. In Portsmouth there is a sleep clinic run by health visitors.

Physiotherapy and occupational therapy

Again we work closely with the therapist to implement the child's programme in the classroom. We receive and share information with parents, hopefully providing consistency in approach and occasionally to discuss the child's likes and dislikes regarding their physiotherapy and occupational therapy programmes!

Transport

How the child comes to school can cause problems it seems, especially during the first and second term, mainly I suspect because of the emotional attachment between mother and child.

Homework

When requested by parents or suggested by staff. This is usually taken from the child's I.E.P and the activities suggested will be to target a specific area of development.

Reviews

These are often quite a new concept for parents. This is not something that happens in mainstream school and parents can be a little baffled by them at first. They do not really know what to expect, as with the general procedure for requests for statements of special educational needs. Often in this sense we are the educators explaining what will happen and just preparing them for what to expect.

To many, parent based issues have very little to do with what is, after all, an educational establishment. However, we pride ourselves in our work with parents and know the significance to the whole family of this extra support.

All families have stress in their lives but having additional problems relating to one of the family having special needs means added pressures.

We therefore also offer:

- support
- listening skills
- reference to other agencies/or support groups
- assistance in writing letters e.g. support of a re-housing application, disability allowance or charitable discretionary awards

We will also liaise with other agencies in crisis times for families and provide contact numbers for other support services.

Parents have been known to request we take their child for an assessment/medical. The reason is that usually the change of environment and routine is potentially very stressful for a child with a communication disorder. Tantrums may occur, and some parents find the whole procedure emotionally upsetting.

Behaviour strategies for siblings will often be requested. Parents' confidence in their parenting ability may have been drastically knocked by already having a child with special needs. Finding the toddler does not respond to the normal parenting interventions can sometimes leave parents in a state of despair.

Occasionally it is simple, the parent has little experience of what parenting skills are. In this case we hope to provide good role models, support, raise self-esteem and educate through Friends of Willows and contact with other parents. Sometimes other agencies will also be involved i.e. social services.

Willows staff arrange visits to other establishments especially when children are due to leave Willows. We set up split placements with mainstream playgroups, schools, day nurseries etc. if the parent, educational psychologist and teacher agree that this is what is required and in the child's best interest. We also have regular trips out to help parents enjoy their child.

The toy library is another support parents can tap into. The travelling toy library visits Willows regularly to change equipment and parents can pop in to borrow it. However, in reality, because children attending Willows come via transport, this service is sadly under used. Staff often take a specific piece of equipment on a home visit if they think a child will benefit from it and simply pick it up again at the next visit.

Emotional support is a very important part of our work and has been actively encouraged within the management structure of Willows at all levels. Parents find the practicalities of day-to-day living with a child with special needs demanding. Emotionally, they are coming to terms with the reality of their child's special needs, and mourning the loss of their individual ideal of what their child/family would be like both short term and long term if their child had been of the socially acceptable 'norm'.

Having discovered just what did go on in those forty-five minute visits, I could answer some of my original questions. What do we do with the information?

- We record the brief content.

- We plan and record children's work/language.

- We use notes for future reference.

- We can identify recurring issues or concerns.

- We can identify staff or parent training needs.

It became clear that there were other issues noted on home visits. Again we could learn from knowing what issues these were and why:

- feeding problems (quite common to us but it was being overlooked)

- social services

- health and hygiene

- safety

- earrings

- pets

And finally, recommendations were to:

- Discuss with the team if there were real benefits to collecting this data realistically. It was agreed to collect the data one term only out of an academic year.

- To print out a termly reminder sheet for 'what's on for parents this month' for staff. Busy schedules meant plugging the Friends of Willows and the toy library were easily overlooked when working on more personal issues with parents. A sheet printed and kept in the home visit file might jog staff's memory.

- Staff also requested speakers on disability allowance, the housing office, and the mental health trust.

And personally what were the benefits for me of doing this research? I found it both interesting and challenging having never attempted anything like it before. It stretched my understanding of working with parents and made me appreciate what we do and what a great place The Willows is to work.

Outreach Work

In February 1999 The Willows was awarded Early Excellence Centre status which provided funds for The Willows to disseminate good practice as identified in our Ofsted Report i.e. working with other agencies as a multi-disciplinary approach, working with parents as partners and working with pupils in a systematic way.

The outreach service was one aspect of this, the training of other professionals in the area another, and the play scheme a third.

The aim was for parents and guardians of children with special needs to:

- Contribute ideas, being developed by Willows and it's outreach service.

- Develop an action plan for developing new initiatives.

- Give advice and information or support to The Willows staff in the form of a working partnership.

- Contribute ideas, skills or practical support in any way that is comfortable or working for each individual person or family.

Figure 1 and Figure 2 show some of our thoughts and ideas on how the service might develop.

When visiting parents in their homes, we found it is useful to tell them how long we will be staying. We also make particular effort with our written material to ensure it is user friendly and easy to understand. The following are 2 examples:

Figure 1

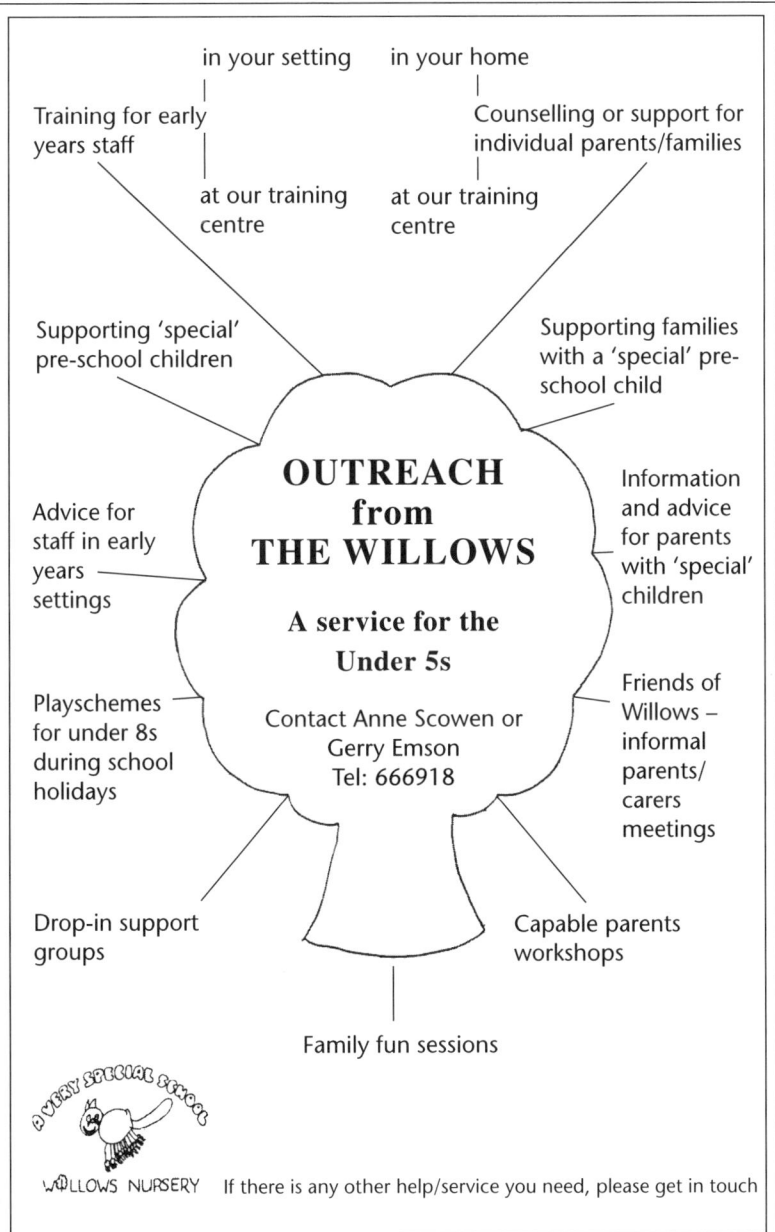

Having concerns about your child/ren?

Are you feeling isolated? Do you want information – help – counselling – support – advice?

Are you experiencing difficulties with a child in your setting?

in your setting

in your home

Training for early years staff

Counselling or support for individual parents/families

at our training centre

at our training centre

Supporting 'special' pre-school children

Supporting families with a 'special' pre-school child

OUTREACH from THE WILLOWS

A service for the Under 5s

Contact Anne Scowen or Gerry Emson Tel: 666918

Information and advice for parents with 'special' children

Advice for staff in early years settings

Playschemes for under 8s during school holidays

Friends of Willows – informal parents/ carers meetings

Drop-in support groups

Capable parents workshops

Family fun sessions

WILLOWS NURSERY   If there is any other help/service you need, please get in touch

Would you like to know more about special needs?

Figure 2

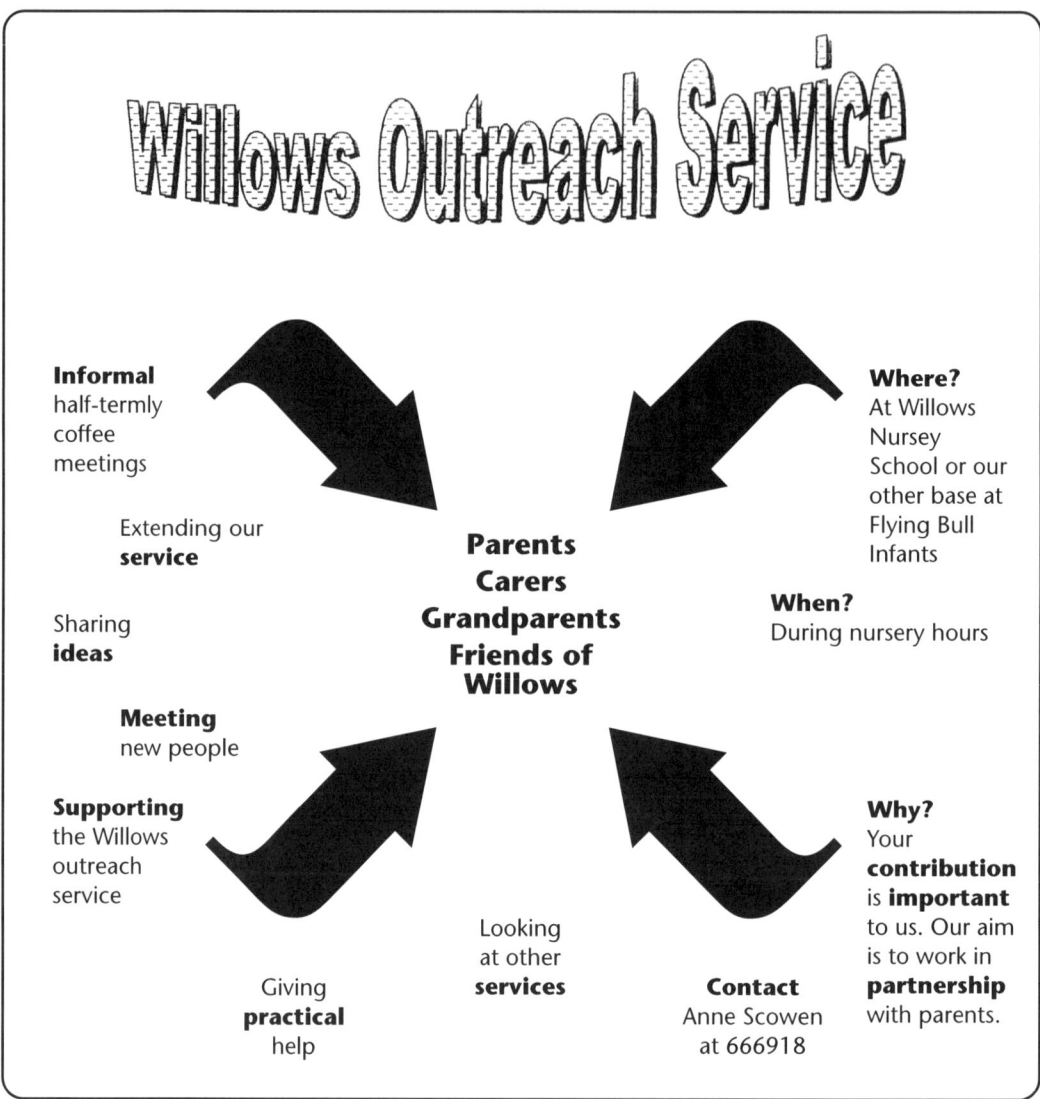

Counselling

Person Centred Counselling at Willows is an approach in gently supporting parents, while they resolve for themselves issues or problems in their lives. It is about giving individual time for parents or carers at home or based at Willows. It is about providing a weekly/fortnightly hourly contact when requested by the parent or carer.

Facts

It is not about telling people how to sort out their lives; it is about:

- building a trusting, working relationship
- empowering parents to make their own decisions
- problem solving
- raising self-esteem

- being in partnership with the parents
- providing role models
- Willows providing support for parents at a deeper level when the need arises

We feel it is the responsibility of the parent or carer to:

- have a commitment to the counselling alliance

- give themselves time to reflect on their thoughts and feelings
- telephone Willows before 9.30 am to cancel appointments where possible
- have a commitment to arrive on time for Willows based counselling sessions

Meriel's Work

This section gives an example of the progress the Friends of Willows scheme has made and how the school evaluates their work.

We give a high priority to the promotion of parent partnership and it is as part of this culture that our Friends of Willows meetings have developed. Meetings for parents have been ongoing for years at The Willows, but were restarted in the spring of 1996 in a more concerted way. I started off with the first of many questionnaires to gauge interest. I asked if parents wanted meetings. If so, was there a preference for informal or more focused groups? I asked about preferred days, times and frequencies and whether child care was an issue.

Based on the response we planned monthly meetings held alternately on mornings and afternoons. People strongly preferred meetings with an invited speaker (18 to 1). Parents preferred topics such as the work of the SALT, our work at Willows, behaviour management, the statementing process and so on.

We started up meetings, publicising them well and providing speakers as requested. Despite the preparation and consultation, attendance was poor. Throughout this time, I continued with surveys. I wanted to get it right.

Then, in October 1998, I decided on a completely new tack – a rather more organic approach. We asked one or two of our ex-

mums if they would host a morning for new parents. It was great! They took over the staff room, sorted out the coffee and cakes but, most importantly, assumed responsibility.

Each meeting since then has followed a similar format. Staff drop in now and again to say hello, but are no longer in the driving seat. The buzz of conversation is a pleasure to hear and several parents have mentioned how good it is to know that they are not alone.

I feel that this is the right approach – parents taking ownership of meetings. There is now personalised and relevant contact between people. I think that whatever direction these gatherings take in the future, the drive for change will rise out of the needs of the parents.

I know that supportive friendships are developing between parents, as advice is sought and found. Can there be a better legacy for the future?

Willows is ever seeking ways in which to improve our service, so we frequently consult with parents, carers and staff about possible new initiatives.

In 1996 we were awarded Investors in People for the quality of our training and also began our acquaintance with the EEL project which enabled us to look in detail at our interactions with the children. The breadth of home visits has increased, as can be seen from Anne's survey and we intend this trend to continue. The Buddy Scheme which Mair has described is gaining impetus and Friends of Willows is continuing successfully.

Late in January 1999 we were pleased to be the recipients of the Chartermark award for which we were nominated by a parent. In February 1998 we were visited by Ofsted who gave us a 'very good' report which said 'The nursery's partnership with parents and the community is outstanding'.

The Willows is now also able to offer much more in the way of special needs training for other schools' staff and improved provision for parent groups or individual families. It is hoped that strong links between all early years providers in the city will be forged so that there will be a seamless service between health, caring services and education for all families whatever their needs.

In addition to external assessments, we continually monitor our work internally. We use questionnaires extensively, for example to parents. We have been asking the advice of parents of new children, and those recently left, about the time of transition. Can we do better? About half of our old customers responded (19 replies out of a possible 40). All rate our procedures effective and two or three respondents made some very heartening comments:

> *I was extremely pleased with the way Willows prepared J. for school.*

> *I was pleased with the way the move was handled. Everyone was very helpful.*

We asked:

Our old customers:

- whether their child went to the school the parent wanted
- if we listened and talked about the move to the parents satisfaction
- did we help with visits to the new school?
- could we have done better?

A selection of new parents:

- if the initial home visit was helpful
- about the user-friendliness (or otherwise) of the parents booklet
- about their first visit to see the school
- if they like home books and newsletters
- if they know about Friends of Willows' meetings
- if they feel worries and concerns are listened to

There was one area for improvement from this information which is to ensure that everyone knows about Thursday newsletters.

College students:

Students who are with us for two weeks or more were asked to complete an evaluation pro forma. This information is collated by one of our classroom assistants who regularly reports to a staff meeting and to governors.

Professional colleagues:

Governors regularly ask visiting professionals to judge our performance via questionnaires.

Fellow early years workers:

Following our Ofsted inspection, Willows teachers were asked to produce a training package. This is aimed at a wide variety of early years workers in the city wanting to know more about working with children with special educational needs. Evaluation sheets (collected after each training day) are analysed and used to inform future training.

As Part of Our In-house Evaluation We Have:

- A suggestion box. To date we have had just one suggestion made, 'please will staff wear name badges'. We now have new badges and fine ourselves 10p if we forget!

- A 'problem' sheet on which to record minor problems, but so far these have not been well used.

- Improved our monitoring of the curriculum, and teachers have developed a monitoring pro forma. We have agreed a consistent frequency of use and an effective reporting system. I foresee that this work will evidence our strengths, inform planning and highlight training needs.

- Curriculum co-ordinators report to a full staff meeting offering support and advice as appropriate. They are also invited to governors' meetings to talk about their particular responsibility.

- Continued to commission the inspection service to comment on our expertise.

- Tried to ensure value for training money. Requests for training are made on a pro forma helpful to access relevance to the School Development Plan. A short presentation is made to a full staff meeting by the person trained.

- Whole school development day. The aim is to develop a strategy for the next five years. All Willows' staff completed a questionnaire evaluating our effectiveness both as trainers and in communicating the values of the school.

For the Future

- Agreement by staff of whole school targets.

- A fact finding mission 'What other services do parents need?' e.g.
  - more playschemes
  - Saturday clubs
  - babysitting service

Conclusion

This chapter highlights the work and ethos of the school in striving to continue to monitor, evaluate and improve quality standards.

The best interests of the child are, and always will be, our overall aim. By working effectively with parents, we are, in most cases, able to ensure:

- the child is well cared for,
- their special needs are met
- the child is able to be happy
- they achieve their potential in all facets of their life.

References

Atkin, J., Bastiani, J., and Goode, J. (1988). *Listening to Parents; An Approach to the Improvement of Home/School Relations*. Beckenham, Kent: Croom Helm.

Bastiani, J. (1989). *Working With Parents: A Whole-school Approach*. Windsor: NFER Nelson.

Bavers, T. (Ed.) (1984). *Management and the Special School*. Beckenham, Kent: Croom Helm.

Bruce, T. (1987). *Early Childhood Education*. London: Hodder and Stoughton.

Bruce, T. (1991). *Time to Play*. London: Hodder and Stoughton.

Cameron, R.J. (Ed.) (1982). *Working Together: Portage in the UK*. London: NFER Nelson.

Clark, M.M. and Cheyne, W. (1979). *Studies in Pre-school Education*. London: Hodder and Stoughton.

Cohen, A. (Ed.) (1988). *Early Education: The Parent's Role*. London: Chapman.

Cohen, L. and Manion, L. (1994). *Research Methods in Education* (4th Edn.). London: Routledge.

Daniels, P. (1994). *Draft Code of Practice 1993 Education Act*. Winchester: HIASS SE.

Dessent, T. (Ed.) (1984). *What is Important About Portage?* Windsor: NFER Nelson.

DFE (1993). *Education Act 1993: Draft Circular on the Development of Social Schools*.

DFE (1994). *Code of Practice on Identification and Assessment of S.E.N.*

Early Years Curriculum Group (1989). *Early Childhood Education*. Stoke-on-Trent: Trentham.

Edwards, V. and Redfern, A. (1988). *At Home in School: Parent Participation in Primary Schools*. London: Routledge.

Education Survey 5 (DATE). *Parent Teacher Relationships in Primary Schools*. London: HMSO/DES.

Furneaux, B. (1988). *Special Parents*. Milton Keynes: Open University Press.

Gelfer, J.I. (1991). Teacher/Parent Partnerships: Enhancing Communications. *Young Children*, Vol. 67; No. 3: pp 164–167.

Gordon, M. (1969). *Practical Parenthood*. Mayflower.

Grant. D. (1989). *Learning Relations*. London: Routledge.

HCC Special Needs Review (1991). *All Our Children: A Summary for Consultation*. Winchester: HCC Educ.

Hopkins, D. (1985). *A Teacher's Guide to Classroom Research*. Milton Keynes: Open University Press.

Hurst, V. (1994). A Review Article: HMI, OFSTED and the Youngest Children in School. *Early Years*, Vol.14; No. 2: pp 42–44.

Isaacs, S. (1968). *The Nursery Years*. London: Routledge and Keegan Paul.

Joyce, B.G. (1987). Parental Involvement: A Model for Program Development. *Rural Special Education Quarterly*, Vol. 8; No. 2: pp 7–13.

Lally, M. (1991). *The Nursery Teacher in Action*. London: Chapman.

Levenstein, P. (1971). Symposium on Parent-Centred Education 2: Learning From and Through Mothers. *Childhood Education*, Vol. 48; No. 4: pp 233–235.

Lewis, I. and Munn, P. (1987). *So You Want to do Research?* Edinburgh: SCRE.

Liedloft, J. (1986). *The Continuum Concept*. Harmondsworth: Penguin.

McConkey, R. (1985). *Working with Parents: A Practical Guide for Teachers and Therapists*. London: Croom Helm.

McGeeney, P. (1969). *Parents are Welcome*. London: Longman.

Miller, S. and Robinson, J. Starting Out. *Special Children*, March 1992, pp 12–13.

Minke, K.M. (1993). The Development of Individualised Family Service Plans: Roles for Parents and Staff. *Journal of Special Education*, Vol. 27; No. 1: pp 82–106.

Mittler, P., Brouillette, R. and Harris, D. (Eds.) (1993). Special Needs Education. In *World Yearbook of Education*.

Plowden, B. (1967). *Children and Their Primary Schools*. HMSO.

Powell, D.R. (1990). Research in Review. Home Visiting in the Early Years. *Young Children*, Vol. 45; No. 6: pp 65–73.

Pugh, G. (1981). *Parents as Partners*. London: National Children's Bureau.

Pugh, G. (Ed.) (1992). *Contemporary Issues in the Early Years*. London: Chapman/National Children's Bureau.

Pugh, G. and De'ath, E. (1984). *The Needs of Parents*. London: MacMillan.

Pugh, G., De'ath, E. and Smith, C. (1994). *Confident Parents, Confident Children*. London: National Children's Bureau.

Raven, J. (1980). *Parents, Teachers and Children*. Sevenoaks: Hodder, Stoughton, SCRE.

Ridell, S. and Brown, S. (Eds.) (1994). *Special Educational Needs Policy in the 1990s*. London: Routledge.

Sharrock, A. (1970). *Home/School Relations*. London: MacMillan.

Siraj-Blatchford, I. (1994). *The Early Years: Laying the Foundations for Racial Equality*. Stoke-on-Trent: Trentham.

Solity, J. (1992). *Special Education*. London: Cassell.

Stobbs, P. (1993). *The Education Act 1993 and Special Educational Needs Highlight* No. 123. London: National Children's Bureau.

Thompson, M. (1994). Head Start for USA. *Child Education*, Vol. 71: No.4.

Tizzard, B. and Hughes, M. (1984). *Young Children Learning, Talking and Thinking at Home and in School*. London: Fontana.

Topping, K.J. (1986). *Parents as Educators*. Beckenham: Croom Helm.

Walters, B. (1993). Swimming with the Tide. *Special Children*, Jan 1993: pp 24–25.

Wheeler, W.P. *et al.* (1993). Facilitating Effective Transition in Early Intervention Services: Parent Involvement. *Rural Special Education Quarterly*, Vol. 12; No. 1: pp 55–60. Theme issue with title 'Early Childhood Special Education'.

White, M., and Cameron, R.J. (1987). *Portage Early Education Programme.* London: NFER Nelson.

White, M., and Cameron, R.J. (Eds.) (1988). *Portage Progress and Possibilities.* London: NFER Nelson.

Whitney, B. (1993). *The Children Act and Schools.* London: Kogan Page.

Wolfendale, S. (Ed.) (1989). *Developing Networks Between School, Home, Community.* London: Cassell.

Conclusion
Hazel Osborn

Partnership with Parents

The preceding chapters give accounts of current experience and work, offering an often moving, and always fascinating mosaic both of working with parents and families, and of being a recipient of such work. The reader may be tempted to only read those chapters which most closely relate to their own experience and perhaps the time available may dictate this. However, reading the whole means that not only is there the exciting possibility of learning about new initiatives or new ways of seeing situations, but also developing, or confirming, an appreciation of the values and issues which remain important whatever and wherever such projects are being undertaken. Additionally, a reading of all the chapters gives the opportunity to make wider connections, and such a reading also gives an indication of how the workers, or those that intervene, are seen, and an opportunity for everyone to have an idea of seeing themselves as others see them.

The Shorter Oxford English Dictionary defines a partner as 'one who has a share or part with another...a partaker...a sharer...an accomplice' and a partnership as 'the fact or condition of being a partner...an association of two or more persons for the carrying on of a business of which they share the expenses, profit and loss'. How closely do these definitions fit the world of the helper and the helped, the intervener and the intervenee? Are there indications of possible pitfalls? If someone is a sharer what exactly does this mean, does everyone have an equal share, and are some even aware that they are partners or sharers? Paul Tosey conveys a feeling of being taken over rather than sharing and moreover of not knowing what the rules of the game are.

However, Frada Feigelson describes a structure where parents are a key part of the process, being an 'integral part of their child's daily life...' and that children are 'perceived as being fundamentally dependent on their parents'. The suggestion, in the dictionary definition, that a partner might be an accomplice suggests a different kind of pitfall, that of the helper becoming so involved in a situation that their help becomes less than useful and indicates the need to occupy the middle ground. Perhaps the idea of a partnership being for the purpose of carrying on a business more usefully suggests an arrangement with a structure and known, written, ground rules. However the phrase 'share the expenses, profit and loss' is a reminder that not all situations go well and that there may be losses as well as profits, in addition to expenses of all kinds, which will have to be accounted for and evaluated.

Working with parents and families in a variety of ways, with the objective of confirming existing strengths and developing new ones, in addition to protecting the vulnerable, must have a history at least as old as that of the helping agencies. A whole literature exists concerning this in a variety of settings. However, each moment in time has its own particular pattern of structures and pressures which makes it relevant and proper to address the work anew, whilst building on the knowledge and experience of the past.

At present we are discovering partnership. Maybe we have not yet reached some acceptance of the fact that most parents must be a form of expert in relation to their own children if only because usually they have spent a great deal more time with them than the worker. The concept of partnership as a sharing conveys some idea of equality, of no one person having all the answers (but of having the responsibility of being clear about the answers that you do have) and above all of listening to the other partners. Starting where the other person is, is very important. In her conclusion Pat Mood states:

> *In the relatively short history of modern palliative care, knowledge and skills have been acquired by careful listening to those parents, and other members of families who are experiencing illness, death and bereavement.*

These ideas are all detailed somewhere in the foregoing chapters . What might be distilled from a reading of all of them? They represent a great richness of ideas and approaches which will have individual resonances for us all. However, I suggest the following might be seen as the crucial issues.

Values

The need to examine, and be aware, of the individuals values, our own and those of others, which influence and guide our work, both work in prospect and that being currently undertaken.

This necessity is present in all the accounts, and clearly articulated by Kate Rose and Anne Savage. There can be a temptation to assume that we are aware of our guiding values and that there is no need to re-examine them. However, in working in partnership with parents, our experience of our own childhood and parents must be a powerful, and to some extent, an inescapable part of the structure of our basic values. This demands an ongoing awareness when working in this arena and in evaluating work in progress. The experience of being parented is common to almost everyone, but at the same time is totally individual. In this lies both the help and the hindrance of experience on which personal values are based.

Shaw and Shaw (1997) clearly recognise the influence of personal values and their significance in self evaluation,

> *…while evaluating in day-to-day practice is seen as a marginal skill, it connects with deeply held personal commitments and value…*

Olsson and Ljunghill (1997) report their study which fascinatingly looks at the personal frames of reference, which they call 'naive theory', that the practitioner, in this case experienced social workers, actually use in their encounters with clients. They suggest that the frames of reference used cannot simply 'be attributed to education, to the directives of political decision makers, to the legislative foundations of the activity, or to the nature of the tasks.' and quoting from Rogers (1965) say:

> *In all forms of care and treatment it is the basic operational philosophy of the practitioner or of the organisation that is decisively important both for the method actually practised, regardless of the theoretical frame of reference or expressed purpose of the intervention…*

In the discussion of their results Olsson and Junghill say that their analysis clearly reveals that 'naive theory' is 'clearly influenced by social and organisational processes within the employing organisation.' An aspect of intervention which is clearly expressed in Tosey's chapter. However, the authors of this study go on to say that the great variation in the workers' approaches suggests other factors in formulating 'naive theories'. They also note that in mapping out the origins of their theories that 'personal experiences had often played the decisive role in the explanatory models (of client's actions) they had adopted, and in their ideas about how to help other people in difficult situations.' They suggest that 'naive theories' are 'unique personal constructions that have been put together during a complicated process in which maturation, education, work organisation and client encounters have all been important'. This indicates a personal responsibility to constantly monitor one's work.

Whilst our basic values may be an abiding influence upon our actions they may also be vulnerable to change with experience, most particularly perhaps in this context, when we add the experience of being a parent to the generally universal experience of being parented. This suggests a need to appreciate the possibility of change in our personal frames of reference in addition to attempting to hold on to an awareness of them. It also strongly suggests the need to be willing to be open to the frames of reference of others, as demonstrated in the chapter from Israel, whilst regularly reviewing one's own frames of reference, particularly in relation to current situations with which one is working.

Personal values rooted in our individual experience have to form the basis of the way we construe the world about us. Whilst this offers a starting point in relating to other people it does not necessarily lead to an instantaneous appreciation of their values. However, without such an appreciation it is hard to consider a meaningful partnership. The need to listen is underlined again, and then to assess, check out and plan the partnership jointly with the partners.

Supervision and Support

If personal values and the resulting attitudes are so influential how can awareness be achieved and monitored? Additionally, how can the worker best meet the possibility of infection by the feelings which are very much a part of the situation in which they are involved? Or indeed of being recruited to the cause of a particular family member?

Rose and Savage say, 'The most fundamental message that we learnt in carrying out this work is that the antagonism and suspicion lay as significantly with the workers as the women'. Co-working offers an opportunity for mutual support and working in partnership, but space to discuss the process with someone with experience of the field might give additional help in standing back from the situation, working with these feelings, as well as connecting the work with the wider world.

The need and value of supervision and support are also emphasised elsewhere in the

preceding chapters. Pat Mood says: 'To remain effective in palliative care a worker needs sound professional supervision, good team leadership and team support.' Peter Ford and Karen Postle give the requirements for membership of the UK College of Family Mediators as training, competence and in receipt of regular supervision. How else might one hold the middle ground?

In order to help constructively, the worker must have the regular opportunity of space in which to share, with a supervisor or consultant, their current experience. Thus an awareness of the influence of their own experience and keeping the balance of partnership in the here and now might be maintained.

Appreciation of the value of regular supervision is not new, Olive Stevenson (1978), commenting upon her research carried out in social service teams said:

> *professional self-awareness remains, in my view, a primary source of protection to the client, which is even more important in the local authority setting than in those which carry less statutory responsibility... for in the last analysis, this (professional development and supervision) is the best protection for clients and transcends formal systems of checks and controls, although these are needed as well.*
>
> (Stevenson, 1978)

It is the suggestion that supervision is the best protection for the client which makes access to it very important in achieving the overall agreed objectives of the work. In this context Peter Sandiford and John Whiteside, in Chapter 8, describe the social work loop system which demonstrates such an approach in current practice.

We are all prone to sticking with our own point of view without review. Although it may seem that access to supervision might sometimes prove difficult, such supervision is of paramount importance in any situation where someone is helping or intervening in the delicate checks and balances of families.

Evaluation and Research

In working with parents at The Willows the usefulness of incorporating evaluation and research into the day-to-day work of a special school is described. It is in fact more than useful, it is essential, in order to keep any work relevant to those upon whom it is focused, as well as ensuring that resources, in particular the workers, are being most usefully employed.

Shaw and Shaw (1997) refer to social workers regarding self-evaluation as an 'add on' for which there is rarely time. The submission above is that regular, structured supervision and consultation is a crucial cornerstone of self-evaluation. However, evaluation of the work undertaken is also crucially a part of supervision/consultation. Evaluation in terms of audit may sound beyond the grasp of the worker in everyday practice, but surely there is an ethical responsibility to constantly check with those with whom you are intervening that the process is understood and can be worked with? This may take both careful listening and in some cases, delicate negotiation, but unless it is undertaken, the work will ultimately be skewed and objectives remain out of reach. Perhaps more importantly, those in receipt of intervention will be left often feeling powerless, confused and angry.

Many in the fields of helping and intervening will say that asking for feedback is a part of their practice and yet there are many on the receiving end who do not seem to find this a part of their experience . Equally, as a manager, I found that in discussing a situation which was problematical to the worker, to ask the question 'What does the client think is happening?' was frequently met with an inability to reply. Often this lack of knowledge, or the lack of an attempt to find out, was a major contributor to the difficulties of the situation.

Why is this apparently basic requirement for feedback so often neglected? It may be that the perception of others as needing help or intervention automatically, in this perception, disempowers them as people able to make a useful contribution to the situation. Gerry Emson quotes Wolfendale as noting that 'parents were seen largely as clients by schools for many years: this blocked true partnership between complementary equals…'

It may be that those who are helping/intervening are afraid that feedback will reflect in a negative way upon their practice, or maybe it will reveal that a cherished project is actually not achieving its objectives. But such a neglect of feedback is surely in total opposition to the concept of partnership. Working together, a sharing of the situation, is a part of the work to be done, difficult as it may sometimes be.

Gerry Emson's account of her research describes a more formal approach to receiving feedback, in addition to allowing an exploration of the current situation and ways forward. Research is not only feedback but also a confirmation of aspects that might hitherto have only been suspected and possibly of discovering totally new scenarios. It is in the discovery of evidence which leads to a change in thinking that much of the value of research lies. However, if research results are incorporated into an ideology, one should also note her statement 'a flexible approach to educational ideology is required'.

Research does not have to be always national and large scale, although that level of research has an important bearing upon policy decisions. However, it does have to be carefully constructed and validated. The account of the research carried out at The Willows also demonstrates the usefulness of a research project where the results could be immediately recognised as relevant and incorporated directly into the work of the school. However, for this to be done there has to be a readiness to assess and accept new ideas. The cultural climate is described by Anne Scowen as The Willows tradition of 'can we improve?'.

Working Together

At the beginning of this chapter I suggested that a reading of all the chapters in this book gives access to impressions of how others might see us. Even if the reader does not easily fit into any of the roles portrayed, they may still gain an appreciation of the very real situations described and the thoughts and feelings of those involved.

Maria Rueggar observes how both social workers and systems operate in relation to families who have been to social services on a number of occasions and on each occasion were seen only once and the case closed. Among the inferences which might be drawn from this are:

- Was a proper assessment made?

- Was there any awareness in social services of the previous occasions when they had been seen?

- Had the family been labelled and thus further thinking about their situation been inhibited?

- Was everyone too busy to hear and work with them and was a decision made regretfully, not to go any further?

- Did the family themselves always somehow defeat approaches and no-one asked why or could this not be resolved?

Maria Rueggar also highlights the usefulness of feedback on a service which may be unaware of the effect of their organisation? This kind of reflection should be seen as one aspect of working together.

The accounts of Mair Dyer and Paul Tosey both give graphic accounts of being on the receiving end of workers and organisations, with very different outcomes. Mair Dyer writes convincingly of being empowered whilst Paul Tosey does not seem to have found this profound experience empowering. Kate Rose and Anne Savage's group spoke of the 'fight'.

Slightly changing the focus, Frada Feilgelson writes of 'the ongoing and special challenge of working collaboratively in therapy with professionals from the juvenile justice and mental health systems…'. Having the accounts of others is always salutary and important and must be listened to responsibly. One can appreciate that certain points of view are most likely to be held by people with certain experiences or with certain roles, but this should not be allowed to lead to their views being dismissed without some consideration. If we are to work in partnership then there must be some appreciation of where the other partners stand.

Mair Dyer, Rosie Nichol Harper and Lisa Lewer all mention the number of different helpers and professionals which might be involved in any one situation. How can they attempt to work together constructively without some appreciation of their roles and the focus of their work?

A reading of the accounts in this book offers an insight into the ways of working of a number of people who have roles in helping/intervening and it therefore offers an opportunity to understand the knowledge, skills and pressures they might bring to situations. Cathy Hill reminds the reader of the range of situations which she encounters and also the range of parental responses to her role. She also describes how a doctor might be frightened. John Stevens emphasises the need to balance the needs of the individual with that of all the others for whom he is responsible. These are examples of the sort of information one acquires all the time but may not be used in thinking about how to work together.

In fact, although many will say how important it is to work together, and government guidelines will constantly remind us of it, the idea that working together is not a marginal activity but requires conscious thought and work to achieve it is somehow often translated into a quasi-social response of 'we all get on well together' without achieving a point where useful discussion which embraces the negatives as well as the positives can be reached. Cathy Hill's observation that 'we have much to learn from each other' is a very important step in this process. Ultimately one would hope to be able to appreciate the focus, understandings and responsibilities of the others in the network whilst at the same time retaining an awareness of ones own focus.

Conclusion

In this chapter I have attempted to reflect upon some of the very important issues which are a part of the preceding chapters. The perceptive reader will identify many gaps and avenues left unexplored. For example, the situation of young carers where usual family patterns of dependence/independence are turned on their head and the difficulty for the family of the worker only having a remit to work with a part of the whole situation. In this situation the social work skill of working with illness as a part of the situation and therefore of working with the parent does not seem to be available. Or the great importance of writing things down, not only the major agreements but the detail of information as in Rosemary Bazley's chapter and the chapter from Israel.

But perhaps the most obvious gap, now that partnership with parents is an expectation in relation to the children's legislation and a requirement in education, is the wide range of family situations where partnership with parents is to be sought. My use of the words 'helping' or 'intervention' might be interpreted as representing alternative words for the same activity or as facets of the same activity, or as opposite ends of a continuum. But any helping is an intervention in someone's life and any intervention must have the objective of helping someone, in this case the child.

In building a partnership it must be clear to everyone what the nature and objective of the intervention is. Partnership with parents in seeking good outcomes for the child would seem an obvious path to follow and yet there appears to be a need for government directives to encourage this path to be followed.

There also appears to be very little published on the subject. However, it is perhaps more likely that there are clues to building partnerships in a variety of sources. I started with the dictionary and all the meanings offered that have a place in our thinking about partnerships. A more complex order of thinking lies in both the literature on family dynamics and in that of building relationships in a professional context.

The existing literature is very valuable, but this book, in publishing descriptions of work being currently undertaken, gives accounts of *how* it might be done and in doing this offers an invaluable view of several different practice realities. One would hope that this is only a beginning and that people might not only be encouraged to search for relevant literature and research, but to look at their own practice and gather information, to better inform others and build their own partnerships.

References

Olsson, E., and Ljunghill, J. (1997). The Practitioner and 'Naive Theory' Social Work Intervention Processes. *British Journal of Social Work*, 27: 931–950.

Rogers, C. (1965). *Client-centred Therapy*. Cambridge, MA: The Riverside Press.

Shaw, I., and Shaw, A. (1997). Keeping Social Work Honest: Evaluating as Profession and Practice. *British Journal of Social Work*, 27: 847–869.

Stevenson, O. (1978). *Social Service Teams: The Practitioner's View*. HMSO.

Useful Names and Addresses

ADR Group
Equity and Law Building
36-38 Baldwin Street
Bristol BS1 1NR
Tel: 0117 925 2090
Fax: 0117 929 4429

Centre for Dispute Resolution
7 St Katherine's Way
London E1 9LB
Tel: 0171 481 4441
Fax: 0171 481 4442

Crossroads: Caring for Carers
10 Regent Place
Rugby
Warwickshire
CV21 2PN
Tel: 01788 573653

Crossroads are the leading provider of practical support for carers with over 200 schemes across England and Wales, and sister organisation in Scotland and Northern Ireland. A range of services have been developed but the core service provided by every scheme is the provision of a trained care attendant to go into the home to give the carer a break.

European Network for Conflict Resolution in Education (ENCORE)
Education Advisory Programme
Friends House
Euston Road
London NW1 2BJ
Tel: 0171 387 3601
Fax: 0171 388 1977

Family Lives
3rd Floor
Chapel House
18 Hatton Place
London EC1N 8RU
Tel: 0171 209 2460
Fax: 0171 209 2461

Family Mediators Association
1 Wyvil court
Wyvil Road
London SW8 2TG
Tel: 0171 720 3336
Fax: 0171 720 7999

Family Rights Group
The Print House
18 Ashwin Street
London E8 3DL
Tel: 0171 923 2628
Fax: 0171 923 2683

The Family Rights Group supports children and families involved with social services by advising families and working with service users, practitioners, researchers and policy makers. FRG works in England and Wales and was established as a charity in 1974.

Our belief, supported by research, is that most children are best looked after within their own family. Where it is not possible for children to live with thier own family, there should be a presumption in favour of some form of contact with the child's family and network, appropriate to the situation.

FRG's Aims

1. *To promote full participation by families in planning and decision-making about their own children.*
2. *To promote full participation by service users and potential service users in the design, delivery and evaluation of local child and family welfare services.*
3. *To develop and improve practice by lawyers, social workers and other relevant groups.*
4. *To campaign for improvements in relevant policy and legislation.*

In order to acheive these aims FRG provides an advice and advocacy service for families; undertakes policy and research projects; runs training courses and conferences and campaigns for changes in legislation, policy and practice.

Mediation UK
Alexander House
Telephone Avenue
Bristol BS1 4BS
Tel: 0117 904 6661
Fax: 0117 904 3331

National Family Mediation
9 Tavistock Place
London
WC1H 9SN
Tel: 0171 383 5993
Fax: 0171 383 5994

Quaker Peace and Service (QPS)
Friends House
Euston Road
London NW1 2BJ
Tel: 0171 387 3601
Fax: 0171 388 1977

Speak Out: The National Network of Peer Mediators
c/o 68 St George's Road
Bolton BL1 2DD
Tel/Fax: 01294 430418

UK College of Family Mediators
24–32 Stephenson Way
London NW1 2HX
Tel: 0171 391 9162
Fax: 0171 391 9165

Parenting Education and Support Forum
National Children's Bureau
8 Wakley Street
London EC1V 8QE
Tel: 0171 843 6099
Fax: 0171 843 6323
e mail: parenting@ncb.org.uk

The Forum is a membership organisation bringing together those concerned with, or working in, the field of preparation, education and support for parents. It promotes a high profile for parenting education, and support of parents growing in knowledge, skill, understanding and personal development. The Forum presses for effective policies and practice at local and national level with the aim of serving the best interests of all children and their families.

The Forum's activities include a newsletter and briefing sheet, an information database, a resource centre, working groups, publications, seminars and conferences to support debate and exchange information.

Children North-East
1a Claremont Street
Newcastle-upon-Tyne
NE2 4AH

Working With Men
320 Commercial Way
London SE15 1QN
Treflloyd@aol.com

Glossary of Terms

Derbyshire Language Scheme. A widely used language programme based on the normal developmental order, consisting of teaching activities linked to an assessment scheme.

Domiciliary therapy. An approach to delivering therapy, in which the sessions take place in the client's home rather than any other setting.

Dysfluent. With disruptions, such as repetitions of words, in the fluent production of speech. Periods of dysfluency are common between the ages of two and seven years.

EEL. The EEL Project at the University of Worcester has developed a framework for evaluating quality which builds upon a knowledge base of effective learning. It is flexible but provides clear principles from which settings can be used for self evaluation around:

- Learning experiences/curriculum.
- Relationships and interaction.
- Equal opportunities.
- Parental partnership, home and community liaison.

Electively mute. A condition where a child does not use the language skills they have in certain situations, for example not talking in nursery or school.

High/Scope. High/Scope is based on the Piagetian theory of 'active learning' and incorporates many features of good practice found in traditional nursery education. The approach is one in which both adult and child plan and initiate activities and actively work together. There is an orderly environment, daily routine, respect and support for children with a plan – do – review cycle.

Makaton. The Makaton programme is a widely used language programme which uses signs, symbols and speech to develop communication skills. The vocabulary used is selected specifically for each client from a staged core vocabulary. Training courses are run for parents and professionals.

Non-directive Therapy. A play-based therapy in which the child chooses the activities and the therapist responds, providing language input appropriate to the child's actions and abilities.

PEEP Peers Early Education Partnership. A literacy project in Oxford working with parents and supporting them as their children's first educators.

Portage. A home teaching programme for pre-school children with developmental difficulties/special needs. Portage workers usually work with parents at home and are employed by the local education authority.

Pragmatic skills. The use of spoken language and understanding of language to interact, to initiate communication, to respond to communication and to achieve different things, such as greeting and requesting.

S.A.L.T. Speech and Language Therapy.

Sign. A standardised hand movement which has the same meaning as a word. The signs used in Makaton in the UK are selected from British sign language.

Statementing procedure. The process of preparing a statement of special education needs, which is the document detailing the educational provision and support required by a child with special needs.

Symbol. A simple, clear, black and white line drawing which has the same meaning as a word.

TEACCH. Training and Education of Autistic and Communication Handicapped Children and Adults.